Socio-Economic Correlates
of Mortality in
Japan and ASEAN

The National Institute for Research Advancement (NIRA) of Japan was founded in 1974 under a special legislation of the Parliament as a result of initiatives taken by representatives from the government, business, labour, and academic communities. NIRA's central purpose is the advancement of interdisciplinary research which seeks viable solutions to the major problems confronting modern society.

The Institute of Southeast Asian Studies was established as an autonomous organization in May 1968. It is a regional research centre for scholars and other specialists concerned with modern Southeast Asia, particularly the multi-faceted problems of stability and security, economic development, and political and social change.

The Institute is governed by a twenty-two-member Board of Trustees comprising nominees from the Singapore Government, the National University of Singapore, the various Chambers of Commerce, and professional and civic organizations. A ten-man Executive Committee oversees day-to-day operations; it is chaired by the Director, the Institute's chief academic and administrative officer.

Socio-Economic Correlates of Mortality in Japan and ASEAN

Edited by
Ng Shui Meng
Institute of Southeast Asian Studies

National Institute for Research Advancement, Japan
and
Institute of Southeast Asian Studies, Singapore

Cataloguing in Publication Data

Socio-economic correlates of mortality in ASEAN and Japan/editor, Ng Shui Meng.
Country reports presented at the Workshop on Socio-economic Correlates of
Mortality Differentials in Japan and ASEAN, Singapore, 30-31 August 1984.
1. Mortality -- Social aspects -- ASEAN -- Congresses.
2. Mortality -- Social aspects -- Japan -- Congresses.
3. Mortality -- Economic aspects -- ASEAN -- Congresses.
4. Mortality -- Economic aspects -- Japan -- Congresses.
I. Ng, Shui Meng.
II. Workshop on Socio-economic Correlates of Mortality Differentials in Japan
   and ASEAN (1984: Singapore)

HB1471 S67   1986

ISBN 9971-988-21-6

Published by
Institute of Southeast Asian Studies
Heng Mui Keng Terrace
Pasir Panjang
Singapore 0511

The responsibility for facts and opinions expressed in this publication rests
exclusively with the contributors and their interpretations do not necessarily
reflect the views or the policy of the Institute or its supporters.

Printed in Singapore by Fu Loong Lithographers Pte Ltd.

CONTENTS

Gabriel C. Alvarez is Senior Lecturer, Department of Sociology at the National University of Singapore. He was elected President of the Philippine Sociological Society in 1978 and has served as consultant in a number of research projects on urban planning and rural development.

Lukman Ismail is Senior Lecturer at the Academy of Statistics, Jakarta, Lecturer in Statistical Methods in Ecological Systems at the University of Indonesia and Chief of Training Section at the Statistical Education and Training Centre, Jakarta.

Ng Shui Meng is Senior Fellow at the Institute of Southeast Asian Studies, Singapore. Her research interests include population and contemporary developments in Indochina. She is currently conducting a study on the Vietnamese community in Laos.

Shinsuke Morio is Deputy Director of the Infectious Diseases Surveillance Division of the Ministry of Health and Welfare in Japan. His current research interests include public health particularly in the prevention of infectious diseases.

Noor Laily binti Dato' Abu Bakar was Director-General at the National Population and Family Development Board. Her current research interests are on women in development and child development.

Suchart Prasithrathsint is Professor of Sociology (Demography) at the National Institute of Development Administration (NIDA). His research interests cover various issues of population and development interactions. He is President of the Thai University Research Association.

Laddawan Rodmanee is Lecturer in Medical and Health Social Sciences at Mahidol University. Her research interests include aspects of medical and health problems and the interactions of health, environment and population.

Budi Soeradji is Chief, Family Planning and Population Bureau, National Development Planning Agency and Director, Academy of Statistics, Central Bureau of Statistics, Jakarta. His current research interests include family planning evaluation, fertility, mortality, and population and development.

Kanikar Sookasame is Assistant Professor of Sociology (Demography) at the National Institute of Development Administration in Thailand. Her research interests include fertility, mortality, migration, and rural-urban development.

Shigesato Takahashi is Research Officer, Division of Population Quality and Human Reproduction, Ministry of Health and Welfare in Japan. His current research interests include demographic changes in Japanese mortality and factors affecting cause structure of mortality in developed countries.

Tey Nai Peng is Assistant Director, Research, Evaluation and Management Information System Division at the National Population and Family Development Board in Malaysia. His current research interests are on population mobility, urbanization and KAP (Knowledge, Attitude and Practice) studies.

LIST OF TABLES

III: Indonesia

IV: Peninsular Malaysia

V: Philippines

VI: Singapore

VII: Thailand

LIST OF FIGURES

V: Philippines

VI: Singapore

VII: Thailand

I SOCIO-ECONOMIC CORRELATES OF MORTALITY IN JAPAN AND ASEAN

Ng Shui Meng

General Mortality Trend in Japan and ASEAN

Historically, there may be limited data to specifically map out the mortality transition of individual societies, but it has generally been agreed that one of the most remarkable developments in contemporary modern demographic history has been that of reduction of mortality levels and a significant prolongation of life. Admittedly, not all societies or segments of societies have participated equally in this mortality revolution. However, it also cannot be denied that mortality differentials at a global level has narrowed substantially.

Mortality levels, like GNP and literacy rates, are often used in the development literature to measure a country's stage of "modernity" or "development". All societies, implicit or explicit, aspire to prolong life and ward off death and take as given that mortality reduction is integral to the modernization process. While no one can argue that mortality reduction is in and of itself desirable and good, our understanding of the linkage between mortality and the so-called process of development is not specific. Historical demographic data drawn largely from Europe suggested that pre-industrial and pre-modern populations were fairly responsive to socio-economic, political and environmental conditions even if these populations were by and large unprotected by modern medicine and public health measures. In other words, while many of the pre-industrial populations were subjected to mortality levels which were high in general, these were not uniform. And sub-populations which enjoyed higher levels of real income, adequate food and clothing and better housing conditions were also able to enjoy longer and better lives (Wrigley 1969, pp. 127, 129). The balance was, however, precarious as any disruption of socio-political or environmental link, would wipe out such gains within a very short period. Hence what marked the mortality pattern of pre-industrial populations were huge

1

fluctuations of mortality through outbreaks of what historical demographers have termed "crises mortality".

Europe's experience of mortality decline had been a slow long-drawn process linked very much to its technological change which brought about the agricultural revolution and then the industrial revolution which in turn helped stabilize the lives of, if not all, then at least some segments of the population. This process spanned a period of more than two hundred years.

Based on the studies on pre-industrial populations of Europe, it was suggested that even in the eighteenth century life expectancy at birth ranged only between thirty to forty years, not significantly different from the previous two or three centuries. These mortality patterns changed in some areas in Europe in the mid-eighteenth century as the benefits of the technological innovations both in the agricultural and the industrial sectors slowly reached larger and larger segments of the population. By 1840, the life expectancy of the population in the most advanced parts of Europe surpassed 40, and it crept up to 45 by 1880 and only reached 50 by the turn of the century. By the 1930s the average life expectancy of the most developed nations broached 60 and by 1950s some countries recorded life expectancies of nearly 70 years (U.N. Population Bulletin No. 6, 1963).

The European experience of mortality decline in the early industrialized countries was not only a very gradual process, it was also age-selective since initial mortality decline was the result of better food and housing and improvement of the economic standard of living. The chief beneficiaries were those in their early adulthood. Improvement of infant mortality and control of diseases for those over 40 or 50 had to await the advancement of medical science and knowledge of public health and sanitation, a development which came later.

Significant medical advancement and the control of mortality though the application of modern medicine and public health practices was largely a twentieth century phenomenon. But once introduced, the acceleration of mortality decline was unprecedented. The greatest beneficiaries of this new technological advance were the developing and industrializing countries outside Europe where mortality reduction telescoped into the time span of a little more than a generation. Many examples of such phenomenal improvement of mortality conditions exist in both Asia and Southeast Asia in the post-World War II period. For example, it took some of the industrialized countries of Europe more than a century to increase life expectancy from 35 to 60, but for many of the developing nations, this feat was achieved in a much shorter time. In many countries in Asia and Southeast Asia the average life expectancy at birth at the beginning of the

2

twentieth century was only around 30 years, by the middle of the twentieth century it had gone up to nearly 50 years and by the 1970s it was above 60 years.

However, with the introduction of the medical factor, mortality reduction was not just dependent upon socio-economic transformation as in the case of the early industrialized countries. The much more clearcut relationship between mortality and socio-economic progress of the earlier period has now become blurred as mortality reduction could be achieved rapidly through the access to life-saving vaccines and other modern "miracle cures" at relatively low economic costs and not necessarily through progress on the socio-economic front. Examples in many Latin American and Asian countries in fact illustrate that mortality decline could take place despite poor or even deteriorating socio-economic conditions (Goldschneider 1971, p. 115). What all this means is that at the global level, regardless of the level of socio-economic progress at the individual or societal level, there has been over the past 50 or so years an increasing narrowing of the mortality gap between developed and developing nations. This narrowing of the mortality gap is commonly referred to as "mortality convergence" in demographic literature. To illustrate this pattern of mortality convergence, some examples are shown in Table 1 and Figure 1.

This pattern of mortality convergence highlights the fact that the study of mortality in contemporary societies has now become more complex which by necessity has to incorporate explanations which take into account technology transfer and technological diffusion in addition to the internal societal dynamics of socio-economic transformation. Of necessity, too, is that the study of mortality has to go beyond the examination of mortality levels (which normally refers to the crude rates of death) to examine the more refined indices of mortality. For example, what is clear even from a cursory perspective is that while the pattern of mortality convergence between developed and developing countries holds true for measures of crude death rates, there is still conspicuous divergence in infant mortality, neo-natal mortality and maternal mortality between the developed and developing nations. The prevention of deaths at infancy for many developing countries has proven more difficult. Extension of health services do help but by itself it is not sufficient. Infant mortality, more so than general mortality, is more closely tied to the overall pattern of living conditions and state of health of all sectors of the population. Increasingly, patterns of differential causes of death have emerged between nations at different stages of economic and social development which have added a new dimension to the study of mortality differentials from a comparative perspective.

3

TABLE 1
Crude Death Rates per 1,000 by Region and Country
in Asia and Southeast Asia, 1950-75

Region and Country	1950-1955	1955-1960	1960-1965	1965-1970	1970-1975
World total	18.3	16.1	14.4	13.1	12.0
More developed region	10.1	9.3	9.0	9.1	9.2
Less developed regions	22.2	19.3	16.8	14.8	13.2
East Asia	19.3	15.5	12.8	10.7	9.1
China	20.1	16.7	13.6	11.2	9.4
Japan	9.4	7.8	7.3	6.9	6.6
Other East Asia	30.0	13.2	11.8	10.1	8.7
Hong Kong	8.9	7.2	6.2	5.5	5.2
Korea	32.0	13.7	12.3	10.6	9.1
Korea, Dem. Peop. Rep. of	32.0	13.3	12.2	11.2	9.4
Korea, Republic of	32.0	13.8	12.4	10.3	8.9
Mongolia	20.5	16.6	13.5	11.2	9.6
Southeast Asia	24.3	22.0	19.7	17.3	15.2
Burma	25.0	23.7	21.0	17.5	15.8
Democratic Kampuchea	25.1	23.1	21.0	19.1	16.9
East Timor	34.5	31.2	28.3	25.3	23.0
Indonesia	26.4	24.4	21.9	19.2	16.7
Lao People's Dem. Rep.	24.9	22.4	22.6	22.8	22.8
Malaysia	19.2	16.4	14.0	11.7	10.2
Philippines	19.2	16.5	14.2	12.2	10.3
Singapore	10.6	8.6	7.1	5.6	5.2
Soc. Rep. of Viet Nam	25.4	23.4	22.4	21.2	19.8
Thailand	21.4	18.1	14.9	12.5	10.5

SOURCE: Abstracted from United Nations, World Population Trends and
Prospects by Country, 1950-2000: Summary report of the 1978
assessment, New York, 1979, Table 2-B.

FIGURE 1
Mortality Convergence 1950–75

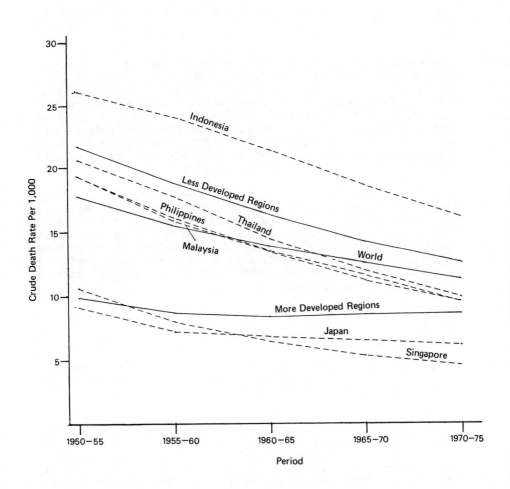

SOURCE: United Nations, <u>World Population Trends and Prospects by Country,</u>
<u>1950-2000: Summary Report of the 1978 Assessment</u>, New York, 1970.
Table 2-B.

To some extent the unprecedented phenonmenon of rapid mortality decline in many developing countries in the post-World War II period has diverted the attention of policy makers and government planners from further investigation into the process and patterns of mortality change in their respective societies. Many take the trend for granted and expect it to continue to decline in this favourable manner into the future as society develops. The assumption is that societal development is unidirectional. Instead, more pressing, as far as the population planners are concerned, is the problem of fertility. Post-war rapid population growth rates magnified Malthusian fears and hence led to the channelling of resources and energy largely towards tackling the problem of over population. This has often been translated into programmes specifically aimed at reducing fertility and controlling family. Hence from the 1960s onwards much of the demographic literature that emerged dealt predominantly on issues related to fertility behaviour with only relatively scant attention paid to mortality.

This state of affairs has changed a little recently. Experience in many developing countries has shown that mortality and fertility are often closely interrelated and in many cases further fertility decline is predicated first upon further mortality reduction. This has led researchers to focus more attention towards the understanding of the dynamics of mortality differentials and in the identification of crucial factors affecting mortality change.

The Mortality Project

The studies in this monograph in part grew out of this felt need to better understand the patterns and process of mortality changes in this part of the world. In particular, it is felt that there are insufficient studies which try to address the issue of mortality in relation to socio-economic development and improvement of environmental and health conditions of the population in these societies. A project to examine the Socio-economic Correlates of Mortality in Japan and the five ASEAN countries of Indonesia, Malaysia, the Philippines, Singapore and Thailand was thus initiated.* The National Institute for Research Advancement (NIRA) of Japan provided the funding and Institute of Southeast Asian Studies (ISEAS) in Singapore co-ordinated the study.

---

*   Brunei was not included because when this project was first conceived, Brunei had not become the sixth member of ASEAN.

Of the six countries, Japan is an industrialized and developed country and in GNP terms it ranks among the top of the countries of the developed world. The ASEAN countries, however, are developing economies, with Singapore perhaps being considered as the more developed and modernized of the five. Population-wise, Japan is probably the most homogenous culturally. The populations of the other five ASEAN countries exhibit great diversity in ethnic, linguistic and religious terms. Because of these differences, it is felt that a project on the study of mortality differentials of these six countries will provide some interesting similarities and contrasts for comparative purposes which would at the same time help cast some light on the process of social transformation and mortality decline within the Asian context compared to the historical experience of western developed nations.

Given the exploratory nature of the project, it was purposely conceived to have only fairly modest objectives. Basically, the project aims first to map out descriptively the changes in mortality patterns and trends of the six countries in the recent period, depending on the availability of data. In addition, the study seeks to examine from a sociological perspective to what extent differential socio-economic factors and environmental conditions including health care and health delivery system and changes in the demographic structure can explain mortality differentials.

Ideally the data required for this kind of study should be at the individual/household level data in which the individual/household's socio-economic background, family conditions, medical history and demographic experience could be examined in relation to the individual/household's mortality experience. However, such data are not easily available. Except for a few societies which historically have had the tradition of keeping family registers, individual household mortality records are difficult to come by. Even in countries with very good vital registration data, the information given in the death certificate is usually too limited to allow for individual level analysis. Sample surveys on mortality are not often attempted because of the obvious constraints of financial resources as well as the difficulty of getting reliable information and a representative sample under conditions of low mortality, for example, in present day Japan and even in many of the ASEAN countries.

However, there are obviously mortality differentials within individual households and socio-economic sub-groups which deserve attention. Some of these variations can be linked to individual level differentials, but there are also variations which are community-level related. No matter how well meaning governments may be, there are always unequal distribution and access to

7

facilities and resource allocation. By and large, rural areas are less well endowed than urban centres in terms of educational, sanitation and medical facilities, but rural areas may also suffer less from problems like urban congestion and air pollution. Mortality differentials are therefore related both to individual as well as community level differences (Preston and Gardner 1976).

In this project the researchers have resorted to studying regional mortality differentials through areal level analysis. The purpose is to explore the relationship between community level socio-economic factors, environmental conditions and community level access to medical facilities/personnel and regional mortality differentials. However, the researchers are also aware of the shortcomings of such analysis as this could lead to problems of ecological fallacy. Hence it has to be stressed that the interpretation of the results has to be tentative. There is also one exception to the use of areal analysis, that is, Singapore. In the case of Singapore, because of its size and dense pattern of settlement and its urbanized nature there is very little regional variation of mortality to speak of. Because of this, Singapore's mode of data analysis is slightly different from the other five countries. Singapore adopts a time series analysis of mortality differentials aimed at exploring how and to what extent socio-economic development over time can explain the pattern of mortality changes.

Because the countries under study are so varied in terms of geographical size, political organization and administrative capacity, the system of data collection, not to mention their quality and validity is bound to be very diverse. This diversity in data sources, availability, organization and reliability was realized and their limitation understood when the project was first conceptualized. However, despite the diversity and various problems with the data, it is still hoped that some valuable information about the individual country's mortality patterns will emerge. The results of the six-country studies are presented in the sections that follow.

Mortality Trends: Crude Death Rates

Summarizing the mortality experience of the six countries, Japan experienced its mortality decline earliest. Although the earlier statistics may not be very reliable, Japanese vital statistics recorded that by 1885 crude death rates in Japan was slightly above 20 per 1,000. The rates fluctuated around that figure for the first two decades of the twentieth century and thereafter

8

declined markedly to about 16.0 per 1,000 in 1941. World War II interrupted the collection of vital statistics and such data became available only with the return of peace.

In the other five ASEAN countries however, mortality levels were generally high in the pre-World War II period. A steady trend of decline in mortality levels occurred only after the war. Of the ASEAN countries, Singapore and Peninsular Malaysia experienced the most rapid post-war decline in crude death rates. For the other countries (Indonesia, Thailand and the Philippines) the decline was much more gradual, accelerating only after the 1960s.

Because mortality decline in Japan had started early, by 1951, the registered Japanese crude death rates had already fallen to around 10 per 1,000. It declined by another 22 per cent between 1951 to 1955 when the recorded crude death rate was 7.8. Thereafter the speed of decline slowed with crude death rates hovering around 6 per 1,000 in the recent decade.

Elsewhere in Singapore and Peninsular Malaysia, the crude death rates in the 1950s were still above 10 per 1,000.

By the late 1950s, the mortality rates of Singapore and Malaysia hovered around 7.0 and 10-12 per 1,000 respectively. The post-independence period witnessed further improvement in the mortality situation. In 1982, the registered crude death rate of both Singapore and Malaysia was 5.2. The low crude death rates in these two countries (lower even than Japan) is reflective of the youthful character of these two populations compared to Japan. As fertility levels in Malaysia and Singapore further decrease, the gradual ageing of the population would bring about a slight reversal of the mortality trend. Crude death rates are expected to rise slightly. In fact this process has already begun in Singapore.

Indonesia, the Philippines and Thailand are all fairly large countries with substantial regional variations in mortality. However, unlike the mortality experience of the countries discussed above, various estimates of crude death rates suggested that mortality decline for these three countries occurred later. In the case of Thailand, for example, while the registered crude death rate was 10.0 by 1950, various demographers have estimated that the crude death rate for that period was probably closer to the range of 15-20 per 1,000. Decline thereafter probably became more rapid and in recent years, crude death rates were around 7.0 per 1,000. Regional mortality variations still exist, with the regions in the North and Northeast experiencing much higher mortality than elsewhere in the kingdom.

9

For Indonesia, the mortality estimates are also only suggestive. Indonesian scholars assert that the mortality conditions in Indonesia actually worsened after 1945 as a result of the war for independence (1946-50). Poor health conditions and the limited supply of food resulted in very poor living conditions especially on the island of Java where the population was most dense and the fighting most serious. Mortality decline started in the early 1950s although it was "very slow and irregular" (see section on Indonesia.)

In the Philippines, estimated crude death rates in the early 1950s were also fairly high (slightly below 20 per 1,000). Lower rates were experienced only from the 1960s. Estimates in the mid-1970s put the national rate around 6.5-7.0 per 1,000. However, there are also significant variations across regions.

Infant Mortality

Measurement in infant mortality which is much more sensitive of the general health and living conditions of the population, show an even more interesting picture across the six countries.

Japan, being the most developed, has expectedly the lowest infant mortality rate. The current registered Infant Mortality Rate (IMR) for Japan is 7.0 per 1,000 live births which is among the lowest in the world. According to the Japanese researchers, further improvement of IMR could not be expected to be very dramatic in the future because of the already very high standard of life enjoyed by ordinary Japanese. The findings showed that although "factors in social life still affect infant mortality rate, the effect of these factors is becoming weak" (see the section on Japan.) This suggests that the causes of infant mortality in Japan today are largely of an endogenous nature and are not easily reduced by manipulation of environmental conditions or improvement of living conditions. Many of the infant deaths could be genetically linked. Further decline may therefore have to depend upon use of corrective or curative measures of ailments which develop at the foetal stage.

In contrast to Japan, some countries in the ASEAN region still exhibit very high levels of infant mortality. In the early 1950s, estimates of IMR showed that in Indonesia probably one to three out of every ten babies died before aged one. By the 1960s, the situation had improved only very slightly. The IMR was estimated to be about 175 per 1,000 live births. The decade of the 1970s, saw IMR being trimmed more rapidly. By the late 1970s, IMR was brought down to close to 100 per 1,000 live births still

10

about 10 times the Japanese rate for the corresponding period and much higher than its ASEAN counterparts. In the case of Indonesia therefore there is still substantial wastage through infant deaths and although various estimates showed that in recent years, general mortality was declining at rates of 3 to 4 per cent per year, much still remains to be done.

As in elsewhere, the Thai researchers also asserted that infant mortality reduction in Thailand in the past few decades can be attributed to the general socio-economic development of the country as well as to the special government programmes in training midwives to provide better maternal and child health services in remote areas. However, compared to Indonesia estimated IMR for Thailand seemed to be lower. Based on survey data, IMR in Thailand in 1964-65 was around 84.3 per 1,000 and 51.9 per 1,000 a decade later (see section on Thailand). This means that the Thai rates are about half that of Indonesia for the same period. The Thai researchers estimated that for Thailand as a whole, IMR in Thailand is currently about 43-47 per 1,000. But like in Indonesia, although the rates of decline in IMR have been fairly impressive in the recent period, substantial regional variations persist.

The present registered IMR in the Philippines is fairly close to that of Thailand (49.1 per 1,000). However, according to the author of the Philippine study, the figure is suspect and would estimate current levels to be between 70-80 infant deaths per 1,000 live births (see section on the Philippines). If these estimates prove correct than in actual fact, the mortality situation in the Philippines would be closer to that of Indonesia rather than Thailand.

Fairing better in terms of infant mortality rate than these three countries are Singapore and Malaysia. In both countries infant mortality rates are quite low now. The IMR for Peninsular Malaysia in 1982 is 19.3, that is about half the Thai rate and one-quarter that of Indonesia and the Philippines. The rate of decline in IMR for Peninsular Malaysia has also been rather impressive. Between 1957 to 1982, IMR in Peninsular Malaysia has declined by 74.4 per cent or at an average annual rate of nearly 3 per cent. In actual fact however, the rate of decline in IMR has been even more rapid in recent years. The findings show that IMR has fallen on an average of 6 per cent per annum for the period 1975-82 as compared to an average of 3.7 per cent per annum during the period 1970-75.

Of all the ASEAN countries, Singapore has reached an IMR level fairly close to that of some of the developed countries in the West. In 1982, the IMR in Singapore was already less than 11 per 1,000 live births. Singapore post-war decline in IMR has also been impressive. Between 1955 and 1975, IMR was trimmed by 71.9 per cent. But between 1975 and 1982, the rate of decline had slowed substantially. It was reduced only from 13.9 to 10.7 per 1,000, a decrease of 23.0 per cent. Given the low rates prevailing, further reduction in infant mortality rates in Singapore, like in Japan, will also be slow.

Expectation of Life

The extension of life is, of course, the hope of every individual, yet long life was until recently out of the reach of most individuals. Less than a hundred years ago in Europe, life expectancy at birth was no more than 40-50 years. Today, in the developed world most people could expect to live on an average 70 or more years. While this is the case in the developed world, there are countries in this part of the world where average life expectancy is still only that of Europe a hundred or more years ago.

Among the six countries under study, long life is already a norm for the Japanese. Present day life expectancy in Japan has surpassed even some of the countries in Europe and has reached 74.2 years for males and 79.7 for females. Much of the elongation of life was essentially a post-war phenomenon. Just before World War II Japanese life expectancy was only slightly above 45 years for males and slightly below 50 for females. During the war years, life expectancy had in fact become worse than pre-war days. This situation was, however, greatly improved once peace returned. In 1955, life expectancy for Japanese males and females alike had gained more than ten years from the previous decade. And according to the Japanese authors of this study, life expectancy improvement was not only due to improvement in infant and child mortality which had already started in the pre-war period but also due to the marked improvement of mortality among young adults. This improvement was attributed to the effective control of infectious diseases through widespread use of antibiotics in medical treatment. In the 20-year period between 1955 and 1975, the Japanese on an average gained another 8 years for males and nearly 9 years for females (71.7 for males and 76.9 for females). Japan has now reached a stage where unless there are breakthroughs in slowing the biological ageing process, further elongation of life will be minimal. What concerns the Japanese now is the problem of ageing rather than further mortality reduction.

Singapore's population whose mortality pattern comes closest to Japan on the whole also enjoys one of the highest expectation of life in Southeast Asia. According to the 1980 census, life expectancy for the population as a whole has already exceeded 70 years. But as is common to most populations, female life expectancy is on the average 4 to 5 years longer than males. In Singapore therefore the average woman has a life expectancy of 74.0 years whereas the average male has a life expectancy of 68.7 years. This means that the difference between life expectancy in Japan and Singapore in the recent period is still more than 5 years for both males and females.

Malaysia's life expectancy does not lag much behind that of Japan and Singapore. By the time Malaysia obtained its independence in 1957, its life expectancy was already close to 60 years (55.8 for males and 58.2 for females). Life expectation continues to improve impressively. Between 1957 to 1979, the average gain in longevity was 11.4 years for males and 14.3 years for females respectively. Compared to its closest neighbour, Singapore, the gap in life expectancy between the two countries is only about one year for males and two years for females.

Compared to Singapore, Malaysia and Japan, the other three countries still lag behind in life expectancy. For Indonesia, for example, average estimated life expectancy in the early 1950s was still in the region of 35 to 38 years, lagging behind that of Singapore and Japan by about 20 years. In other words, longevity of Indonesians in the 1950s was only comparable to that of pre-industrial Europe in the late eighteenth century.

The situation in Thailand and the Philippines is somewhat better than Indonesia. In both the Philippines and Thailand, present expectation of life has exceeded 60 years (62 years for the Philippines, and 61.1 for Thai males and 64.9 for Thai females). In both countries, gains in longevity were most rapid only after the 1950s.

In all these countries, there are still gains to be attained, gains which are expected to follow further economic and social development including the improvement in the control of diseases and the extension of health care and public health services especially to the more remote areas where the population may not have the benefit of easy access to medical and health care and basic information about preventive medicine.

Causes of Death

The analysis of causes of death becomes particularly important as the mortality pattern of a society changes rapidly. The structure of death causes also undergoes interesting transformation and to

13

some extent mirrors the changing living conditions of a society at the macro and micro levels.

However, the difficulty in carrying out in-depth analysis of causes of death stems again from the difficulty in getting fairly systematic and reliable data. In newly developing countries where vital registration data are already grossly incomplete and of dubious reliability, it is not surprising that causes of death data are only of limited use. In remote rural areas where even the sick are not necessarily tended by medical doctors or trained personnel, the causes of deaths are generally unknown or very crudely categorized as "infection", "fevers", "old age" or some other vague malady. Because of the nature of the data, good analysis of causes of death are often lacking. Even if available, these tend to be related to small studies conducted by hospitals.

All the countries included in the study seemed to have gone through a phase when deaths were largely caused by infectious diseases like diphtheria, cholera, typhoid, tuberculosis or influenza, which until the invention of antibiotics and vaccines had claimed numerous lives especially of the young. With the invention of such vaccines, and their relatively cheap production and easy application, many of these killer diseases have been brought under control even in very poor and remote corners of the world.

In Japan, by 1955, infectious diseases of these kind were eliminated as main causes of death. In the countries in Southeast Asia, although these infectious diseases are no longer such dreaded diseases as in the past, their total elimination has not been achieved in the more remote countryside. Even in Singapore for example, infective and parasitic diseases as late as 1970 still accounted for 6.8 per cent of all deaths and of which 4.3 per cent were due to tuberculosis.

Peninsular Malaysia's data on causes of death though available are very deficient. In 1980, only 37.5 per cent of total deaths were medically certified, the others being classified under the category "other known causes of deaths". Although the data and the classification leave much to be desired, it is also clear that Malaysia's causes of death structure is reflective of a developing country where despite the control and steady decline of infectious and parasitic diseases, the diseases are not completely eliminated.

A similar picture applies also to the Philippines. But for the Philippines because its development level still lags behind Singapore and Malaysia, diseases like pneumonia and tuberculosis were until fairly recently still serious causes of death. Another

14

catch-all category "nutritional deficiencies" is also listed as an important cause of death.

In Japan, as early as 1955, the so-called "modern" killers -- cerebro-vascular diseases, malignant neoplasms and heart diseases -- were already ranked as the three main causes of death. These diseases tended to affect more mature adults and older persons. This shift in the causes of death structure in the case of Japan underlines its faster progress in its development process as well as a shift in the population structure in which adults and the old are more predominant than people in younger age groups.

From the causes of death information available for Singapore, Malaysia and the Philippines, we can only draw the general conclusions that in the past decade, there has been a structural shift in the causes of deaths towards degenerative and chronic diseases like heart diseases, cerebro-vascular diseases and malignant neoplasms.

In Singapore beginning from 1970, malignant neoplasms, heart and hypertensive diseases were already the leading causes of death with cerebro-vascular diseases taking fourth position. Diseases of the respiratory system has remained in the third position. Between 1970-82, deaths through heart diseases and malignant neoplasms increased at a very steep rate jumping from 16.6 per cent and 15.2 per cent for heart diseases and malignant neoplasms in 1970 to 22.4 per cent and 21.2 per cent respectively in 1982. Death through diseases of the respiratory system has also continued to increase as a percentage of total deaths. The share of deaths through cerebro-vascular diseases has been rather stable and it has dropped in the last few years. The share of deaths through accidents, poisonings and violence, the fifth leading cause of death has also remained fairly stable (see section on Singapore.)

In Malaysia, up until 1977, diseases of early infancy had ranked as the leading cause of death indicating that childhood deaths still account for a large proportion of Malaysia's mortality. However since 1980, that position is now occupied by heart diseases with diseases of early infancy falling to the second position. In 1980, deaths caused by heart diseases accounted for 16.4 per cent of total deaths in Malaysia. Death caused by accidents was ranked third with the fourth and fifth position taken by cardio-vascular diseases and neoplasms respectively (cardio-vascular diseases: 7.9 per cent; neoplasms: 7.8 per cent of total deaths). (See section on Malaysia.)

In the case of the Philippines, pneumonia is still the leading killer followed by heart diseases and respiratory tuberculosis in 1978. Over the years, however, there is a clear indication that while pneumonia and tuberculosis have declined, deaths through heart disease and malignant neoplasms have increased. Between 1970-75, data on cause of specific death rates in the Philippines showed that there had been a drop of 13.64 per cent in deaths through pneumonia whereas there was an increase of 59.7 per cent in deaths through heart diseases. The corresponding figures for the period between 1975-78 are -3.5 per cent for pneumonia and +32.2 per cent for heart diseases. As for deaths caused by neoplasms, the trend also showed one of increase throughout the 1960-78 period.

The findings show that in the countries in Southeast Asia, with the exception of Singapore, there is still a substantial proportion of deaths caused by diseases which afflict the very young. These are diseases related more to low standard of living, poverty, inadequate health care and poor sanitation. These diseases, unlike those which affect people in adult life are more easily amended through eradication of poverty, better public health practices and access to health facilities. Knowledge about preventive medicine, nutrition and general sanitation can improve the situation quite dramatically. This is certainly an area for attention by policy makers and the individual country's health planners.

References

Barclay, George W. Techniques and Population Analysis. New York: John Wiley & Sons, Inc., 1958.

Cohen, Jacob and Patricia Cohen. Applied Multiple Regression/Correlation Analysis for the Behavioral Science. New Jersey: LEA Publishers, 1975.

Goldscheider, Calvin. Population Modernization and Social Structure. Boston: Little, Brown & Co., 1971.

Preston, S.H., and R. Gardner. "Factors Influencing Mortality Levels in Asia: International Comparisons and a Japanese Case Study". Paper presented at the Seventh Summer Seminar in Population, East-West Center, Honolulu, 1976.

Ueda Kozo. Recent Trends of Mortality in Asian Countries. Tokyo: SEAMIC Publications No. 34, 1983.

United Nations. Department of Social Affairs, Population Division. Foetal, Infant and Early Childhood Mortality, Vols. 1 and 2. Population Studies No. 13. New York, 1954.

_____. U.N. Population Bulletin, No. 6, 1963.

United Nations. <u>World Population Trend and Prospects by Country</u>, 1950-2000. New York, 1979.

_____. <u>Levels and Trends of Mortality since 1950</u>. New York, 1982.

Wrigley, E.A. <u>An Introduction of English Historical Demographic from the Sixteenth to the Nineteenth Centuries</u>. London: Weidenfeld and Nicolson, 1966.

World Health Organization. <u>Mortality in South and East Asia: A Review of Changing Trends and Patterns, 1950-1970</u>. Manila, 1982.

Shinsuke Morio and
Shigesato Takahashi

Mortality Trends in Japan

It was in 1872 that the first modernized vital statistics were
released by the central government in Japan. The crude death rate
in that year was 11.6 per 1,000. This rate gradually increased
thereafter exceeding 20.0 per 1,000 in 1885, and remained almost
stable until 1915. In the year 1898, the first life expectancy
was calculated from the vital statistics by the central
government. The life expectancy for males in that year was 42.8
years, and that for females was 44.3 years. The life expectancy
increased very gradually and became 44.3 years for males and 44.8
years for females in 1913.

The crude death rate temporarily exhibited an increasing
trend from 1916 to 1920, but gradually decreased by 1943. The
highest crude death rate was recorded as 27.3 in 1918, and the
lowest was 16.0 in 1941. The life expectancy rose more markedly
after 1913, and became 46.9 and 49.6 years for males and females
respectively in 1936, which were the highest figures attained
before World War II.

The decrease of the crude death rate from 1921 to 1943 and
the elongation of the life expectancy from 1898 to 1936 were
mainly brought about by the decrease of infant and child mortality
rates. The main causes of death in those days were infectious
diseases, such as pneumonia, bronchitis, tuberculosis and so
forth. The improvement in the living conditions, the development
of medical care and public health following the economic growth
since the Meiji Restoration (in 1868) reduced deaths from the
above mentioned diseases.

After World War II, the crude mortality rate continued to
decrease, and became less than 10.0 in 1951 and 7.8 in 1955.
Immediately after World War II, life expectancy was temporarily

18

shorter than that of the pre-war days, but it soon recovered, and exceeded 50 years for males and females alike. The life expectancy in 1947 was 50.1 and 54.0 years for males and females respectively and reached 63.6 and 67.8 years respectively in 1955.

The improvement of mortality conditions in the post-war period was brought about not only by the decrease of infant and child mortality as in the pre-war era but also as a result of substantial decrease of mortality among young adults. This decrease of death in infants, children, and young adults was brought about by the decrease of deaths due to infectious diseases in these age groups following the widespread use of antibiotics in medical treatment. In fact, deaths due to infectious diseases were no longer considered one of the main causes of death since 1955. Instead by 1955 the three main causes of death were cerebro-vascular diseases, malignant neoplasms and heart diseases.

However, the rate of decline in crude death rates slowed after 1955. The crude death rate was 6.3 in 1975 and 6.0 in 1982. The steepest rate of decline in crude death rate occurred mainly between 1947 and 1955. Two main reasons account for this phenomenon. Firstly, as mentioned before, infectious diseases were eliminated from the main causes of death in 1955, and cerebro-vascular diseases, malignant neoplasms, and heart diseases became the main causes of death after that time. There were antibiotics for infectious diseases, but there were no drugs especially effective for these chronic diseases. Even with new medicines, it is still considered a challenge to decrease deaths caused by these diseases. Secondly, there has been an increasing proportion of older people in the population. As the population ages, the overall ratio of deaths also increases in relation to the total population. Thus, the rate of the decline of crude death rates for the population as a whole also decreases. Life expectancy, however, which is affected mainly by mortality in infants and children but little by mortality in the older age groups has continued to improve since 1955. The life expectancy in 1975 was 71.7 for males, and 76.9 for females, and in 1982, it was 74.2 for males, and 79.7 for females. Japanese life expectancy figures are among the highest in the world (Shigetmatsu and Nagai 1982).

Mortality Rates by Sex and Age Group

It is well known that there are remarkable differences in the mortality rates between males and females, and also by age group. Generally, the mortality rate of females is lower than that of males, and the rate calculated by age group is higher among the newborn and gradually decreases, bottoming out in the early stage of teens, and then gradually increases again.

Before World War II, the mortality rate in Japan calculated by age group showed very high figures in the infant period, reaching a minimum among 10-15 years old and increasing again after aged 20. The age specific death rates therefore exhibited a typical U-shaped pattern. However, in the post-war period the curvature of the mortality rate by age has become a J-shaped pattern owing to the decrease of the mortality rate by age among infants and children compared to other age groups. This J-shaped pattern became more pronounced after 1960, and has continued until today.

The calculation of the mortality rate by sex and age group shows that the mortality rates for males are higher than that for females in all age groups, but the curvature of the mortality rate by age groups shows a similar pattern for both sexes indicating that except for the variation in levels, the schedule of deaths by age is almost similar for males and females since 1981 (World Health Organization 1982).

The age pattern of mortality has changed over time since the pre-war period and hence the age group which affected and lengthened Japan's life expectancy has also changed correspondingly. As a result, the age group which contributed most to lengthen life expectancy in Japan was the infant group in both males and females in the 1960s. However, by the early half of the 1970s, the main contributing group was the 50-64 age group for males, and the 75 and above age group in females. In the latter half of the 1970s, it was the 65-74 age group in males, and the 75 and above age group in females which accounted for the increase in the life expectancy of the population as a whole.

Differentials in Mortality among Socio-economic Sub-populations

Differentials in mortality among socio-economic sub-populations are one of the major topics in the study of demography and public health (Kitagawa 1977). Since sub-populations are characterized by socio-economic features, each sub-population tends to have some differences in their health and mortality conditions. For example, a sub-population located in a rural area may have different accessibility to medical facilities compared with a sub-population in an urban area. Obviously in Japan like in most other countries, medical facilities are more highly utilized in urban areas compared to that of rural areas. This means that

20

factors associated with medical facilities may highly correlate to the level of mortality among communities.

Even if the level of resources for medical facilities are equally available among communities, some other possible differentials still remain. For example, initial care of the sick may be taken at home. This means that the level of knowledge of ways to treat diseases would be very important among individuals or families. Some differentials in mortality could occur as a result of differential levels of knowledge of diet habits and other health practices under such circumstances. Therefore, differentials in mortality rates will appear due to factors both at the community and individual levels (Preston and Gardner 1976).

It is possible to identify some of the determining factors that affect mortality based on the analysis of differentials in mortality among socio-economic sub-populations. In this analysis, we will examine several socio-economic variables that can reasonably be related to health and mortality conditions. These include level of mother's education, urban/rural residence and occupational status.

Sources of Data

Data used in this study are from the Japanese vital statistics and the Japanese National Fertility Survey. In the Japanese vital statistics only death by occupation, marital status, and place of occurrence and cause of death are shown. Although there are some limitations in the vital statistics, it still gives us adequate information to examine the structure of mortality and the age pattern of mortality. Since the death rate by socio-economic variables is limited in the vital statistics, we have supplemented the mortality information with data collected from the National Fertility Survey.

Methodology

In this study, the authors used two different procedures for the analysis. If there are vital statistics which were tabulated by socio-economic status, we mainly used the age-standardized death rates as the measurement of mortality. In addition, because of the limitations of the vital statistics, we also analysed mortality by using the indirect estimation technique (Brass 1975).

21

The method of estimation of infant and child mortality used here is the later version of the indirect estimation technique that was developed by J. Trussell (United Nations 1983). It is possible to calculate separately by sex the probability of dying from birth to a specified age of infancy. But as the number of deaths among mothers was quite small, we have calculated child mortality, q(a), for both sexes combined. There are two types of methods available for estimating infant and child mortality. These are the estimations based on data classified by marriage duration and also by age of mothers. In this study, we used the technique based on marriage duration because the number of births and the number of deaths among younger women were very small.

Differentials in Mortality among Occupational Groups

Table 1 contains mortality data for males by major occupational categories from 1965 to 1980 in Japan. The age-standardized death rate by occupational groups is based on the age distribution of working males in 1965. It should be noted that some rates are relatively high because of the problem of small numbers in certain occupational categories, like that of managers and officials in 1975 and miners and quarrymen in 1980.

It is very clear that for all years those in non-manual occupations experience lower mortality than those in manual occupations. In 1965, the category of manager and officials showed the lowest age-standardized death rate (355.8 per 100,000 population) compared to that of other occupational categories in the same year. This was followed by the occupational group of service workers (409.2). In contrast, the occupation of miners and quarrymen showed the highest rate; about three times higher than that for the occupation category of managers and officials. The mortality ratio between the category of miners and quarrymen and that of managers and officials remained quite consistent over the years except for 1980. The very high standardized death rate for the category miners and quarrymen in 1980 is probably due to the problem of small numbers. The same problem applies to the category of managers and officials in 1975 where an abnormally high rate was shown for that year. If the age-standardized death rate was calculated by another procedure, the age-standardized death rate for managers and officials in 1975 would have been about 270 per 100,000 population rather than 730.1.

It can be concluded that differentials in mortality among occupational groups still exist in Japan, even if the level of age-standardized death rate substantially declined from high to low in the last 15 years. The categories of occupations that show

a higher age-standardized death rate are identical to specific
industrial sectors. These are the sectors of primary industry and
secondary industry. It is very clear that occupational hazards
tend to be higher in industrial sectors as compared to the other
sectors. However, the distribution of population among
occupations has been changed throughout the period. Therefore,
the change of overall age-standardized death rate may be
attributed in part to the changes in the occupational structure in
Japan.

TABLE 1
Age-standardized Death Rate by Occupation

Occupational Categories	Age-standardized Death Rate			
	1965	1970	1975	1980
Total working population	639.3	482.7	387.2	340.4
Professional and technical	528.9	424.2	354.5	371.3
Managers and officials	355.8	281.7	730.1	237.0
Clerical	463.2	432.4	338.2	276.3
Sales	552.6	537.7	441.1	372.6
Farmers, lumbermen and fishermen	802.4	621.6	526.7	465.0
Miners and quarrymen	1152.0	949.9	734.9	1548.9
Transport and communications	657.4	527.6	431.7	418.5
Craftsmen, productions process workers and labourers	567.1	400.8	315.5	239.2
Service workers	409.2	499.9	369.7	471.4
Protective service workers	-	276.6	238.3	207.9

SOURCE: Ministry of Health and Welfare, Vital Statistics by Occupation
and Industry, Special Report on Vital Statistics, various years.

It is noted that there has been an increase in the proportion
of people in occupations with lower age-standardized death rates
in later years compared with that for the occupations with
relatively higher rates. The percentage of population for the
category of professional and technical workers increased from 5.5
per cent in 1965 to 8.6 per cent in 1980. The proportion of
population for the category of managers and officials also
increased from 13.1 per cent in 1965 to 16.5 per cent in 1980. In
contrast, the proportion of population in the occupations of
farmers, lumbermen and fishermen decreased from 24.5 per cent in
1965 to 10.8 per cent in 1980. Therefore, it can be stated that

23

the rapid decline of overall age-standardized death rate during the last 15 years is attributable to the improvement in mortality conditions as well as changes in the occupational structure in Japan.

The age-specific death rates by various causes of death are available from vital statistics. The classification of causes of death used here is according to the International Classification of Diseases. Here we used four leading causes of death based on the B-Lists of the Seventh and Eighth Revisions of the International Lists of Diseases and Causes of Death (World Health Organization 1965). The causes of death in this study are used here as follows:

(1) Cerebro-vascular Diseases; B5, and B6

(2) Malignant neoplasms; B19

(3) Heart diseases; B26, B28-29

(4) Accidents; BE47-49

Table 2 shows the age-standardized death rates for males by leading causes of death and by occupation for selected years.

The age-standardized death rate among these four causes varies widely with occupational categories. In particular, there are substantial differences in the age-standardized death rate from accidents between those in lower status occupations and those in higher status occupations. Those in the category of managers and officials for example, have the lowest age-standardized death rate from accidents (22.2) in 1970, as compared to that of the category of miners and quarrymen (329.9). The age-standardized death rate from accidents is almost 15 times larger than that for the category of managers and officials. In 1975, the same tendency can be seen. The age-standardized death rate from accident for the category of miners and quarrymen exceeds that for professionals and technicians by 9 times.

Relatively high death rates from accidents can also be found in the occupations of farmers, transport, and communications. The age-standardized death rate from accidents for these occupations is relatively higher than that for the working population as a whole for all years, but the differentials of age-standardized death rate are more pronounced in the earlier years than in the later years.

It can be concluded that differentials in the age-standardized death rate from accidents among occupations still exist in Japan, but the overall level of mortality from this cause

TABLE 2

Age-standardized Death Rate from Various Causes of Death by Occupation, Selected Years

Occupational Categories	Causes of Death											
	Malignant neoplasms			Heart diseases			Cerebro-vascular diseases			Accidents		
	1970	1975	1980	1970	1975	1980	1970	1975	1980	1970	1975	1980
Total working population	107.4	99.9	102.2	53.4	47.4	51.1	110.4	77.2	57.1	70.5	47.2	37.9
Professional and technical	102.5	95.6	121.3	55.5	50.5	62.1	90.1	67.3	59.5	46.2	27.9	25.5
Managers and officials	84.3	88.4	84.7	34.6	35.4	37.2	51.5	44.1	34.3	22.2	183.7	13.2
Clerical	123.4	107.0	100.1	52.0	43.6	42.4	78.1	54.3	39.0	45.1	30.6	22.7
Sales	131.9	123.7	119.0	65.6	58.9	57.0	115.7	86.4	62.4	57.6	37.9	29.7
Farmers, lumbermen and fishermen	122.4	116.4	117.6	63.7	58.6	65.0	152.8	110.6	77.1	93.1	78.0	75.4
Miners and quarrymen	155.0	143.2	393.2	59.8	49.0	219.8	170.0	102.6	245.2	329.9	251.3	260.3
Transport and communications	126.4	108.9	132.3	49.9	46.6	53.6	99.3	77.4	67.0	120.4	74.4	57.5
Craftsmen, production process workers and labourers	85.2	79.2	67.6	40.6	35.6	34.1	84.2	60.2	38.0	79.6	50.3	37.0
Service workers	108.9	88.8	136.7	59.3	48.8	36.3	110.4	72.2	80.7	59.0	39.8	40.5
Protective service workers	72.2	73.4	65.5	35.2	31.3	36.3	53.2	43.1	32.9	42.8	29.8	23.5

SOURCE: Ministry of Health and Welfare, Vital Statistics by Occupation and Industry, Special Report of Vital Statistics, various years.

has declined sharply. This means that while the hazardous factors among occupations were reduced from 1970 to 1980 there has still been not much reduction of differentials in occupation mortality from accidents.

Death from cerebro-vascular diseases also shows significant differences among occupations. The ratio of death rate from cerebro-vascular diseases between high status occupations to low status occupations was about 3.3 in 1970 and 2.6 in 1975. Its ratio in 1980 was 7.5 but this level of ratio can be inaccurate because of the small number of cases in the occupation category of miners and quarrymen. The differentials in cerebro-vascular diseases among occupations is suspected to have been reduced from 1970 to 1980.

The causes of death from malignant neoplasms and from heart diseases show a different tendency compared with the causes of death from cerebro-vascular diseases and accidents. These two causes of death have relatively small differentials among occupations, and the changes of age-standardized death rates from these causes of death from 1970 to 1980 were quite small. The ratio of deaths from malignant neoplasms and heart diseases between high to low occupational status was 2.1 for malignant neoplasms and 1.7 for heart diseases in 1970. In 1975, its ratio was shown as 2.0 for the malignant neoplasms and 1.9 for heart diseases. In 1980, there was again a problem of "small number of cases", and the actual ratio is suspected to be similar to that of 1975.

The general conclusion is that despite the overall reduction in mortality, substantial mortality differentials among occupational groups especially from deaths caused by accidents and cerebro-vascular diseases continue to exist.

Regional Differences in Japanese Mortality

Regional differences in mortality still exist in Japan. Table 3 shows age-standardized death rates from selected causes of death by the urban/rural residents between 1965 and 1980. In this table, the categories for the urban/rural residents are defined as follows: (1) urban residents are those living in cities, and (2) rural residents are those living outside of city limits.

The differentials in mortality between urban and rural residents can be seen over the entire period. The overall ratio in age-standardized death rate between rural and urban residents is 1.08 in 1965, 1.08 in 1970, 1.05 in 1975, and 1.03 in 1980. It

26

TABLE 3

Age-standardized Death Rate from Various Causes of Death, Selected Years

Age-standardized Death Rate

Causes of Death	1965			1970			1975			1980		
	Urban (1)	Rural (2)	Ratio (2)/(1)	Urban (1)	Rural (2)	Ratio (2)/(1)	Urban (1)	Rural (2)	Ratio (2)/(1)	Urban (1)	Rural (2)	Ratio (2)/(1)
All causes	651.9	702.3	1.08	569.9	614.5	1.08	476.6	501.3	1.05	409.9	423.6	1.03
Cerebro-vascular diseases	157.8	172.2	1.09	125.5	141.6	1.13	111.2	121.1	1.09	84.1	90.8	1.08
Malignant neoplasms	104.1	97.3	0.94	90.1	81.8	0.91	97.9	91.9	0.94	98.9	91.7	0.92
Heart diseases	70.3	73.9	1.05	69.1	70.5	1.02	65.7	65.8	1.00	66.6	67.3	1.01
Accidents	49.0	62.6	1.28	28.0	34.6	1.24	39.5	53.5	1.35	33.1	45.7	1.38

SOURCE: Ministry of Health and Welfare, Vital Statistics -- Special Issue for the Regional Report for the Vital Statistics, various years.

is observed that the degree of differentials in mortality changed very little from 1965 to 1980. However, the levels of age-standardized death rate decline substantially in both the urban and rural areas.

It is possible to identify from the figures in Table 3 differentials in causes of death between urban and rural residents which are indicative of the social, economic, and environmental differences between regions. For example, the cerebro-vascular diseases are highly correlated with air temperature and dietary habits. Infectious diseases are highly associated with the inferior sanitation and poor water systems.

Four leading causes of death are shown in Table 3. For the cerebro-vascular diseases, the ratio of deaths between rural and urban residents as in 1965 shows 1.09, similar to the ratio for all causes. The ratio over the years also appear to be fairly stable. A similarly stable pattern of differentials appears also for deaths caused by malignant neoplasms and heart diseases. Only for deaths through accidents are higher ratios between rural and urban residents found.

Indirect Estimates of Child Mortality

Using the data from National Fertility Survey for the urban/rural residents and Brass's technique of indirect estimation it is possible to estimate child mortality by rural/urban residence. The definition of rural/urban residence here differs from the preceding definition. The category of urban in the Eighth National Fertility Survey adopts the definition used in the Japanese Census. In the Japanese Census, regional characteristics are represented by the DID index (Densely Inhabited District). DID is defined as an area within a <u>shi</u> (city), <u>machi</u> (town) or <u>mura</u> (village) that is composed of a group of contiguous enumerated districts each of which has a population density of about 4,000 inhabitants or more per km^2. In this analysis, therefore, urban residents are those who are living in the DID areas, and rural residents are those who live in non-DID areas.

In Table 4, the estimated child mortality, q(a), of the rural/urban residents is shown. The estimated values for all can be compared with the life table's q(a). The average value of the life table's probability of dying from birth to aged 2 was about 0.0100 during the decade from 1970 for both males and females. Judging from the estimated value of 0.0269, it was an over-estimation. But q(3) and q(5) were estimated fairly well. The

28

q(3) and q(5) values in the official life tables were 0.0103 and 0.0113.

The probabilities of dying from birth to any subsequent age indicate higher values for non-DID areas. It means that children born in urban areas tend to have a smaller risk of dying compared with those born in rural areas. However, the ratios are less than 1.3 for all probabilities above q(2). This means that the differentials in childhood mortality between the rural/urban residents are not large. However, differentials in mortality during childhood still exist in Japan.

Mortality Differentials by Education

There is no doubt that changes of socio-economic conditions in society influence the level of mortality. In this sense, the differentials in mortality among sub-populations also changed due to changes in the socio-economic characteristics of the sub-populations. Mother's education may be considered one of the most important factors for the child mortality because the knowledge of primary health care is highly correlated with child mortality. For example, if the sanitation and medical facilities are highly utilized in a community, the differences in mortality among individuals may be related to the level of mother's knowledge of primary health care. Therefore, some of the differentials in mortality can be explained by the level of mother's education. In this section, the change in childhood mortality differentials by education will be analysed using data from the Second, Sixth and Eighth National Fertility Surveys (NFS).

TABLE 4
**Estimate of Child Mortality, q(a), by Rural/Urban Residence
based on the Eighth National Fertility Survey Data**

| q(a) | Total | Place of Residence | | Ratio (1)/(2) |
		Non-DID area (1)	DID area (2)	
q(2)	0.0269	0.0310	0.0238	1.30
q(3)	0.0134	0.0145	0.0127	1.14
q(5)	0.0199	0.0223	0.0182	1.23
q(10)	0.0189	0.0205	0.0176	1.16
q(15)	0.0359	0.0371	0.0344	1.08

29

The definitions of the categories of mother's education are as follows: (1) "lower" -- for mothers who did not obtain a senior high school education but had graduated from junior high school; (2) "higher" -- for mothers who graduated from senior high school and above.

Table 5 shows the child mortality differentials by mother's education based on the 1952 (Second) National Fertility Survey data.

The estimated probability of dying from birth to aged 2 is 0.0457, 0.0650 from birth to aged 3, 0.0905 from birth to aged 5, and 0.1156 from birth to aged 10. The results of this estimation compare fairly well with the life table's probabilities q(a). The 1952 life table's values of q(2) are 0.0562 for both sexes, 0.627 for q(3) and 0.0887 for q(4). The rates between those observed from the life table and from estimation are not very different.

The results show a negative relationship between mother's and child mortality, except for q(3). The ratios observed area 1.28 for q(2), 0.99 for q(3), 1.13 for q(5) and 1.14 for q(10). The lower ratio for q(3) requires further investigation before we can speculate on the reason for this discrepancy. In any case, the basic tendency is that there is a marked childhood mortality differential by mother's education.

TABLE 5

Estimate of Child Mortality, q(a), by the Mother's Educational Qualification, based on the Second National Fertility Survey Data

| q(a) | Total | Educational Group | | Ratio (1)/(2) |
		Lower (1)	Higher (2)	
q(2)	0.0457	0.0477	0.0372	1.28
⌐(3)	0.0650	0.0641	0.0647	0.99
q(5)	0.0905	0.0927	0.0815	1.13
q(10)	0.1156	0.1187	0.1038	1.14
q(15)	0.1294	0.1363	0.0894	1.52
q(20)	0.1843	0.1885	0.1499	1.25

NOTE: Definitions of categories for educational groups are as follows:

"Lower" : the length of schooling in under 10 years
"Higher": the length of schooling in 10 years or more

30

The result of the estimation based on the 1972 (Sixth) Fertility Survey also showed basically the same tendency (see Table 6).

All of the values for q(a) are relatively low for both groups compared with the q(a) values estimated from the 1952 Fertility Survey. It is obvious that Japanese infant and child mortality has declined rapidly after World War II. However, childhood mortality differentials between the two educational categories can still be observed. The ratios exceeded 1.0 for all values of q(a) from birth. The ratios are also higher for the younger ages than for the older ages. Also, comparison of the ratios between 1952 and 1972 show that the ratios for the younger ages are larger for the latter period than for the former.

In Table 7, the values of q(a) are estimated from the 1982 (Eighth) National Fertility Survey.

Again the 1982 NFS estimates for q(a), except for the values of q(2), are very close to the values from the 1982 life tables. This exception might again be due to the problem of small samples. The number of babies' death from the marriage duration of 0 to 4 is only 15, whereas the number of births for the same duration was 75. In any case, differentials in childhood mortality between the two educational groups continue to exist even in this latest National Fertility Survey.

TABLE 6

Estimate of Child Mortality, q(a), by the Mother's Educational Group, based on the Sixth National Fertility Survey Data

| q(a) | Total | Educational Group | | Ratio (1)/(2) |
		Lower (1)	Higher (2)	
q(2)	0.0338	0.0479	0.0266	1.80
q(3)	0.0371	0.0474	0.0276	1.72
q(5)	0.0474	0.0507	0.0443	1.14
q(10)	0.0495	0.0511	0.0476	1.07
q(15)	0.0615	0.0620	0.0587	1.06

NOTE: Category of education defined as follows:

"Lower" : for the mothers who graduated junior high school
"Higher": for the mothers who graduated senior high school and above.

31

It is possible to say that since sanitation and medical facilities are highly utilized in Japan, the mothers' knowledge about how to avoid the risks of disease has become much more important. This is one of the main reasons why such differentials in mortality persists. But, of course, there are other factors including the close association between mother's education and income, and mother's education and residence. The women with higher education tend to have higher income, and therefore they have more access to medical facilities compared to those with lower education and lower income. Higher educational attainment is also related to place of residence. Higher education rates in urban areas are relatively high compared to that of rural areas. Hence women with higher education also tend to live in areas with highly developed medical and sanitary facilities.

TABLE 7
Estimate of Child Mortality, q(a), by the Mother's Educational Group, based on the Eighth National Fertility Survey Data

| q(a) | Total | Educational Group | | Ratio (1)/(2) |
		Lower (1)	Higher (2)	
q(2)	0.0269	0.0441	0.0235	1.88
q(3)	0.0134	0.0186	0.0128	1.45
q(5)	0.0199	0.0191	0.0198	0.96
q(10)	0.0189	0.0201	0.0176	1.14
q(15)	0.0359	0.0397	0.0303	1.31

Multivariate Analysis of Mortality Differentials

Until recent years, various two-variable statistical methods had been used to show causal associations in health and demographic events (Rosenwaike et al. 1980). However, with the progress of knowledge in the areas of public health, demography and statistical knowledge, these statistical methods have come to be regarded as unsatisfactory for the study of causal associations. Instead of two-variable methods, multivariate analyses have come to be utilized in attempting to isolate more precisely the relationships between variables (Wingard et al. 1982; Iwamoto et al. 1981). The present studies are the first to utilize multivariate analysis to examine the relationship between infant mortality and socio-economic factors.

The main purpose of the study is to identify those factors in social life that affect infant mortality for the decade 1970-80.

The variables used in the study based on government statistics inlcude:

1. INFANT   -- infant mortality rate;

2. MEANTMP   -- yearly mean air temperature;

3. LOWTMP   -- lowest air temperature;

4. POPUL   -- population per square kilometre of inhabitable area;

5. DID   -- population density in densely inhabited districts;

6. JUVENIL   -- ratio of the juvenile population;

7. AGEING   -- ageing index;

8. BIRTH   -- crude birth rate;

9. WATER   -- ratio of population covered by a water supply system;

10. DIFFUSE   -- diffusion rate;

11. SEWAGE   -- ratio of population benefiting from the sewer system;

12. INSTITUTE -- medical institutions per 100,000 persons;

13. BED   -- beds per 100,000 persons;

14. PHYSICIAN -- physicians per 100,000 persons;

15. NURSE   -- clinical nurses and assistant clinical nurses per 100,000 persons;

16. CENTRE   -- health centres per 100,000 persons;

17. HNURSE   -- public health nurses per 100,000 persons;

18. EMRGNCY   -- emergency hospitals and general clinics per 100,000 persons;

19. STAY   -- average days of stay of hospitalized patients;

20. INSPECT   -- ratio of persons inspected by public health
               officials for geriatric diseases;

21. BENEFIT   -- rate of persons issued old-age medical
               beneficiaries certificates;

22. BABY   -- ratio of babies 2,500g or less among all
               live births;

23. WEIGHT   -- mean weight of live births;

24. MEDBTH   -- ratio of births in medical institutions
               among all live births;

25. MOTHER   -- mean age of mothers at delivery;

26. THIRD   -- ratio of third births or over among all
               live births;

27. WORK   -- rate of working women in the 20-44 years
               age category;

28. INCOME   -- prefectural per capita income;

29. LIVEXP   -- monthly living expenditure per worker's
               household;

30. MEDEXP   -- monthly medical care expenditure per
               worker's household;

31. RATEXP   -- ratio of medical care in monthly living
               expenditure;

32. NONPRI   -- ratio of persons employed in non-primary
               industries;

33. TERTIA   -- ratio of persons employed in tertiary
               industry;

34. HIGHSCL   -- percentage of persons whose last completed
               educational level was senior high school
               and above;

35. JUNRCOL   -- ratio of persons whose last completed
               educational level was junior college,
               technical college and above;

36. WHIGHSCH   -- ratio of women whose last completed
               educational level was senior high school
               and above;

34

37. WJUNRCOL -- ratio of women whose last completed
                educational level was junior college,
                technical college and above;

38. ADVANCE   -- ratio of senior high school graduates
                following an advanced course;

39. NUCLEI   -- ratio of nuclear households;

40. GRR   -- gross reproduction rate;

41. NRR   -- net reproduction rate;

All data were collected by the prefectural governments in
1970, 1975 and 1980. However, the 1970 data labelled as BENEFIT,
INCOME, LIVEXP, MEDEXP, and RATEXP were not available because
these were not collected at that time.

Methodology

In this study, hierarchical regression analysis and the stepwise
regression analysis were utilized. As a first step, the
independent variables were divided into groups. They were:
(1) the natural environment factors group, (2) the demographic
factors group, (3) environment hygiene factors group, (4) public
health factors group, (5) infant health factors group,
(6) economic factors group, (7) social factors group and
(8) reproduction factors group. The dependent variables were
infant mortality rate and crude death rate.

The natural environment factors group included MEANTMP and
LOWTMP. The demographic factors group included POPUL, DID,
JUVENIL, AGEING and BIRTH. The environment hygiene factors group
included WATER, DIFFUSE, and SEWAGE. The public health factors
group included INSTITUTE, BED, PHYSICIAN, NURSE, CENTRE, HNURSE,
EMRGNCY, STAY, INSPECT and BENEFIT. The infant health factors
group included BABY, WEIGHT, MEDBTH, MOTHER, THIRD and WORK. The
economic factors group included NONPRI, TERTIA, HIGHSCL, JUNRCOL,
WHIGHSCL, WJUNRCOL, ADVANCE and NUCLEI. The reproduction factors
group included GRR and NRR.

Among the various variables, one predictor variable which
showed the strongest correlation (zero-order correlation)
coefficient with infant mortality (INFANT) was selected as the
representative variable of the group. Eight predictor variables
were selected as the representative variables of the eight groups.

35

Then, hierarchical regression analysis was applied in order to estimate the relative importance of the eight selected factors in affecting infant mortality.

Finally, the stepwise regression was also applied to identify which among the eight factors have the greatest explanatory power for infant mortality in Japan. In order to satisfy the requirements of stepwise regression five principal assumptions (univariate randomness, independence, linearity, homoscedasticity, and normal distribution) were tested by graphical analysis of residuals. The probability 0.05 was used to assess the partial F statistic for each variable present in the regression model. Interactions among representative variables were ignored in order to simplify the regression model. Before carrying out the analysis, the data were also checked by examining the means, standard deviations, and maximums and minimums.

Findings

The number of prefectures included in the study was 46 in 1970, 47 in 1975, and 47 in 1980 (data from 1970 do not cover Okinawa Prefecture). Table 8 shows the means, standard deviations, minimums, and maximums of infant mortality for 1970, 1975 and 1980. Okayama Prefecture showed the lowest infant mortality rate (10.830) and Iwate Prefecture the maximum (18.390) in 1970. Fukuoka Prefecture and Yamanashi Prefecture registered the lowest infant mortality rate and Kagawa Prefecture and Shimane Prefecture the highest in 1975 and 1980 respectively. The mean infant mortality rate in 1980 was 54.3 per cent of the 1970 figure. The standard deviation and range of infant mortality decreased between 1970 and 1980. These changes may indicate not only an improvement of many of the conditions which were associated with infant

TABLE 8

Mean and Standard Deviation of Infant Mortality Rate in 1970, 1975, 1980

	1970	1975	1980
Mean	14.223	10.548	7.722
S.D.	1.926	1.416	0.947
Mini.	10.830	7.993	5.315
Max.	18.390	13.772	9.539

mortality, but also a narrowing of the differences of these conditions among prefectures over time.

Means, standard deviations, minimums, and maximums of the 40 predictor variables were shown in Table 9. Means of MEANTMP, LOWTMP, JUVENIL, INSTITUTE, CENTRE, EMRGNCY, STAY, BENEFIT, WEIGHT, MOTHER, THIRD, WORK, RATEXP, ADVANCE, and NUCLEI were fairly stable in 1970, 1975 and 1980. Means of POPUL, DID, AGEING, WATER, DIFFUSE, SEWAGE, BED, PHYSICIAN, NURSE, HNURSE, INSPECT, MEDBTH, INCOME, LIVEXP, MEDEXP, NONPRI, TERTIA, HIGHSCH, and JUNRCOL increased from 1970 to 1980. And means of BIRTH, BABY, WHIGHSCL, WJUNRCOL, GRR, and NRR also increased from 1970 to 1980.

In order to select predictor variables to enter the hierarchical regression analysis and the stepwise regression, correlation coefficients between INFANT and 40 predictor variables were calculated for each year (see Appendices 1-22). In 1970, INFANT had the strongest correlation with MEANTMP ($r = 0.460$) in the natural environment factors group, JUVENIL ($r = 0.848$) in the demographic factors group, STAY ($r = 0.702$) in the public health factors group, BABY ($r = 0.805$) in the infant health factors group, INCOME ($r = -0.901$) in the economic factors group, NUCLEI ($r = 0.521$) in the social factors group, and GRR ($r = 0.696$) in the reproduction factors group, DIFFUSE (-0.266) in the environment hygiene factors group was not significant at the 0.05 level (Table 10).

In 1975, INFANT had the strongest correlation with DID ($r = -0.448$) in the demographic factors group, WATER ($r = -0.512$) in the environment hygiene factors group, STAY ($r = 0.327$) in the public health factors group, MOTHER ($r = -0.373$) in the infant health factors group, INCOME ($r = -0.572$) in the economic factors group, NONPRI ($r = -0.544$) in the social factors group, and GRR ($r = 0.279$) in the reproduction factors group. MEAN (-0.056) in the natural environment factors group was not significant at the 0.05 level (Table 10).

In 1980, INFANT had the strongest correlation with DID ($r = -0.377$) in the demographic factors group, WATER ($r= -0.563$) in the environment hygiene factors group, HNURSE ($r = 0.319$) in the public health factors group, MEDBTH ($r = -0.365$) in the infant health factors group, INCOME ($r = -0.466$) in the economic factors group, NONPRI ($r = -0.594$) in the social factors group and GRR ($r = 0.251$) in the reproduction factors group (Table 3). Again there was no variable in the natural environment factors which had a significant correlation with INFANT (Table 10).

The hierarchical regression analysis of infant mortality in 1970 showed that prefectural per capita income (INCOME) and

TABLE 9
Means of 40 Predictor Variables in 1970, 1975, 1980

Groups	Variables	1970	1975	1980
Natural environment factors	MEANTMP	13.983	14.615	14.096
	LOWTMP	-2.028	-0.649	-0.911
Demographic factors	POPUL	1179.6	1221.2	1287.5
	DID	39.524	42.647	45.389
	JUVENIL	35.694	35.952	34.706
	AGEING	33.769	38.139	45.084
	BIRTH	17.335	16.540	13.600
Environment hygiene factors	WATER	72.938	83.121	88.172
	DIFFUSE	10.974	13.968	17.384
	SEWAGE	47.604	71.834	80.123
Public health factors	INSTITUTE	73.054	71.824	73.207
	BED	1367.1	1470.2	1613.1
	PHYSICIAN	108.24	111.45	124.92
	NURSE	279.61	346.85	450.48
	CENTRE	0.903	0.859	0.818
	HNURSE	16.605	17.633	18.578
	EMRGNCY	4.371	4.265	4.447
	STAY	45.460	45.526	46.603
	INSPECT	8.363	8.7874	10.295
	BENEFIT	-	5.1438	6.070
Infant health factors	BABY	6.825	5.850	5.656
	WEIGHT	3.179	3.205	3.189
	MEDBTH	83.654	91.038	95.566
	MOTHER	27.322	27.213	27.942
	THIRD	17.761	16.228	18.766
	WORK	62.693	57.487	60.266
Economic factors	INCOME	-0.733	0.000	0.242
	LIVEXP	-	12.020	12.395
	MEDEXP	-	8.280	8.611
	RATEXP	-	2.32	2.23
Social factors	NONPRI	73.935	80.912	84.942
	TERTIA	43.533	49.211	52.834
	HIGHSCL	21.017	24.311	27.905
	JUNRCOL	2.409	3.129	3.841
	WHIGHSCL	10.983	9.162	7.662
	WJUNRCOL	2.346	1.562	0.880
	ADVANCE	25.765	32.766	30.404
	NUCLEI	60.451	61.075	60.608
Reproduction factors	GRR	1.011	0.974	0.889
	NRR	0.982	0.953	0.874

- : no datum

TABLE 10

Correlation Coefficients between Infant Mortality Rate (1970, 1975, 1980)
and Predictor Variables in 1970, 1975, 1980

Groups	1970	1975	1980
Natural environment factors	0.460* (MEANTMP)	-0.056 (MEANTMP)	-0.217 (LOWTMP)
Demographic factors	0.848* (JUVENIL)	-0.448* (DID)	-0.377* (DID)
Environment hygiene factors	-0.226 (DIFFUSE)	-0.512* (WATER)	-0.563* (WATER)
Public health factors	0.702* (STAY)	0.327* (STAY)	0.319* (HNURSE)
Infant health factors	0.805* (BABY)	-0.373* (MOTHER)	-0.365* (MEDBTH)
Economic factors	-0.901* (INCOME)	-0.572* (INCOME)	-0.466* (INCOME)
Social factors	0.521* (NUCLEI)	-0.544* (NONPRI)	-0.594* (NONPRI)
Reproduction factors	0.696* (GRR)	0.279* (GRR)	0.251* (GRR)

* Significant at 0.05 level.

yearly mean air temperature (MEANTMP) had a negative relationship with infant mortality, while ratio of babies 2,500g or less among all live births (BABY), and ratio of juvenile population (JUVENIL) had a positive relationship. Based on the R^2 values, economic factors (INCOME in this case) seemed to have the strongest effect on infant mortality. R^2 increment after the inclusion of the other variables was only less than 10 per cent of the total variance (Table 11).

The hierarchical regression analysis of infant mortality in 1975 showed that prefectural per capita income (INCOME), ratio of population covered by a water supply system (WATER), mean age of mothers at delivery (MOTHER), and ratio of persons employed in non-primary industries (NONPRI) had a negative relationship with infant mortality, while ratio of population in densely inhabited districts (DID) and gross reproduction rate (GRR) had a positive relationship. INCOME again appeared to have the strongest impact on infant mortality (Table 12).

The hierarchical regression analysis of infant mortality in 1980 showed that ratio of persons employed in non-primary industries (NONPRI), ratio of population covered by a water system (WATER), ratio of births in medical institutions among all live births (MEDBTH), public health nurses per 100,000 population (HNURSE), and prefectural per capita income (INCOME) had a negative relationship with infant mortality, while ratio of population in densely inhabited districts (DID) and gross

TABLE 11

Hierarchical Regression Analysis of Infant Mortality Rate, 1970

Independent Variables	Step			
	1	2	3	4
	Beta Coefficients			
INCOME	-0.777	-0.694	-0.602	-0.509
BABY		0.190	0.323	0.319
MEANTMP			-0.189	-0.191
JUVENIL				0.131
R^2	0.777	0.796	0.809	0.814

All beta coefficients were significant at 0.05 level.

reproduction rate (GRR) had a positive relationship. According to the value of R^2 social factors R-square (NONPRI in this case) might be most salient in explaining infant mortality rate in 1980 (Table 13).

TABLE 12
Hierarchical Regression Analysis of Infant Mortality Rate, 1975

Independent Variables	Step					
	1	2	3	4	5	6
	Beta Coefficients					
INCOME	-0.572	-0.414	-0.403	-0.585	-0.497	-0.376
WATER		-0.274	-0.211	-0.288	-0.321	-0.268
MOTHER			-0.154	-0.221	-0.251	-0.265
DID				0.315	0.323	0.391
GRR					0.125	0.167
NONPRI						-0.216
R^2	0.572	0.614	0.629	0.650	0.658	0.663

All beta coefficients were significant at 0.05 level.

TABLE 13
Hierarchical Regression Analysis of Infant Mortality Rate, 1980

Independent Variables	Step						
	1	2	3	4	5	6	7
	Beta Coefficients						
NONPRI	-0.594	-0.391	-0.672	-0.623	-0.691	-0.671	-0.629
WATER		-0.292	-0.325	-0.299	-0.287	-0.308	-0.318
DID			0.372	0.342	0.324	0.357	0.364
MEDBTH				-0.130	-0.110	-0.101	-0.096
HNURSE					-0.093	-0.086	-0.079
GRR						0.061	0.044
INCOME							-0.058
R^2	0.594	0.630	0.665	0.676	0.678	0.680	0.681

All beta coefficients were significant at 0.05 level.

41

Stepwise Regression Analysis

The selected regression model using the stepwise regression analysis on INFANT for 1970 were the following seven representative variables: MEANTMP, JUVENIL, STAY, BABY, INCOME, NUCLEI, and GRR.

The Stepwise Regression analysis for 1970 indicated that two main factors affected the infant mortality rate (see Table 14). They were INCOME (prefectural income per capita) and BABY (rate of babies of 2,500g or less among all live births). The higher INCOME became the lower INFANT and the higher BABY became the higher INFANT. The total R^2 was 63.3 per cent and the F statistic for the null hypothesis of no significant "linear" regression was 37.142 and was highly significant ($p < 0.01$).

The selected regression model using stepwise regression analysis on INFANT for 1975 were the following seven representative variables: DID, WATER, STAY, MOTHER, INCOME, NONPRI, AND GRR.

The regression model indicated that WATER (ratio of population covered by water supply system), MOTHER (mean age of mother at delivery) and INCOME (prefectural per capita income)

TABLE 14
Stepwise Regression Results and Analysis of Variance in 1970

Variables	Coefficient	Std. Error	Beta Coefficient
Constant	4.686		
BABY	0.671	0.362	0.190
INCOME	-6.767	1.003	-0.694

Source	d.f.	S.S.	M.S.	F-Ratio	R-Square
Regression	2	108.072	54.036	37.142**	0.633
Error	43	62.558	1.455		
Total	45	170.630			

** $p < 0.01$

affected infant mortality (see Table 15). All these three factors had a negative relationship with infant mortality. Total variance explained by all the variables were 39.6 per cent.

For 1980, the stepwise regression model used the following seven representative variables: DID, WATER, HNURSE, MEDBTH, INCOME, NONPRI, and GRR.

The regression model indicated that DID, WATER and NONPRI had the strongest influence on infant mortality rate (see Table 16.) Among these three variables DID had a positive relationship with infant mortality while INCOME and WATER had a negative relationship. The total variance explained by the model was 44.2 per cent and the partial F was significant at the 0.01 level.

The findings indicate that improvement in socio-economic conditions did have an impact on infant mortality. A comparison among the regression models in 1970, 1975 and 1980 indicated that (1) the economic factor was a major factor affecting INFANT in 1970 and 1975, but the extent of its effect decreased from 1970 to 1975. By 1980 it was no longer so significant; (2) the infant health factor was significant for INFANT in 1970 and 1975, but not

TABLE 15
Stepwise Regression Results and Analysis of Variance in 1975

Variables	Coefficient	Std. Error	Beta Coefficient
Constant	28.116		
WATER	-0.030	0.022	-0.211
MOTHER	-0.553	0.479	-0.154
INCOME	-4.364	1.574	-0.403

Source	d.f.	S.S.	M.S.	F-Ratio	R-Square
Regression	3	37.290	12.430	9.379[**]	0.396
Error	43	56.987	1.325		
Total	46	94.277			

[**] $p < 0.01$

significant in 1980; (3) the environment factor became significant for INFANT in 1975 and 1980; (4) the increase in population density became of positive significance (increasing INFANT) in 1980; and (5) infant mortality in 1980 was less affected by factors in social life and became more stable than in former years.

TABLE 16
Stepwise Regression Results and Analysis of Variance in 1980

Variables	Coefficient	Std. Error	Beta Coefficient
Constant	18.079		
DID	0.019	0.010	0.372
WATER	-0.038	0.019	-0.325
NONPRI	-0.092	0.030	-0.672

Source	d.f.	S.S.	M.S.	F-Ratio	R-Square
Regression	3	18.240	6.080	11.367**	0.442
Error	43	23.000	0.535		
Total	45	41.240			

** $p < 0.01$

Conclusion

This study utilized two types of analyses; indirect estimation method as exemplified by the Trussell method, and multivariate analysis. The data base on which these two types of analyses were based are different. In the Trussell analysis, the data utilized were individual level data. The collected data covered only 0.05 per cent of all couples in Japan. But in the multivariate analysis, the data were prefectural level data. This method may suffer from problems of ecological fallacy. Hence caution must be taken when interpreting the results. These differences in the data base may sometimes produce inconsistency or contradiction in the results of the two analyses. In this study, too, there are also a few inconsistencies or contradictions. This suggests that

44

more studies utilizing both individual level data and prefectural level data should be done in order to provide a better understanding of the mortality pattern in Japan.

The conclusions which can be drawn from the Trussell analysis are:

1. People in the non-manual occupations tend to experience a lower age-standardized death rate than those in the manual group in 1965, 1975 and 1980.

2. The rapid decline of overall age-standardized death rate during the last 15 years could be attributed jointly to an improvement in mortality as well as to changes in the occupational structure in Japan. A lesser proportion of the population is in manual occupations today than 15 years ago.

3. Differentials in age-standardized death rate from accidents among occupations still exist in Japan in 1980, but the level of mortality has declined sharply.

4. There are differentials in child mortality rate by mothers' education 1952, 1972 and 1982; the more highly educated mothers tended to have relatively lower child mortality, and the educational factor is relatively more important today than in the past.

The conclusions drawn from the multivariate analysis are:

1. The effect of prefectural per capita income on infant mortality rate decreased from 1970 to 1975, and became relatively unimportant in 1980.

2. The effect of life style (indicated by ratio of persons employed in non-primary industries in this analysis) became the main factor affecting infant mortality rate in 1980.

3. The type of water supply system, which is indicative of environmental hygiene, was still an important factor for infant mortality rate today.

4. The mean age of mothers at delivery and the birth of babies were important factors in 1970 and 1975. This might suggest that the standard of medication in the 1970s was still relatively low in some parts of Japan such that the poor physical condition of babies often resulted in death.

45

5. Social factors declined in importance in explaining differentials in infant mortality over the period from 1970 to 1980. This is so because infant mortality has already reached a very low and stable level in the recent period. Further improvements in socio-economic conditions may only have small incremental effects on improving infant mortality in the case of Japan.

Judging from these conclusions, one can say that in countries where infant mortality rates are about 10.0-15.0 per 1,000 live births, improvement of medical facilities in communities, upgrading of women's education, and improvement of environmental conditions, especially the availability of piped water supply are important factors to reduce infant mortality rate. Infant mortality rate in Japan is about 7.0 per 1,000 today, and factors in social life still exert some effect on infant mortality. However, the effect of these factors is becoming weaker and one may not expect that infant mortality will substantially decline in the future.

APPENDIX 1
Correlation Matrix among Natural Environment Factors
in 1970

	INFANT	MEANTMP	LOWTMP
INFANT	1.000		
MEANTMP	0.460*	1.000	
LOWTMP	-0.209	0.559*	1.000

* $p < 0.05$

APPENDIX 2
Correlation Matrix among Demographic Factors in 1970

	INFANT	POPUL	DID	JUVENIL	AGEING	BIRTH
INFANT	1.000					
POPUL	-0.247*	1.000				
DID	-0.181	0.818*	1.000			
JUVENIL	0.848*	-0.124	0.057	1.000		
AGEING	0.513*	-0.277*	-0.277*	0.396*	1.000	
BIRTH	0.285*	0.476*	0.818*	0.549*	0.002	1.000

* $p < 0.05$

APPENDIX 3
Correlation Matrix among Environment Hygience Factors
in 1970

	INFANT	WATER	DIFFUSE	SEWAGE
INFANT	1.000			
WATER	0.132	1.000		
DIFFUSE	-0.226	0.623*	1.000	
SEWAGE	0.032	0.512*	0.500*	1.000

* $p < 0.05$

APPENDIX 4

Correlations Matrix among Public Health Factors in 1970

	INFANT	INSTITUTE	BED	PHYSICIAN	NURSE	CENTRE	HNURSE	EMERGNCY	STAY	INSPECT
INFANT	1.000									
INSTITUTE	0.39*	1.000								
BED	0.57*	0.63*	1.00							
PHYSICIAN	0.30*	0.90*	0.65*	1.00						
NURSE	0.47*	0.70*	0.88*	0.69*	1.00					
CENTRE	0.60*	0.63*	0.76*	0.54*	0.73*	1.00				
HNURSE	0.54*	0.26*	0.56*	0.60*	0.62*		1.00			
EMERGNCY	0.17	0.18	0.10	0.14	0.09	0.13	-0.12	1.00		
STAY	0.70*	0.55*	0.79*	0.55*	0.66*	0.62*	0.43*	0.04	1.00	
INSPECT	0.30*	0.18	0.36*	0.08	0.31*	0.56*	0.51*	0.04	0.21	1.00

* $p < 0.05$

APPENDIX 5
Correlation Matrix among Infant Health Factors in 1970

	INFANT	BABY	WEIGHT	MEDBTH	MOTHER	THIRD	WORK
INFANT	1.000						
BABY	0.805*	1.000					
WEIGHT	0.731*	0.869*	1.000				
MEDBTH	0.500*	0.713*	0.857*	1.000			
MOTHER	0.716*	0.857*	0.993*	0.869*	1.000		
THIRD	0.758*	0.684*	0.564*	0.234*	0.596*	1.000	
WORK	0.428*	0.262*	0.105	0.065	0.084	0.342*	1.000

* $p < 0.05$

APPENDIX 6
Correlation Matrix among Social Factors in 1970

	INFANT	NONPRI	TERTIA	HIGHSCL	JUNRCOL	WHIGHSCL	WJUNRCOL	ADVANCE	NUCLEI
INFANT	1.000								
NONPRI	0.16	1.00							
TERTIA	0.36*	0.85*	1.00						
HIGHSCL	0.13	0.88*	0.81*	1.00					
JUNRCOL	-0.04	0.84*	0.80*	0.88*	1.00				
WHIGHSCL	0.28*	0.78*	0.70*	0.82*	0.69*	1.00			
WJUNRCOL	-0.06	0.81*	0.67*	0.83*	0.89*	0.83*	1.00		
ADVANCE	0.12	0.82*	0.69*	0.78*	0.74*	0.53*	0.72*	1.00	
NUCLEI	0.52*	0.83*	0.87*	0.76*	0.66*	0.80*	0.65*	0.61*	1.00

* $p < 0.05$

APPENDIX 7
Correlation Matrix among Reproduction Factors
in 1970

	INFANT	GRR	NRR
INFANT	1.000		
GRR	0.696*	1.000	
NRR	0.685*	0.999*	1.000

* $p < 0.05$

APPENDIX 8
Correlation Matrix among Natural Environmental
Factors in 1975

	INFANT	MEANTMP	LOWTMP
INFANT	1.000		
MEANTMP	-0.056	1.000	
LOWTMP	-0.029	0.961*	1.000

* $p < 0.05$

APPENDIX 9

Correlation Matrix among Demographic Factors in 1975

	INFANT	POPUL	DID	JUVENIL	AGEING	BIRTH
INFANT	1.000					
POPUL	-0.378*	1.000				
DID	-0.448*	0.819*	1.000			
JUVENIL	0.144	-0.081	0.128	1.000		
AGEING	0.149	-0.453*	-0.671*	-0.579*	1.000	
BIRTH	-0.166	0.287*	0.518*	0.754*	-0.831*	1.000

* $p < 0.05$

APPENDIX 10

Correlation Matrix among Environment Hygiene Factors in 1975

	INFANT	WATER	DIFFUSE	SEWAGE
INFANT	1.000			
WATER	-0.512*	1.000		
DIFFUSE	-0.381*	0.646*	1.000	
SEWAGE	-0.191	0.428*	0.430*	1.000

* $p < 0.05$

APPENDIX 11

Correlation Matrix among Public Health Factors in 1975

	INFANT	INSTITUTE	BED	PHYSICIAN	NURSE	CENTRE	HNURSE	EMRGNCY	STAY	INSPECT	BENEFIT
INFANT	1.00										
INSTITUTE	-0.25*	1.00									
BED	0.22	0.54*	1.00								
PHYSICIAN	-0.21	0.82*	0.56*	1.00							
NURSE	0.19	0.65*	0.85*	0.60*	1.00						
CENTRE	0.20	0.47*	0.70*	0.35*	0.72*	1.00					
HNURSE	0.29*	0.12	0.50*	0.02	0.56*	0.63*	1.00				
EMRGNCY	0.07	0.13	0.18	0.07	0.11	0.12	-0.99*	1.00			
STAY	0.33*	0.41*	0.72*	0.39*	0.67*	0.53*	0.30*	0.06	1.00		
INSPECT	0.01	0.28*	0.53*	0.22*	0.42*	0.63*	0.36*	0.21	0.31	1.00	
BENEFIT	0.26*	0.35*	0.50*	0.17	0.60*	0.72*	0.66*	0.17	0.51*	0.50*	1.00

* $p < 0.05$

APPENDIX 12

Correlation Matrix among Infant Health Factors in 1975

	INFANT	BABY	WEIGHT	MEDBTH	MOTHER	THIRD	WORK
INFANT	1.000						
BABY	0.308*	1.000					
WEIGHT	0.199	-0.639*	1.000				
MEDBTH	-0.287*	-0.213	-0.077	1.000			
MOTHER	-0.373*	-0.005	-0.204	-0.066	1.000		
THIRD	0.370*	0.667*	-0.291*	-0.508*	0.121	1.000	
WORK	0.243	-0.014	-0.078	0.026	-0.476*	0.167	1.000

* $p < 0.05$

APPENDIX 13

Correlation Matrix among Economic Factors in 1975

	INFANT	INCOME	LIVEXP	MEDEXP	RATEXP
INFANT	1.000				
INCOME	-0.572*	1.000			
LIVEXP	-0.516*	0.325*	1.000		
MEDEXP	-0.431*	0.541*	0.375*	1.000	
RATEXP	0.317	-0.454*	-0.089	-0.952*	1.000

* $p < 0.05$

APPENDIX 14

Correlation Matrix among Social Factors in 1975

	INFANT	NONPRI	TERTIA	HIGHSCL	JUNRCOL	WHIGHSCL	WJUNRCOL	ADVANCE	NUCLEI
INFANT	1.00								
NONPRI	-0.54*	1.00							
TERTIA	-0.26*	0.64*	1.00						
HIGHSCL	-0.47*	0.51*	0.24	1.00					
JUNRCOL	-0.53*	0.74*	0.57*	0.77*	1.00				
WHIGHSCL	-0.44*	0.60*	0.43*	0.94*	0.80*	1.00			
WJUNRCOL	-0.52*	0.82*	0.66*	0.66*	0.95*	0.74*	1.00		
ADVANCE	-0.44*	0.69*	0.35*	0.56*	0.66*	0.52*	0.72*	1.00	
NUCLEI	0.17	0.55*	0.60*	0.33*	0.48*	0.48*	0.56*	0.29*	1.00

* $p < 0.05$

APPENDIX 15
Correlation Matrix among Reproduction Factors
in 1975

	INFANT	GRR	NRR
INFANT	1.000		
GRR	0.279*	1.000	
NRR	0.258*	0.999*	1.000

* $p < 0.05$

APPENDIX 16
Correlation Matrix among Natural Environmental
Factors in 1980

	INFANT	MEANTMP	LOWTMP
INFANT	1.000		
MEANTMP	−0.180	1.000	
LOWTMP	−0.217	0.949*	1.000

* $p < 0.05$

APPENDIX 17
Correlation Matrix among Demographic Factors in 1980

	INFANT	POPUL	DID	JUVENIL	AGEING	BIRTH
INFANT	1.000					
POPUL	−0.353*	1.000				
DID	−0.377*	0.810*	1.000			
JUVENIL	−0.271*	0.130	0.349*	1.000		
AGEING	0.272*	−0.497*	−0.714*	1.000		
BIRTH	0.042	−0.134	0.028	0.633*	−0.475*	1.000

* $p < 0.05$

APPENDIX 18

Correlation Matrix among Public Health Factors in 1980

	INFANT	INSTITUTE	BED	PHYSICIAN	NURSE	CENTRE	HNURSE	EMRGNCY	STAY	INSPECT	BENEFIT
INFANT	1.00										
INSTITUTE	-0.13	1.00									
BED	0.16	0.54*	1.00								
PHYSICIAN	-0.12	0.83*	0.54*	1.00							
NURSE	0.18	0.61*	0.88*	0.56*	1.00						
CENTRE	0.26*	0.50*	0.73*	0.33*	0.73*	1.00					
HNURSE	0.32*	0.14	0.50*	0.04	0.59*	0.62*	1.00				
EMRGNCY	-0.01	0.05	0.15	0.03	0.06	0.08	-0.03	1.00			
STAY	0.27*	0.42*	0.80*	0.33*	0.75*	0.55*	0.29*	0.06	1.00		
INSPECT	-0.06	0.24	0.49*	0.02	0.45*	0.57*	0.30*	0.08	0.54*	1.00	
BENEFIT	0.28*	0.35*	0.56*	0.17	0.64*	0.69*	0.69*	0.16	0.46*	0.47*	1.00

* $p < 0.05$

APPENDIX 19
Correlation Matrix among Infant Health Factors in 1980

	INFANT	BABY	WEIGHT	MEDBTH	MOTHER	THIRD	WORK
INFANT	1.000						
BABY	0.138	1.000					
WEIGHT	0.155	-0.802*	1.000				
MEDBTH	-0.365*	-0.183	-0.019	1.000			
MOTHER	-0.172	-0.017	-0.198	0.020	1.000		
THIRD	0.251*	0.490*	-0.215*	-0.491*	-0.156	1.000	
WORK	0.131	-0.077*	0.095	0.073	-0.523*	0.223	1.000

* $p < 0.05$

APPENDIX 20
Correlation Matrix among Economic Factors in 1980

	INFANT	INCOME	LIVEXP	MEDEXP	RATEXP
INFANT	1.000				
INCOME	-0.466*	1.000			
LIVEXP	-0.269*	0.382*	1.000		
MEDEXP	-0.211	0.386*	0.122	1.000	
RATEXP	-0.079	0.202	-0.302*	0.904*	1.000

* $p < 0.05$

APPENDIX 21
Correlation Matrix among Social Factors in 1980

	INFANT	NONPRI	TERTIA	HIGHSCL	JUNRCOL	WHIGHSCL	WJUNRCOL	ADVANCE	NUCLEI
INFANT	1.00								
NONPRI	-0.59*	1.00							
TERTIA	-0.25	0.58*	1.00						
HIGHSCL	-0.34*	0.53*	0.35*	1.00					
JUNRCOL	-0.41*	0.80*	0.66*	0.68*	1.00				
WHIGHSCL	-0.35*	0.50*	0.42*	0.89*	0.69*	1.00			
WJUNRCOL	-0.40*	0.72*	0.64*	0.63*	0.90*	0.78*	1.00		
ADVANCE	-0.40*	0.59*	0.30*	0.52*	0.64*	0.63*	0.64*	1.00	
NUCLEI	-0.09	0.50*	0.59*	0.35*	0.51*	0.25	0.35*	0.29*	1.00

* $p < 0.05$

APPENDIX 22
Correlation Matrix among Reproduction
Factors in 1980

	INFANT	GRR	NRR
INFANT	1.000		
GRR	0.251*	1.000	
NRR	0.235	0.999*	1.000

* $p < 0.05$

References

Brass, W. <u>Method for Estimating Fertility and Mortality from Limited and Defected data</u>. Chapel Hill: Carolina Population Center, University of North Carolina, 1975.

Caldwell, J.C. "Education as a Factor in Mortality Decline: An Examination of Nigerian Data". <u>Proceedings of the Meeting on Socio-Economic Determinants and Consequences of Mortality</u>, Mexico City, 19-25 June 1979.

Hadley, J., and A. Osei. "Does Income Affect Mortality? An Analysis of the Effects of Different Types of Income on Age/Sex/Race-Specific Mortality Rates in the United States". In <u>Medical Care</u>, vol. XX, no. 9 (1982): 901-14.

House, S.H., C. Robbins and L.H. Metzner. "The Association of Social Relationships and Activities with Mortality: Prospective Evidence from the Tecumseh Community Study". <u>American Journal of Epidemiology</u>, vol. 116, no. 1 (1982): 123-40.

Inaba, U., H. Takagi and H. Yanai. "Waga Kuni ni okeru Buibetsu Ganshiboritsu no Chiriteki Bunpu nin kansuru Inshibunseki". <u>Japanese Journal of Public Health</u>, vol. 26, no. 2 (1979): 67-75 [in Japanese].

Iwamoto, M., H. Dodo, J. Yoneda and Y. Ueda. "A Study of the Death Rate in Japan based on Cause and Social Environment -- Application of Multivariate Statistical Analysis". <u>Japanese Journal of Hygiene</u>, vol. 36, no. 4 (1981): 678-86 [in Japanese].

Japan. Ministry of Health and Welfare. Special report of vital statistics, various years.

Katabami, J. and I. Kaneko. "A Study on the Differences of Incidence of Spontaneous Foetal Deaths at Prefectural Level (1)". <u>Japanese Journal of Public Health</u>, vol. 25, no. 6 (1978): 319-25 [in Japanese].

Kitagawa, E.M. "On Mortality". <u>Demography</u>, no. 14, (1977): 381-89.

_____ and P.M. Hauser. <u>Differential Mortality in the United States: A Study of Socio-Economic Epidemiology</u>. Cambridge, Mass.: Harvard University Press, 1973.

Mare, R. "Socio-Economic Effects on Child Mortality in the United States". <u>American Journal of Public Health</u>, vol. 72, no. 6 (1982): 539-47.

Preston, S.H. and R. Gardner. "Factors Influencing Mortality Levels in Asia: International Comparisons and a Japanese Case Study". Paper presented at the Seventh Summer Seminar in Population, East-West Center, Honolulu, 1976.

Rosenwaike, I., N. Yaffe and P. Sagi. "The Recent Decline in Mortality of the Extreme Aged: An Analysis of Statistical Data". American Journal of Public Health, vol. 70, no. 10 (1980): 1074-80.

Shigematsu, I. and M. Nagai. "Factors Associated with the Decline of Mortality in Japan". In Mortality in South and East Asia: A Review of Changing Trends and Patterns, 1950-1970. Manila: World Health Organization, 1982.

United Nations. Levels and Trends of Mortality since 1950. New York, 1982.

_____. Manual X: Indirect Technique for Demographic Estimation. New York, 1983.

_____ and WHO. "UN/WHO Meeting on Socio-Economic Determinants and Consequences of Mortality, Mexico City, June 1979". In Population Bulletin of United Nations, No. 13, 1980.

Wingard, L.D., F.L. Berkmann and J.R. Brand. "A Multivariate Analysis of Health-Related Practices, A Nine-Year Mortality Follow-up of the Alameda Community Study". American Journal of Epidemiology, vol. 116, no. 5 (1982): 765-75.

World Health Organization. Mortality in South and East Asia: A Review of Changing Trends and Patterns, 1950-1970, Manila, 1982.

III SOCIO-ECONOMIC CORRELATES OF MORTALITY IN INDONESIA

Budi Soeradji and
Lukman Ismail

Introduction

Infant and child mortality is commonly considered as an indicator of health status of the population. Since the degree of infant and mortality is also highly associated with the socio-economic condition of the population, the rate of infant and child mortality is also used as an indicator of the population well-being.

An infant is exposed to his environment by the time he is born. Before that, during the gestation period, his survivorship is entirely influenced and determined by the biological factors of the parents and other environmental-biological factors operating through the mother. For example, poverty will result in malnourishment of the mother during pregnancy which may in turn affect the health of the baby.

In general, factors influencing infant and child mortality are classifiable into two major groups. The first group of factors relate to those carried over by the baby when he is born. These factors are inherited from the parents during conception or from the mother during pregnancy. These factors are known as endogenous factors or causes of infant death. The second group consists of factors associated with the external environment and living circumstances and are known as exogeneous factors or causes of death. Ideally, differentiations of those two groups of factors are possible through statistical analysis. In practice, however, this endeavour is very difficult. In developing countries, in particular, the quality of data is often low and the availability of the data is also scanty (United Nations 1973).

As a person grows older, the endogeneous causes of death weaken while the exogeneous factors exert a stronger influence. This theoretical argument is not perfectly found in everyday life.

About a quarter of the post neo-natal deaths are caused by exogenous factors during the neo-natal period. In other words, the number of exogeneous infant deaths is about 1¼ times the number of the post neo-natal deaths (Burgeois 1952). This illustrates that environmental factors are still very significant in affecting infant mortality. The quality and condition of environment such as hygiene, sanitation, and other socio-economic conditions determine the level of mortality of the population, in particular infants and children.

When infant mortality is high, the ratio between the number of neo-natal deaths and the number of post neo-natal deaths is also high. This high ratio changes under conditions of declining infant mortality rate. This pattern will continue until the environmental factors are under control and the proportion of neo-natal deaths becomes dominant. At this stage, the infant deaths are more likely to be influenced by endogenous factors (Keyfitz 1977).

Indonesia as well as most developing countries is still far from reaching the condition described above. What is being experienced in Indonesia is that high rates of infant mortality and large differentials according to social strata as indicated by place of residence, region, income and other socio-economic characteristics still prevail. An understanding of these differences would help find ways of reducing such differences. This is an important step towards reducing the high level of mortality, particularly infant and child mortality rates currently experienced in Indonesia.

Mortality Level in Indonesia

Because of data limitation, in terms of content and coverage, in the vital registration in Indonesia, infant mortality rates have so far been estimated indirectly from the Population Census and Survey data. Two population censuses, 1971 and 1980, and several surveys such as the Intercensal Population Survey 1976, Fertility Mortality Survey 1973, and the National Socio-Economic Survey 1979 yielded somewhat consistent estimates of infant mortality rates. These sources also indicate similar patterns of differentiation of infant mortality according to some population characteristics such as region (province), place of residence (urban and rural), sex, and socio-economic status. These sources, furthermore, con- sistently indicate a tendency of mortality decline in Indonesia.

Going back to the years before 1950, rough estimates were that crude death rate was between 28 to 35 per 1,000 population and life expectancy at birth was no more than 30 to 35 years (Nitisastro 1970). In the 1940s, the death incidence was high due to the outbreak of World War II (1943-45) and the war for Independence (1946-50). During that period, the health condition of the population was very poor. The supply of food was very limited if not insufficient and large numbers of males were sent for hard labour in remote areas where many never came back. Under such hardships, mortality increased while fertility declined. The conditions were worse in Java than in the other islands.

In the early 1950s, the mortality rate was still high but it started to decline although the decline was very slow and irregular. This declining mortality was probably due to the return of more peaceful life in Indonesia. The irregularity of the mortality decline, however, was caused by epidemics of smallpox and malaria in some areas. It was estimated that life expectancy at birth at that time was between 35 to 38 years (Heligman 1975), while the infant mortality rate was estimated at between 100 and 300 per 1,000 live births.

Population data from which estimates of infant mortality rates can be derived started to increase after 1960. From the quality point of view, the earlier data were more deficient due to the problems of the design and the low quality of responses in the data collection, census and survey instrument.

In 1960, the infant mortality rate was estimated to be 175 per 1,000 live births while it was 150 in 1965 (Hull and Sunaryo 1978). The estimate for 1975 was 110 (McDonald 1978) which reduced to 107 in 1977 (Soemantri 1983). Based on these analyses, it is clear that there has been a decline in mortality in Indonesia, with the rate of decline at about 3 to 4 per cent per year. It has also been argued that the decline in mortality rate is attributed to improvement of socio-economic conditions among the population. Additionally, better health conditions among the population might have also contributed to the mortality decline.

The degree of the decline in mortality rate has been shown to vary from one province to another (Soemantri 1983 and Soeradji 1983). The most rapid decline is found in Jakarta and Sumatra while it is relatively slow in Kalimantan, Yogyakarta, and East Java. From the studies, it has also been reported that mortality rate varies with socio-economic characteristics such as place of residence, level of education, literacy rate, occupation, and housing conditions.

Conceptual Framework of Mortality Studies

Death is seldom caused by a single factor. It is the outcome of multiple factors acting concurrently upon the biological and physical environments in which we live. Studies of causal relationships of mortality are therefore often difficult because we are unable to identify all the variables which indirectly or directly cause death. In social science research in the field of mortality, socio-economic factors such as education, income, occupation, place of residence, and other related social variables are often posited to be related to mortality, including infant and child mortality. However, in much of these research, it is still unclear how and to what extent socio-economic factors actually influence mortality. In bio-medical research on mortality, for example, attention is often focused only on biological factors or their proxies which influence the incidence of death and or prevalence of a disease. In this field of research, socio-economic factors are usually ignored or only given scant attention.

Considering the respective inadequacies of the social and bio-medical approaches to the study of mortality, a combination of both models may overcome their individual weaknesses in providing explanations of the determinant factors of mortality, and in the case of this study, infant and child mortality. Mosley (1982) proposed a model which essentially combined both approaches in the study of mortality (see Figure 1). In this model, Mosley classifies all biological factors into five categories: maternal factors, nutrition, environmental contamination, accident, and personal disease control factors. He claims that all socio-economic factors will influence mortality through these biological factors. In other words, biological factors function as intermediate variables through which other factors influence mortality.

Mosley (1983), furthermore, illustrates in a more simplified form the mechanism through which the influence of those five intermediate variables act upon child and infant mortality (see Figure 2). The model identifies the relevant social practices that are related to each of the five categories of intermediate variables. It is to be noted that the intermediate variable "nutrient availability" is modulated by the physiological factors of the person concerned, namely appetite, absorption, and metabolism. Similarly, the risks related to the intermediate variable "environmental contamination" are influenced by the person's resistance to infection. In this latter case, the resistance may be decreased by injuries or immaturity at birth, or increased by vaccines. In this model, the author introduces a concept of social synergy meaning that the same social determinant, for example, poverty can operate independently on

65

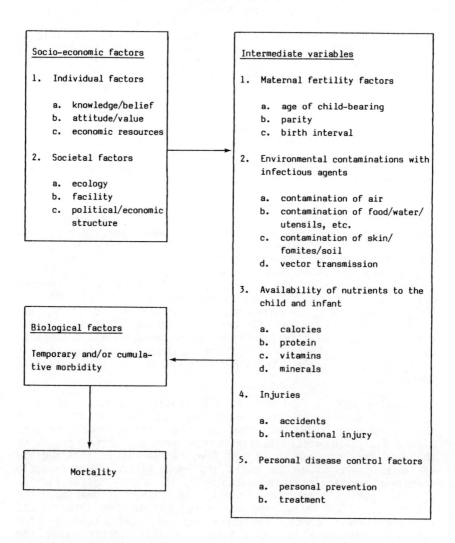

FIGURE 1
Mosley's Framework for the Study of Factors Influencing
Infant and Child Mortality

SOURCE: Mosley (1982).

66

FIGURE 2
Conceptual Model Showing Basic Operations of the Five Intermediate
Variables and their Household Social Determinants Leading to
Child Morbidity and Mortality

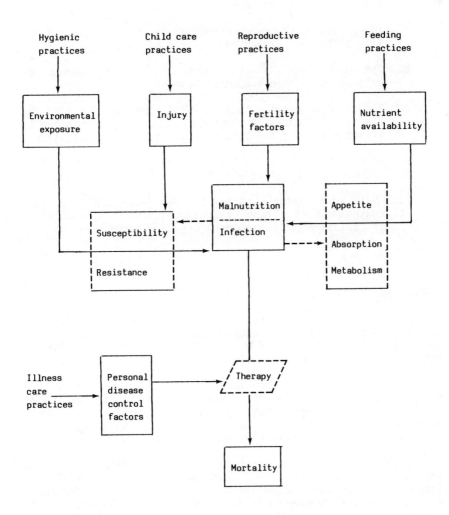

SOURCE: Mosley (1982).

67

more than one intermediate variable to influence the risk of infant mortality, resulting in a combined risk that is more than would be expected by the simple sum of the operation of each intermediate variable. For example, a child from a poor family tends to have insufficient food, greater exposure to infection, and less likely to have modern health treatment when he gets sick.

The models mentioned are based on the following assumptions:

a. In a good environmental condition, 98 per cent of the live births will reach their fifth birthday.

b. The reduction of the survivorship is caused by unfavourable socio-economic factors.

c. The socio-economic factors will operate through the biological factors or intermediate variables in order to affect the child and infant mortality of the population.

d. Morbidity experience of a child may be temporary but it may have a cumulative effect.

e. Child and infant mortality is generally the last consequence of a cumulative experience of morbidity and it is less often caused by a single disease.

Objectives of the Study

A review of the mortality studies conducted in Indonesia indicated that the majority have been concentrated on the level and trend of mortality, particularly infant and childhood mortality. Some of these studies, however, have dealt with mortality differentials employing a single differentiating factor. Such studies have a major shortcoming, namely they do not examine the joint effects of factors in influencing the differentials of mortality level. It is recognized, however, that mortality is jointly affected by multiple factors. Moreover, such studies fail to elaborate the mechanism by which factors influence mortality.

Given the above considerations, it is the major purpose of this study to investigate the determinants of infant mortality in Indonesia. Such studies, we feel will add to the knowledge about a very important phenomenon in the Indonesian population, as well as contribute towards better development planning formulations in Indonesia, in particular in the area of population and health development planning. The value of such contribution becomes more significant in the current development plan* in Indonesia because the Government of Indonesia has specifically expressed the need to accelerate the reduction of infant mortality rate so as to increase the physical quality of life of the Indonesian population.

In identifying the factors which influence mortality, special attention will be given in this study to the role of health variables. As far as possible, the effects of health factors in affecting the level of mortality will be partialled out from other factors so as to determine its unique contribution on mortality differentials.

At this stage, it is necessary to note that this study has two major shortcomings. First, it only covers Java and Bali. From the geographical point of view, Java and Bali constitute about 7 per cent of the land area of Indonesia but about two-thirds of the population of Indonesia.

The second major shortcoming of this study is that it relies upon secondary data and hence the selection of the factors for study is dictated by data availability.

Despite these shortcomings, we believe that no such detailed study on mortality has been conducted in Indonesia before and we hope that this will help break new ground in mortality analysis for Indonesia.

Methodology

Unit of Analysis

In this study we are confining it to the examination of differentials in infant mortality. In studying this phenomenon, we can either use individuals or a cluster of individuals such as region or community as the unit of analysis. In deciding the type of units of analysis to be employed, there are several considerations to be taken into account; data measurement and data availability as well as the relative importance of the two types of study results for development planning.

---

*   The Fourth Five-Year Development Plan, 1983-88.

69

In the recent Population Censuses and Surveys, efforts have been directed to collect information on the number of births classified by the survivorship of the children. Some population censuses and surveys have also tried to have further breakdown of such information by the timing of the events: last births or births during a specified reference period. Given this information, a mortality study can employ individuals as units of analysis with the proportion of deceased children as the dependent variable. However, it is felt that high recall lapses on the number and timing of deceased children may cause serious errors in the analysis. If we confine to births for a specified reference period, say one year, the sample for the analysis may also become too small for a study with few independent variables.

The employment of individuals as units of analysis in mortality studies seems to be more appropriate when the source of the data is not the result of population censuses or surveys but rather service statistics such as death records or vital registration. These sources, however, often have very limited information.

Even given the data limitation, mortality studies using individuals as units of analysis may still be possible provided the number of factors to be observed is very small, say about three variables. However, this will not be too useful if we are interested in the inter-relationship between variables.

Considering the above problems, it was therefore decided that areal level analysis will be used.

Administratively, Indonesia is divided into 27 provinces. Each province is further divided into regencies constituting kabupatens and kotamadyas. There are 299 regencies in Indonesia out of which 114 regencies are in Java and Bali. Each regency is divided into kecamatans (districts). Finally, each kecamatan is further divided into kelurahans in kotamadya and desas in kabupaten. Both terms are equivalent to villages.

Public administration constituting executive, judicial and legislative agencies are found down to the kabupaten level. The head of a regency or kabupaten is also considered the lowest level administrator in charge of development. Hence, it is quite appropriate to employ the regency as the unit of analysis for this study.

FIGURE 3
Diagram of Administrative Divisions in Indonesia

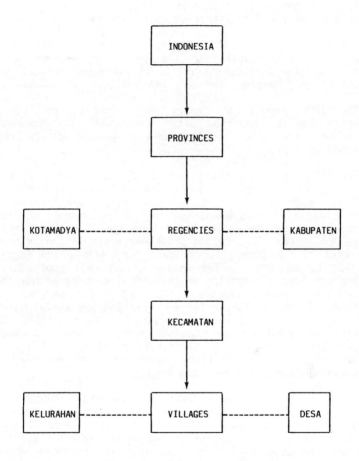

NOTE: Total number of provinces   : 27
       Total number of regencies   : 299
       Total number of kecamatans : 3,260
       Total number of villages   : 63,000

SOURCE: Mosley (1982).

71

Sources of Data

As was indicated before, most estimates of infant mortality rates available for Indonesia so far have been derived from the results of Population Censuses or Surveys. This is primarily due to the imperfection of vital registration in Indonesia.

For the purpose of this study, most of the statistics are derived from the results of the 1980 Population Census of Indonesia and the service statistics of the Department of Health. The last source, however, has very limited types of data.

The 1980 Population Census of Indonesia is the third Population Census conducted after Indonesia's independence in 1946. The post-independence nation-wide census was in 1960 and the second in 1971.

The 1980 Population Census was conducted in two phases. The first phase was a complete enumeration of the population. Basic information such as name of head of household, number of household members classified into broad age categories, number of disabled persons, schooling status for population aged 7-12 years and land area was collected. The second phase was a sample census covering 5 per cent of the population (except for Jakarta and Yogyakarta which was 10 per cent). The sample census collected additional and more detailed information or individual members of households. The individual data collected include age, sex, marital status, education, migration, labour force participation, age at marriage, fertility, and family planning practices. The household charac-teristics collected include housing conditions such as number of rooms, number of buildings in the compound (if applicable), number of households in the building, possession of durable goods, environmental sanitation and land area.

The sample census was designed such that it can produce efficient estimates at regency level. Although this purpose was generally met there were still some problems when it came to estimating certain variables which had small numbers. Events like death do pose such a problem especially in provinces where the population is small. Therefore not all statistics can be produced with tolerable efficiency at regency level especially if they are for small provinces. This is one of the major reasons why we have confined our study to the more populous provinces of Java and Bali where the estimated mortality rates are more reliable.

With the assistance and collaboration of the Indonesian Central Bureau of Statistics, we are able to have access to the raw data of the 1980 Population Census. Tabulations for calculating various rates are worked out by the Bureau of Data Processing and Presentation of the Central Bureau of Statistics.

Certain types of data vital for our study, like health or social services statistics are not available from the census. These have to be obtained from statistics collected by the Department of Health. Not all the statistics are available at the regency level. For regency level data, we were able only to obtain data on the number of medical doctors, number of midwives, number of assistants to midwives (nurses), and number of Public Health Centres (Pusat Kesehatan Masyarakat or PUSKESMAS).

Estimation of Infant Mortality Rate

In the questionnaire of the Sample Census of the 1980 Population Census, questions on women's fertility were included. These were:

a. Number of children born alive who are still living in the household;

b. Number of children born alive who are staying away;

c. Number of children born alive who have died;

d. Date of last birth;

e. Survivorship of the last birth.

From the first three questions, the proportion of live births which have died classified by successive age group of mothers can be derived. This information then becomes the basis for the calculation of the indirect estimates of infant mortality rates. Utomo (1983) in this context, however, argues that the employment of such information for calculating mortality rate has several shortcomings, namely:

a. The data only cover the survivorship of children whose mothers are still alive at the time of census taking. If the mortality rate of children whose mothers have died is different from that of those who are alive, the estimates will carry some bias;

b. Experience also indicates that there is usually a tendency for under-reporting of deceased children;

c. Still-births are sometimes reported as mortality of live births.

73

Despite the shortcomings he, nonetheless, indicates that the child survivorship information in the 1980 Census are quite consistent. Hence, the utilization of the information for calculating the infant mortality rate is quite justified.

Two other problems which need consideration in the estimation of infant mortality rate using indirect methods are the choice of a suitable technique and the choice of an appropriate regional model life table.

Soemantri (1983) has applied three methods on four sets of Indonesian data to estimate infant mortality. The techniques applied are: the Brass technique (1968), the Trussell technique (1973) and the Sullivan technique (1972) while the four sets of data are the results of 1971 Population Census, 1976 Intercensal Population Survey, 1979 National Socio-Survey and 1980 Population Census. The results of the estimations are presented in Table 1.

The estimations resulted from the Brass and Trussell techniques differ between 1 and 4 per cent where the Trussell technique tends to produce higher estimates. Between the Sullivan and the Trussell technique, the differences are not consistent. Given these slight differences in the estimations, we may conclude that any method would be quite appropriate. Given this finding and the fact that Trussell technique has been commonly used in Indonesia, we are in favour of employing Trussell technique to estimate the infant mortality rates for this study.

As for choosing an appropriate regional Model Life Table, Sinquefield and Kartoyo (1977) have argued at one time that the Indonesian pattern of mortality is more closely approximated by the South Model. McDonald (1978), contended that the West pattern was more appropriate given the scanty data available for Indonesia. Soemantri (1983) in response to this problem, tested both the South and West Model Life Tables on the same four different sets of data as referred to before (see Table 2).

Table 2 indicates that the application of West Model Life Table gives slightly higher mortality estimates than those of the South Model. The differences vary between 2 to 7 per cent. It should also be noted that the differences have narrowed with the decline in infant mortality. Since we are employing the 1980 Population Census data for estimating the infant mortality rates, we have decided to use the West Model Life Table which has also been used in most mortality studies in Indonesia, including the official statistics published by the Indonesian Central Bureau of Statistics (1984).

Although we consider the Mosley conceptual framework appropriate for the study of infant mortality, it cannot be

74

TABLE 1

Estimated Values of $_2q_0$ Based on Different Sets of Data on Techniques of Estimation

Data Sources	Technique			Ratio	
	Brass	Sullivan	Trussell	(1)/(3)	(2)/(3)
	(1)	(2)	(3)	(4)	(5)
1971 Population Census	0.175	0.179	0.180	0.97	0.99
1976 Intercensal Population Census	0.136	0.139	0.138	0.99	1.01
1979 National Socio-economic Survey	0.127	0.130	0.130	0.98	1.01
1980 Population Census	0.130	0.133	0.135	0.96	0.99

SOURCE: Soemantri, "Pola Perkembangan dan Perbandingan Daerah Angka Kematian Bayi" (Trend and Regional Differentials of Infant Mortality Rates), 1983.

TABLE 2

Estimated Values of q_0 Based on Different Sets of Data and Regions of Life Table Model

Life Table Model	1971 Population Census	1976 Intercensal Population Census	1979 National Socio-Economic Survey	1980 Population Census
West Model	0.144	0.114	0.108	0.109
South Model	0.134	0.111	0.106	0.103
Ratio	1.07	1.03	1.02	1.02

SOURCE: Soemantri, "Pola Perkembangan dan Perbandingan Daerah Angka Kematian Bayi" (Trend and Regional Differentials of Infant Mortality Rates), 1983.

totally adopted for this study given the limitations and lack of availability of some data. As such, we could only use a modified version of the Mosley model. The operational framework we used finally for this study is shown in Figure 4. It can be seen from the figure that although the variables we use do not correspond entirely to the variables in Mosley's model, its approach is fundamentally similar. The assumptions of the model are that socio-economic factors influence biological and health factors to affect morbidity and mortality levels.

In this study, it is assumed that population density and the size of a village will to some extent influence the degree of "crowdedness" in a community which may induce or impede the spread of contagious diseases. At the same time the larger the population and higher the density the greater the accessibility of medical services as these are more likely to be concentrated in the more urbanized parts of the country.

Similarly, other socio-economic factors such as the level of literacy, education, level of urbanization, ability to speak the national language and employment in non-traditional jobs, may also be indicative of the level of modernization. The more modern the society, the more likely people would accept innovative ideas and development including modern medical treatment. This will result in lower morbidity and mortality rates.

The level of education in this case is measured as the percentage of school-going-age population who are still in school. The selection of this criteria as a measure of education is based on several reasons. Education was made compulsory in Indonesia only in 1984. Hence large numbers of children did not go to school. The general level of educational attainment is also low. In 1980, only 32 per cent of the entire Indonesian population aged 10 years and over had completed primary school.

Ability to speak the national language, Bahasa Indonesia, is measured as the proportion of population 10 years and over who are able to speak Indonesian language. The more people can speak the Indonesian language the better will they be able to receive and understand messages conveyed through the government-run communication and motivation programmes. The effect of this variable on mortality level is expected to be similar to that of communication exposure which is measured as the proportion of households possessing radio and television. This last variable, however, is also a measure of the welfare of the population.

The economic indicator is represented by the female labour force participation rate, the female employment rate, type of farming and size of farm. The higher the economic status of the population in the regency, the higher the ability of the

76

FIGURE 4

**Operational Framework for the Study on the Determinants
of Infant Mortality in Java and Bali**

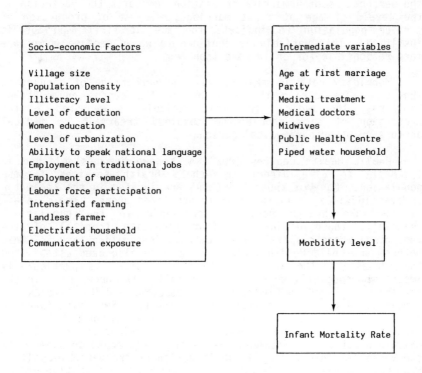

SOURCE: Mosley (1983).

population to spend money for health treatment. Under this assumption, the economic status of the population will have influence on health prevention and treatment which consequently will have an effect on the level of mortality.

In this study, age at first marriage is measured by the proportion of married (female) population aged 15-24. Although the 1980 Population Census collects information on age at first marriage, the reliability of the data particularly for the older generation is probably low. The census also reported quite a high proportion of non-response for this question. Since variation in the percentages of unmarried population indicates the variation in the levels of age at first marriage, the use of proportion of married population to indicate the age at first marriage is justified. This variable is confined to women because women are more responsible for child care than men.

Morbidity rate is measured as the percentage of population who were sick during the week before the census enumeration. Similarly, the medical treatment variable is measured as the proportion of sick people who obtained treatment by medical doctors or other paramedical personnel.

Public Health Centres (PUSKESMAS) have been established in Indonesia to give direct and cheap health services to the population. Many of these PUSKESMAS are located in the kecamatan or even in villages in the densely populated areas. The main aim is to make health services accessible to the population, especially those living far from the city (capital of the kabupaten) where hospitals are located. In addition to PUSKESMAS, Mothers and Child Health (MCH) clinics have also been established in Indonesia. The availability of the latter is particularly important especially where infant mortality is concerned. In the variables included in Figure 4, the PUSKESMAS and MCH clinics are combined. The reason is that many of the PUSKESMAS also function as MCH clinics and vice versa. It is also often difficult to separate PUSKESMAS which do not offer MCH services and MCH clinics which are not also PUSKESMAS. Hence it is easier to combine these two variables into a single public health centre variable. It is hypothesized that this variable will have high contributive effect to the explanation of variation in the infant mortality rates among regencies.

Similarly, it is expected that paramedical personnel will also have an important effect on the variations in infant mortality rates. This variable includes the number of midwives and assistants to midwives who are working at the PUSKESMAS or MCH clincis. These hypotheses will be tested when we analyse the data.

The percentage of households with piped water represents the contamination of water variable in the Mosley scheme. (See Appendix 1 for list of variables.)

Correlation of Variables

In the initial stage of analysis, the variables are assessed through the examinations of the zero order correlation between the 22 independent variables and the dependent variable, infant mortality rate. The correlation coefficients and the significance levels of the 22 variables are presented in Table 3. Among the 14 socio-economic variables, we find that 11 of them are significantly different from zero at the 5 per cent level of significance. Out of eight intermediate variables (including morbidity), seven variables have levels of significance of less than 5 per cent.

We note, however, that the average number of living children is one of the sources of information employed in the calculation of infant mortality rate using the Trussell method. Hence, the inclusion of this variable will raise the problem of auto-correlation between the independent variable and the dependent variable. Accordingly, we prefer to eliminate this variable as one of the predictors of infant mortality rate.

From the above examinations on the correlation coefficients, we conclude that 17 variables constituting 11 background variables and six intermediate variables should be examined further for multi-collinearity effects. This can be done by investigating the relative values of the correlation coefficients. Variables with very high correlation coefficients should be dropped from the analysis.

Table 4 presents the correlation matrix of the 17 variables. We find two variables with very high correlation coefficients with other variables. These two variables are the proportion of urban residence and the ability to speak the national language (NATLANG). Accordingly, these two variables are eliminated from the analysis.

Regression Coefficients

As this study is aimed at analysing the influences of several factors on infant mortality rate, multiple regression analysis is

79

TABLE 3

Correlation Coefficients of Variables with Infant Mortality Rate and their Significance Levels

Variables	Correlation Coefficient	Significance Level
Background factors		
1. Village Size (VILSIZE)	-.1212	.099
2. Population Density (DENSITY)	-.2800	.001
3. Level of Education (EDLEV)	-.6373	.000
4. Level of Urbanization (URBRES)	-.3020	.001
5. Female Illiteracy Level (ILIT)	.3175	.001
6. Women's Education (WEDUC)	-.4368	.000
7. Ability to Speak National Language (NATLANG)	-.2812	.002
8. Female Employment in Traditional Occupation (TRAD)	.2928	.001
9. Female Labour Force Participation Rate (LFPR)	-.2497	.004
10. Women Employment Rate (EMPRATE)	-.1630	.042
11. Household with Electricity (ELECHH)	-.2497	.004
12. Communication Exposure (COMM)	-.4414	.000
13. Intensified Farming (INFARM)	.0695	.231
14. Landless Farmer (NOLND)	.0548	.281
Intermediate variables		
1. Proportion of Married Women aged 15-24 (PROPMAR)	.6035	.000
2. Average Number of Living Children (LIVCHILD)	.1755	.031
3. Medical Treatment (MEDTR)	.1574	.047
4. Number of Doctors (DOCTOR)	-.2756	.002
5. Number of Midwives (MIDWIVES)	-.3452	.000
6. Public Health Centre (PHC)	-.0506	.296
7. Households with Piped Water (PIPEDHH)	-.2197	.009
8. Morbidity Level (MORBID)	.3772	.000

80

TABLE 4

Correlation Matrix of Variables Influencing Infant Mortality Rate

Variables	1	2	3	4	5	6	7	8	9	10	11	12	13	14	15	16	17
1. DENSITY	*																
2. EDLEV	0.36	*															
3. URBRES	0.71	0.47	*														
4. ILIT	-0.51	-0.67	-0.65	*													
5. NATLANG	0.59	0.54	0.76	-0.83	*												
6. EMPLY	-0.17	-0.12	0.20	0.05	-0.15	*											
7. LEPR	0.30	0.08	0.40	0.40	-0.47	0.46	*										
8. WEDUC	0.77	0.53	0.91	-0.61	0.75	-0.15	-0.30	*									
9. ELECHH	0.73	0.46	0.97	-0.67	0.72	0.19	-0.45	0.86	*								
10. COMM	0.68	0.63	0.85	-0.70	0.84	-0.19	-0.30	0.89	0.82	*							
11. TRAD	-0.63	0.49	-0.89	0.54	-0.72	0.25	0.37	-0.85	-0.45	0.80	*						
12. PROPMAR	-0.49	-0.64	-0.59	0.40	-0.47	-0.04	-0.17	-0.72	-0.51	0.68	0.63	*					
13. MEDTR	0.24	0.15	0.36	-0.46	0.43	-0.15	-0.38	0.27	0.39	-0.19	-0.31	-0.08	*				
14. DOCTOR	0.61	0.47	0.75	-0.50	0.53	-0.13	-0.19	0.72	0.76	0.66	-0.68	-0.61	0.29	*			
15. MIDWIVES	0.49	0.48	0.66	-0.34	0.45	-0.04	-0.06	0.63	0.65	0.58	-0.63	-0.63	0.22	0.85	*		
16. PIPEDHH	0.50	0.32	0.68	-0.43	0.56	-0.22	-0.28	0.63	0.68	0.65	-0.61	-0.43	0.29	0.42	0.40	*	
17. MORBID	0.08	0.08	-0.08	0.19	-0.31	0.25	-0.14	-0.40	0.06	0.22	-0.14	0.17	0.92	0.11	0.03	0.12	*

used to investigate the relationship of each variable by taking into account the effects of other variables. First, the partial regression coefficients resulting from stepwise regression are examined. The examination is conducted independently for each block of variables; background and intermediate variables.

The summary of the regression equation of background variables on infant mortality rate is presented in the first part of Table 5. In order to select the variables to be included in subsequent stages of analysis, the values of the standardized regression coefficients and the R^2 change of each variable are examined. Those with small or meaningless contribution in the explanation of variations in the dependent variable will be excluded in subsequent analysis.

Out of the nine background variables, level of education has the most important contribution to the explanation of variation in infant mortality rates among regencies in Java and Bali. Women employment, on the other hand, does not have very meaningful contribution at all. Its F-value is very small such that it is not even included in the computation of the regression equation by the computer programme. We may also note that female illiteracy level, communication exposure, population density and female employment in traditional occupations are insignificant even at the 10 per cent level of significance. Female labour force participation rate and households with electricity are not significant at the 5 per cent level but they are significant at 10 per cent level of significance. Only educational level and women education are highly significant. In order to keep more variables for further analysis, the variables which are significant at 10 per cent level of significance are retained. Hence, the variables to be included in further analysis are: level of education, labour force participation rate, women education and households with electricity. Another variable, female employment in traditional occupations, is also retained as it has been found to have implications on infant mortality even if it is found not to be significant in this instance.

As for the pattern of relationship between intermediate variables and infant mortality rate, it is found that proportion of married women aged 15-24 years, morbidity level and medical treatment are significantly associated with infant mortality rate while the rest of the three variables are not. Following our previous criterion of variable selection, only the first three variables are included in subsequent analysis. However, since a secondary objective of this study is to examine the impact of health facilities on infant mortality, we will also include the number of doctors and midwives for further analysis even though these variables did not show significant relationships with the dependent variable. Thus, based on the previous analysis, the

TABLE 5

Partial Regression Coefficients of Background and Intermediate Variables with Infant Mortality Rate

Variables	Standardized Regression Coefficient	R^2 Change
Background Variables		
1. Level of Education	-.576*	40.616
2. Female Labour Force Participation	-.160**	4.033
3. Women Education	-.619*	4.687
4. Household with Electricity	.250**	2.586
5. Female Employment in Traditional Work	-.214	0.738
6. Female Illiteracy Level	-.127	0.416
7. Communication Exposure	-.052	0.044
8. Population Density	.014	0.007
9. Women Employment	-	-
Intermediate Variables		
1. Proportion of Married Women aged 15-24	.461*	36.419
2. Morbidity	.867*	7.765
3. Medical Treatment	-.633*	3.357
4. Number of Doctors	.101	0.412
5. Households with Piped Water	.031	0.066
6. Number of Midwives	.028	0.020

* Significant at 5 per cent.
** Significant at 10 per cent.

number of variables to be further analysed has been reduced to five background and five intermediate variables as shown in the revised operational framework in Figure 5.

Effects of Socio-economic Variables

In this section hierarchical regression analysis is used first on the set of socio-economic variables and then on the intermediate variables to establish the contributive effect of each variable on infant mortality net of the other variables. Table 6 shows the results of hierarchical regression analysis of the five socio-economic variables on infant mortality. The five socio-economic variables, level of education, women education, female labour force participation, female employment in traditional work or occupations, households with electricity, can be grouped into three groups constituting the education, economic and housing condition variables.

It is recalled that the level of education is defined as the proportion or the percentage of school-going-age population who are still in school. Since educational level is still low in Indonesia, differences in the proportions of school-age population who are in school among regencies can be considered as indicative of the differences in the level of education of the population in general. Generally parents who have achieved higher levels of education will have greater intention of sending their children to school. Consequently, areas with a more educated population will have higher proportion of school-age population who are in school.

Another indication which can be derived from these differences is that education is often linked to social well-being. The higher the social well-being of the region, the more likely the children are sent to and kept in school. With high social well-being, we may also expect that the population will have better nutrition. As a consequence, these regions will have lower infant mortality rates.

The data for Java and Bali indeed supported the above contention. The simple correlation coefficient between the level of education and infant mortality rate is shown to be -0.64 which is significant at the 5 per cent level of significance (see Table 6). The results from the hierarchical analysis furthermore show that the effects of educational level on mortality incidence among infants are still significant after accounting for the effects of other socio-economic variables.

FIGURE 5

Revised Operational Framework for the Study of Socio-economic
Correlates of Infant Mortality Rate in Java and Bali

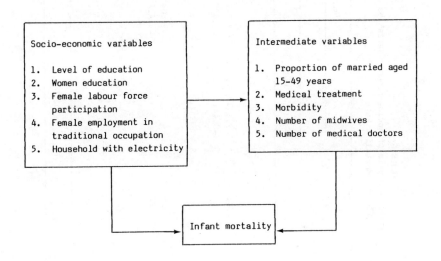

TABLE 6
Hierarchical Regression Analysis of Socio-economic Variables on Infant Mortality Rate

Independent Variables	Simple Correlation	Regression 1 b	Regression 1 Beta	Regression 2 b	Regression 2 Beta	Regression 3 b	Regression 3 Beta
Education							
1. Level of Education	-.64	-2.354	-.564	-2.061	-.494	-2.131	-.511
2. Women's Education	-.44	-0.441	-.138	-1.479	-.464	-2.020	-.634
Economic							
3. Female Labour Force Participation	-.25			-0.804	-.259	-0.623	-.201
4. Female Employment in Traditional Occupation	.29			-0.327	-.249	-0.230	-.176
Housing Condition							
5. Households with Electricity	-.25					0.423	.299
R^2 (in %)		42.00		50.94		52.66	

Another education variable, women's level of education, defined as the proportion of women aged 15-49 years who have completed at least junior high school, is also very significant in explaining variation in infant mortality. In fact, this variable is thought to be even more sensitive to infant mortality than the general education variable since the survival of an infant is very much linked to the quality of mother's care. Women with higher education may have better knowledge of child care and give more attention to child health and treatment and prevention like immunization. Also, women with higher educational level are also more likely to be economically better off and can afford more help to take care of the child. Hence, we expect children of women with higher education will experience less child and infant diseases. Consequently, the regions with more highly educated will also have lower infant mortality.

This negative association is confirmed by our data shown in Table 6. The zero order correlation between women education and infant mortality level is -.44. The association between these variables and infant mortality remains even when the effects of other socio-economic variables -- individually or altogether -- are taken into account.

The economic indicators included in the analysis are female labour force participation and female employment in traditional occupations. The female labour force participation is defined as the percentage of women aged 10 years and above who are in the labour force. This variable has been considered as an important economic variable in other demographic studies. A region with high female labour force participation rate suggests that more women are working and earning income. Hence, the economic status of women in these regions are likely to be higher. Under this condition, it is expected that these regions will have lower infant mortality rates.

Indeed our data gain support in this hypothesis (see Table 6). The zero order correlation between female labour force participation and infant mortality is -0.25. When the effects of the educational variables are controlled for, the partial regression coefficient of this variable is still high (-0.804) and is still significant at the 5 per cent level of significance. This is also true when the effects of all the socio-economic variables are taken into account.

The variable female employment in traditional occupations in this study is defined as female employment in agriculture and retail trades. This variable is commonly used to indicate the level of modernization of a society. The higher the level of development the less people will be employed in traditional occupations. The higher the level of development experienced in a society or community the lower also the lower infant mortality. Hence, we expect a positive association between proportion of women involved in traditional occupations and infant mortality.

This expectation is borne out by our data although the relationship between female employment in traditional occupations and infant mortality level is not very strong. However, this relationship, after controlling for the effects of education aspects and labour force participation, remains significant at the 5 per cent level of significance. However, when the last variable, households with electricity, is also included, the relationship between female employment in traditional occupation and infant mortality rate becomes insignficant. It is also noted that there is a sign change in this relationship from a positive to a negative direction when the effects of the other variables, individually or altogether, are accounted for.

Electricity is still considered in Indonesia as an "expensive and luxury good". The 1980 Population Census reported that only 13.8 per cent of the households in Java and Bali had electricity as the source of lighting. The majority of households were still using kerosene. Hence, households with electricity tend to have higher socio-economic status than those without electricity. This may in turn be linked to more sanitary and healthier household conditions. These arguments purport a hypothesis that the more households with electricity in the region, the higher economic status of the region and the healthier the household environment of the region, the lower the infant mortality incidence.

The above hypothesis seems to be supported by our data. The simple correlation coefficient between percentage of households with electricity and infant mortality rate is 0.25 which is significant at the 5 per cent level of significance. After taking into account the effects of the other socio-economic variables, we find that the partial regression coefficient (0.423) is still significant. Note, however, that the direction of association is reversed after accounting for the other variables.

Our discussion thus far indicates that the five socio-economic variables behave as expected. However, when all the socio-economic variables have been included in the analysis, we find that the direction of the relationship of the female employment in traditional occupations and households with electricity changes. Furthermore, the relationship between female employment in traditional occupation and infant mortality rate becomes insignificant.

From the R^2 statistic, we find that the socio-economic variables are able to account for 52.7 per cent of the variations in infant mortality rates among kabupaten (see last row of Table

6). The two education variables by themselves account for 42 per cent of the variance in infant mortality. When economic variables are included in the analysis, the explaining power increases to 50.9 per cent. Finally, when housing condition represented by households with electricity is added into the model, the explaining power increases by 1.9 per cent. This increment seems to be relatively insignificant. At this point, we may conclude that the education variables seem to be important in explaining the differences in infant mortality rates among kabupaten in Java and Bali. The F ratio is also significant at the 5 per cent level.

Effects of Intermediate Variables

In the previous discussions, we have reduced the number of intermediate variables to five. The regression coefficients resulting from the hierarchical regression equation of these five variables on infant mortality rates are presented in Table 7.

The first variable included in the equation is proportion of married women, defined as the percentage of women aged 15-24 years married in the 1980 census. This measure is associated with age at first marriage. The higher percentage of married women in this age group indicates that the regency has lower age at first marriage for women. Low age at first marriage has been shown to be associated with higher risk of child losses (Soeradji 1981). Hence, low age at first marriage is associated with higher child mortality and infant mortality. Consequently, a positive relationship between proportion married and infant mortality level is expected.

This contention is supported by our data in Table 7. The zero order correlation shows a figure of 0.60 which is considerably high. This variable alone, is able to explain 36.4 per cent of the variations in infant mortality rates among regencies. However, after controlling for the effects of the health variables, the partial regression coefficient is considerably reduced (from 1.313 to 0.890). The standardized regression coefficient (beta), for example, is also reduced from 0.603 to 0.409. But when health facilities variables are also included in the regression, the regression coefficient increases slightly. This indicates that there is a spurious effect from health facilities variables on infant mortality rates.

Two health condition variables, morbidity and medical treatment, are included in the equation. Morbidity is defined as the percentage of population who had reported to be sick during the week before census taking. A person will be considered as

TABLE 7
Hierarchical Regression Analysis of Intermediate Variables on Infant Mortality Rate

Independent Variables	Simple Correlation	Regression 1 b	1 Beta	2 b	2 Beta	3 b	3 Beta
Maternal							
1. Proportion of Married Women	.60	1.313	.603	.890	.409	.990	.455
Health Condition							
2. Medical Treatment	.16			-1.563	-.594	-1.613	-.613
3. Morbidity	.38			15.982	.854	15.957	.852
Health Facilities							
4. Number of Midwives	-.33					-1.547	-.027
5. Number of Medical Doctors	-.28					10.620	.106
R^2 (in %)		36.4		47.54		47.97	

being sick in the census if the person is not able to go to work or he is not able to do his regular job. Under this definition, a regency with a high morbidity rate is deemed to have an unfavourable health condition. Accordingly, we may expect that the higher morbidity rate, the higher the infant mortality rate. In other words, we expect a positive relationship between these two variables.

These results show a zero order correlation coefficient of 0.38 between morbidity and infant mortality rate. The standardized regression coefficient of morbidity rate on infant mortality rate after controlling for the effects of medical treatment is found to be 1.507. When proportion married is also accounted for as a control variable, we find a partial regression coefficient of 0.854, that is, a reduction in the partial regression coefficient by about half. The inclusion of the health facilities variables, however, does not change the relationship significantly.

Unlike morbidity rate, the medical treatment variable reversed its direction of association with infant mortality when the effects of other variables are controlled. There is a positive correlation (.16) between medical treatment and infant mortality but when the effects of the other variables are accounted for, the direction of association becomes negative.

Although when we first tested the relationship between the health facilities variables (number of midwives and number of medical doctors) and infant mortality rate they are found to be insignificant, these variables are found to be significant in the hierarchical regression analysis at the 5 per cent level. A plausible explanation for this discrepancy could be linked to the placement of midwives and medical doctors in the regencies. In general regencies with larger numbers of population are more likely to have more midwives and doctors. In this study, we have defined the variables as the number of midwives and doctors per 10,000 population. The variation of the values across regencies is probably quite small which makes the variable less sensitive to the variability of the infant mortality rate.

Summarizing the results, it is shown that the proportion of married women alone explains 36.4 per cent of the variation in infant mortality rates among regencies. When health condition variables, morbidity rate and medical treatment are included in the regression, the predicting power increases to 47.54 per cent. This indicates an increment of about 11.1 per cent of explained variance in infant mortality rates among regencies in Java and Bali areas. The increment, however, is only about 0.4 per cent when health facilities variables are included in the regression which shows the relative insignificant effects of number of midwives and medical doctors.

Joint Effects of Socio-economic and Intermediate Variables

In the next stage of analysis, the socio-economic and intermediate variables are included together in one regression model. The inclusion of variables, is performed in a hierarchical order with the variables classified under socio-economic, maternal, health condition and health facilities variables. The computed regression coefficients are presented in Table 8.

It is important to examine the regression coefficients (b, and beta) for all the variables and across the regression equations. When we compare the regression coefficients of the socio-economic variables, for example, across the regression equations it is evident that the values of the regression coefficients decline as the effects of the other sets of variables are introduced. When only socio-economic variables are entered into the regression (regression 1), the regression coefficient (beta) for level of education is -0.511. This value decreases to -0.464 when proportion of married women is included. The beta value declines further when the health condition and health facilities variables are taken into account. The exception seems to be the variable female employment in traditional occupations. The beta value for this variable in fact increases when the other variables are included in the regression.

This pattern indicates that the effects of socio-economic variables on infant mortality rate are mediated through the maternal, health condition and health facilities variables.

Comparing the values of the regression coefficients for the intermediate variables in Table 8 (regressions 2, 3 and 4) with the ones in Table 7, we find that the effects of the intermediate variables on infant mortality rate are substantially reduced when the effects of socio-economic variables are controlled for. For proportion of married women, for example, the regression coefficient is 0.603 (Table 7, regression 1). When we control for socio-economic variables, the beta value for proportion of married women is almost reduced to one-third (.203, Table 8, regression 2). And when we control for socio-economic and health and health facilities variables, the beta value is further reduced to 0.152 (Table 8, regression 4). A similar pattern is found for the morbidity variable.

TABLE 8

Hierarchical Regression Analysis of Infant Mortality Rate

Independent Variables	Simple Correlation	Regression 1		Regression 2		Regression 3		Regression 4	
		b	Beta	b	Beta	b	Beta	b	Beta
Socio-economic									
1. Level of Education	-.64	-2.131	-.511	-1.936	-.464	-1.759	-.422	-1.771	-.424
2. Women Education	-.44	-2.020	-.634	-1.555	-.488	-1.312	-.412	-1.328	-.417
3. Female Labour Force Participation	-.25	-0.623	-.201	-0.410	-.132	-0.231	-.074	-0.227	-.073
4. Female Employment in Traditional Occupation	+.29	-0.230	-.176	-0.307	-.234	-0.257	-.196	-0.280	-.213
5. Households with Electricity	-.25	-0.423	.299	0.335	.237	0.234	.166	0.116	.082
Maternal									
6. Proportion of Married Women 15-49	.60			0.442	.203	0.254	.117	0.330	.152
Health Condition									
7. Medical Treatment	.16					-0.822	-.312	-0.754	-.286
8. Morbidity	.38					10.146	.542	0.952	.509
Health Facilities									
9. Midwives	-.33							-5.550	-.098
10. Medical Doctors	-.28							20.553	.204

The above findings therefore show that the intermediate variables are less sensitive in affecting infant mortality rates as compared to the socio-economic variables. In other words, the differences in the rates of infant mortality among regencies in Java and Bali are largely influenced by the differences in the levels of socio-economic status.

The regression coefficient indicates the change in the value of the dependent variable resulting from the changes in the values of the predictors or independent variables. Hence the values of the regression coefficients are indicative of the relative strength of the effects of the predictor variables in influencing the values of the dependent variable (in this case infant mortality). Note that standardized regression coefficient (beta) is more suitable for this purpose than the unstandardized regression coefficient (b).

Looking at the last column of Table 8 when all the variables are included in the regression, morbidity rate has the highest beta value (0.509) followed by the level of education (-0.424) and women educator (-0.417). The smallest value is shown for female labour force participation rate (-0.073) followed by households with electricity (0.082). These lead us to conclude that morbidity rate has the strongest effect on infant mortality rate while labour force participation rate has the weakest effect.

Another way of utilizing the results of the multiple regression analysis is to examine the values of the coefficient of determination (R^2) and the multiple correlation coefficient. The first statistic indicates the proportion of variance in infant mortality rates explained by the variables included in the regression equation. The education variables alone account for 42 per cent of the explained variance in infant mortality (see Table 9). The predictive power increases as other variables are included in the model. When economic variables are added to the education variables, the model explains 51 per cent of the variance in infant mortality rates, an increase of about 8 per cent of explained variance. The increment in R^2 when households with electricity and proportion of married women are included in the model is much smaller (1.7 per cent and 1.1 per cent respectively).

From the findings, we find that education, economic and health condition variables are the most salient variables in explaining variance in infant mortality rates. All the ten variables taken together are able to explain 60.27 per cent of the variance on infant mortality rates. This figure is considered quite substantial.

TABLE 9

Coefficient of Determination and Multiple Correlation Coefficient of Hierarchical Regression Analysis on Infant Mortality Rate

Variables in the Model	R-Squared	Multiple Correlation Coefficient	F-Ratio
1. Education	41.995	0.648	40.181
2. (1) + Economic	50.944	0.714	28.299
3. (2) + Household with Electricity	53.661	0.726	24.028
4. (3) + Proportion Married	53.704	0.733	20.687
5. (4) + Health Condition	59.423	0.771	19.221
5. (5) + Health Facilities	60.270	0.776	15.625

TABLE 10

R^2 of Each Variable by Mode of Regression Analysis on Infant Mortality Rate

Variables	Stepwise		Hierarchical	
	Order of inclusion	R^2	Order of inclusion	R^2
Level of Education	1	40.62	1	40.62
Women Education	6	0.66	1	1.38
Labour Force Participation Rate	8	0.37	2	7.34
Employment in Traditional Occupation	7	1.61	2	1.61
Household with Electricity	10	0.09	3	1.72
Proportion Married	3	4.38	4	1.04
Medical Treatment	5	0.89	5	0.82
Morbidity Level	2	10.67	5	4.90
Midwives	9	0.20	6	0.03
Medical Doctors	4	0.79	6	0.82

95

Alternative Mode of Analysis

The hierarchical mode of regression analysis assumes a predetermined causal relationship among variables in effecting infant mortality rates. This is then reflected in the hierarchical ordering of the variables introduced in the regression equations. In the analysis, we assume that some of the effects of socio-economic variables on infant mortality are mediated through the intermediate variables. These last mentioned variables are assumed to have direct effects on infant mortality rates.

Although these assumptions are generally acceptable, our hierarchical ordering of the variables may not match the actual situation.

Moreover, it is well known that the values of R^2 for individual variables depend on the order of inclusion into the equation. A variable which is introduced first will in general have higher values of R^2 than the variables entered later.

An alternative method is to let the ordering of the variables be determined by their statistical importance. The variances with the highest effects on infant mortality rate will be included first in the regression equation. In other words, the inclusion of variables in the regression equation is based on the relative importance of each variable on the dependent variable. This mode of analysis is called stepwise regression analysis. The R^2 of the stepwise regression analysis are shown in Table 10 so as to provide comparison with the R^2 of the hierarchical analysis.

It can be seen from the figures in Table 10 that in both stepwise and hierarchical regression, level of education has the highest effects on infant mortality accounting for 40.6 per cent of the explained variance. In the stepwise regression analysis, the second highest effect is shown for morbidity level, followed by proportion married. The other variables do not contribute much to the explained variance of infant mortality rates.

Summary and Conclusion

The 1980 Population Census of Indonesia indicates that the estimated population growth rate in the 1970s is 2.32 per cent which is higher than the projected rate of 2.08 per cent. This phenomenon is disturbing considering the fact that the family planning programme has been launched since 1970. More interesting too is that studies have shown that fertility and birth rates did decline over the same period. Mamas (1983), for example, reported that fertility rate has declined at the rate of 1.8 per cent annually. This rate of decline is considered fairly rapid. If birth rate has been declining, what then explains the higher growth rate in the 1970s over that for the 1960s?

The reason is largely found in the decline in mortality. The Central Bureau of Statistics (1983) reported that there has been a decline of 23 per cent in mortality rates between 1971 and 1980. This gives an annual rate of decline of about 2.5 per cent. The annual rate of decline in fertility rate, however, has been estimated to be only 1.8 per cent. This indicates that mortality rates during the 1970s have been declining faster than fertility rates. Since migration rate can largely be ignored, the higher rate of decline in mortality than in fertility accounts for the increase in the Indonesian population growth rate.

The rapid decline in mortality, including infant mortality, corresponds to the aim of the Indonesian Government to reduce nation-wide mortality. Hence in recent years, there has been an increase in research interest in identifying the factors which influence mortality. Some studies in this direction have been conducted in Indonesia. However, these studies often fail to give the holistic picture for the understanding of mortality differentials because they often focus only on a limited number of variables. To fully understand this demographic phenomenon the design of the study must be more comprehensive.

But this is not always easy given the shortcoming of available data. However, the study reported here tries to provide a more comprehensive analysis of the determinants of infant mortality. Taken into account the reliability and the availability of data, the study is only confined to Java and Bali which comprise about two-thirds of the Indonesian population. In order to provide some useful information for population and health development planning, the study employs the regency as the unit of analysis as administratively that is the lowest level for development planning.

Although the study initially tried to cover a large number of variables, the final analysis on the differentials in infant mortality rates is confined to 10 variables constituting two education, two economic, one housing condition, one maternal, two health condition, and two health personnel variables.

Contrary to expectation, the number of public health centres do not have any significant effect on infant mortality. The zero order correlation between the number of health centres per 10,000 population and infant mortality rate is reported to be -0.05 which is insignificantly correlated. There are several possible

97

explanations for this phenomenon. First, public health centres have only been recently established. This means that public health centres have not yet been maximally utilized by the population. Furthermore, some of these public health centres may not be easily accessible. The final reason is that it is probably too early to expect that public health centres would have any effect on infant mortality. Given time, they may play a greater role in reducing infant mortality in the population.

The number of health personnel, midwives and medical doctors, is shown to be significantly correlated with infant mortality rate. However, when the relationship is controlled by other variables, the association becomes insignificant. We suspect that this is due to the placement of health personnel which is proportional to the total population. It is also regretted that the study could not include the number of traditional midwives and the number of mother and child health care centres since these two variables are probably more directly related to the delivery of the babies as well as to the health care of the infants.

Because of the above shortcomings, this study is unable to cast much light on the relative importance of the health programme in influencing infant mortality and is hence not very useful in providing any meaningful information for health development planning as was originally intended.

Our analysis, however, indicates that level of education is the most powerful variable explaining the differences in infant mortality rates among regencies in Java and Bali areas. Also, the analysis shows that women's education is significantly associated with infant mortality level. This suggests the relative importance of education in reducing infant mortality. Given the present government's programme to improve the level of education and the fact that the level of education in Indonesia is still low, the beneficial effects of improvement of education in infant mortality can be substantial.

The government's effort to provide more job opportunities for women and to place greater emphasis on the role of women in development are also likely to have a beneficial impact on the level of infant mortality. As more women work in the modern sector the greater would be the likelihood for infant mortality to be reduced. Similar arguments are valid for increasing the age at first marriage. Delaying age at first marriage will help accelerate the reduction in mortality rates, particularly among children and infants.

This study also indicates that the health condition of the population is significantly associated with infant mortality rate. The healthier a regency is, the less likely is the regency to have

98

a high infant mortality rate. We may note in this context that health condition of the population is primarily related to its better socio-economic status which is linked to a better nutritional condition in the population.

The results of this study may provide some indications for future studies. The study needs to be expanded to cover variables that are directly related to infant mortality incidence such as the number of traditional midwives. They are more important than modern midwives because in Indonesia they are the ones who attend the majority of deliveries. The number of children who obtain immunization and the number of people who obtain mother and child health care are also important variables. These variables are needed to assess the role that health improvement programmes play in the reduction of infant mortality rate. Also, it is suggested that in order that these programmes be successful, they should be easily accessible by all socio-economic strata of the population.

So far, this study shows that socio-economic variables are important in determining the level of infant mortality rates. But socio-economic progress should also go hand-in-hand with health improvement programmes. This study, however, does indicate that the prospects for further reduction in infant mortality in Indonesia is good. This is because many of the government programmes are aimed at improving the socio-economic status and the general health of the population.

List of Variables

1. Village size (VILSIZE)   - Average total population per village.

2. Population Density (DENSITY)   - Total number of population per square kilometre.

3. Level of Education (EDLEV)   - Proportion of school-going-age population who are still in school.

4. Level of Urbanization (URBERS) - Percentage of population residing in urban areas as classified by the 1980 Population Census.

5. Female Illiteracy Level (ILIT) - Proportion of women who are illiterate.

6. Women Education (WEDUC)   - Percentage of female population aged 15-49 years who have completed junior high school.

7. Ability to speak National Language (NATLANG)   - Proportion of population who are able to speak the national language, Bahasa Indonesia.

8. Female Employment in Traditional Occupation (TRAD) - Percentage of female population who are employed in traditional occupation.

9. Female Labour Force Participation (LFPR)   - Percentage of female population aged 10+ years who are in the labour force.

10. Women Employment Rate (EMPLY) - Percentage of female population who are employed to female population who are in the labour force.

11. Households with Electricity (ELECHH)   - Percentage of households with electricity as source of lighting.

12. Communication Exposure (COMM) - Percentage of households possessing televisions or radios.

13. Intensified Farming (INFAM) - Percentage of farm areas under intensive production programme.

14. Landless Farmers (LANDLESS) - Percentage of farming households without farm land.

15. Proportion of Married Women (PROPMAR) - Percentage of female population aged 15-24 who have been married.

16. Average Number of Children (LIVCHILD) - Average number of children born alive who are still living.

17. Medical Treatment (MEDTR) - Percentage of population who are sick during a week before the Census and getting treatment from medical facilities.

18. Medical Doctors (DOCTORS) - Number of medical doctors per 10,000 population.

19. Midwives (MIDW) - Number of midwives per 10,000 population.

20. Public Health Centre (PHC) - Number of public health centres per 10,000 population.

21. Households with piped water (PIPEDHH) - Percentage of households with piped water as source of drinking water.

References

Bourgeois Pichat J. "An Analysis of Infant Mortality". In Population Bulletin No. 2. New York: United Nations, Department of Social Affairs, Population Division, ST/SOA/Ser. N/2, 1952.

Brass, William and Ansley Coale. "Methods of Analysis and Estimation". In The Demography of Tropical Africa, ed. W. Brass. Princeton: Princeton University Press, 1968.

Heligman, Larry. Levels and Trends of Mortality in Indonesia, 1961-1971. Washington: International Statistical Program Center, 1975.

Hull, Terence and Sunaryo. Levels and Trends of Infant and Child Mortality in Indonesia. Yogyakarta: Pusat Penelitian dan Studi Kependudukan, 1978.

Indonesia. Proyeksi Penduduk Indonesia. Indonesian Population Projection, Jakarta: Biro Pusat Statistik, 1983.

_____. Proyeksi Penduduk per Propinsi (Population Projection by Province). Jakarta: Biro Pusat Statistik, 1983.

_____. Rencana Pembangunan Lima Tahun Keempat, 1983-1988 (Fourth Five-Year Development Plan, 1983-1988). Jakarta, 1983.

Keyfitz, Nathan. "Cause of Death in Future Mortality". Paper presented at the International Population Conference, Mexico City, 1977.

Mamas. "Tren dan Variasi Angka Kelahiran Menurut Propinsi" (Trends and Variations in Birth Rates by Province). Paper presented at the Seminar on Fertility in Indonesia, Jakarta, 1983.

Martokoesoemo, Budi S. "Marriage and Divorce in Indonesia". Ph.D. dissertation, University of Chicago, 1979.

Mosley, W. Henry. "Social Determinants of Infant and Child Mortality: Some Considerations for an Analytical Framework". Paper presented at a conference on Health and Mortality in Infancy and Early Childhood, Cairo, 1980.

_____. "Consideration for a Conceptual Framework for the Study of Child Survival". Mimeographed. Jakarta: Ford Foundation, 1982.

_____. "Will Primary Health Care Reduce Infant and Child Mortality?" Paper presented at Seminar on Social Policy, Health Policy and Mortality Prospect, Paris, 1983.

McDonald, Peter. "The Age Pattern of Mortality in Indonesia: A Comment". In Majalah Demografi Indonesia, No. 9, V, 1978.

102

Nitisastro, Widjojo. Population Trends in Indonesia. Cornell: Cornell University Press, 1970.

Sinquefield, Jeanne C. and Azwini Kartoyo. "Using Retrospective Mortality Data to Test the Applicability of Model Life Tables for Indonesia". In Majalah Demografi Indonesia, 4 (7), 1977.

Soemantri, Suharsono. "Pola Perkembangan dan Perbandingan Daerah Angka Kematian Bayi" (Trends and Regional Differentials of Infant Mortality Rates). Paper presented at the Seminar on Infant Mortality Rate in Indonesia, Jakarta, 1983.

Soemantri et al. "Berbagai Indikator Sistem Kesehatan Nasional Yang Dapat Diberikan oleh Sensus Penduduk 1980". (Some Indicators of National Health System Derivable from the 1980 Population Census). Paper presented at a Seminar at the Research and Development Board, Department of Health, Jakarta, 1982.

Soeradji, Budi. "Patterns and Consequences of Age at First Marriage". Paper presented at workshop ASEAN-Population Project, Baguio City, 1981.

_____. "Population Trend and Policy in Indonesia". Paper presented at NIRA-ISEAS Joint Seminar on Population Problems and Fertility in ASEAN Countries, Tokyo, 1983.

Sullivan, Jeremiah M. "Models for the Estimation of the Probability of Dying Between Birth and Exact Ages of Childhood". In Population Studies, 26 (1), 1972.

Trussell, T. James. "A Re-estimation of the Brass Techniques for Determining Childhood Survivorship Rates". In Population Studies, 29 (1), 1975.

United Nations. "Determinants and Consequences of Population Trends". In Population Studies Series, No. 50, 1973.

Utomo, Budi. "Prospek Angka Kematian Bayi dan Anak di Indonesia Menjelang Tahun 2000" (Infant and Childhood Mortality Rates in the Year 2000). Paper presented at third meeting of Indonesian Demography Association, 1983.

Utomo, Budi et al. "Infant and Child Mortality in Indonesia: What do we know and where do we go from here?" Mimeographed, n.d.

Tey Nai Peng and
Noor Laily binti Dato' Abu Bakar

INTRODUCTION

Demographic Situation

The population of Malaysia has been growing at about 2.5 per cent
per annum for the most part of the present century. The total
population was estimated at 13.7 million in the 1980 Population
Census, of which 83.2 per cent were in Peninsular Malaysia, 7.3
per cent in Sabah and 9.5 per cent in Sarawak. The country is a
land with great diversity of ethnicity and culture. In Peninsular
Malaysia the Malays made up 55.3 per cent of the population,
Chinese 33.8 per cent, Indian 10.2 per cent and other 0.7 per
cent.

Between 1970 and 1980 the urban population of Malaysia grew
at 4.7 per cent per year, while the rural population grew by only
1.2 per cent per year, resulting in a significant increase in
urban population from 29 per cent to 37.2 per cent. This was
largely brought about by net migration from rural to urban areas,
natural increase and changes in administrative urban boundaries
(Khoo 1983).

Since the enforcement of tight restriction in immigration in
1947, the population has stabilized in terms of the age and sex
distribution. The proportion of persons below the age of 15 fell
from 45 per cent in 1970 to 39 per cent in 1980, while the
proportion of persons aged 60 and over increased only marginally
from 5 per cent to 6 per cent during the intercensal period.

The crude birth rate for Peninsular Malaysia had declined by
30 per cent since independence from 46.2 per 1,000 in 1957 to 32.3

104

in 1982. However, such decline had slowed in the 1970s and the crude birth rate has been hovering around 30 per 1,000 population.

Mortality rate in the late 1940s was estimated at around 15 per 1,000 population. Since the early 1950s there has been a consistent downward trend in mortality. By 1960, the crude death rate was slightly above 9 per 1,000 population and by 1982 it had reached a low 5.2. This has been brought about by improvement in the standard of living as well as health care services.

Health Programme

The Ministry of Health is responsible for the provision of a comprehensive and easily accessible medical and health services. The concept of primary health care through the Rural Health Programme has been implemented since 1961. Over the years, the country has developed the basic health infrastructure and expanded the medical services to include a wide range of preventive, nutrition and sanitation activities to cover both the urban and the rural areas. Such activities were directed to provide an integrated medical, dental and maternal and child health services.

In implementing the Rural Health Service Programme, a network of one main health centre, four health sub-centres and 20 midwife clinics-cum-quarters were established to cover every 50,000 population.

The Patient Care Programme located at the General and District Hospitals is run concurrent to the Public Health Service Programme. The general hospitals, located in each of the 14 states, provide both out-patient and in-patient service care for the population it serves, as well as cases referred from the district hospitals and health centres. Despite the rather extensive network of peripheral health stations, patient care services, however, still face several constraints such as shortage of beds and insufficient trained personnel. Plans are underway to rectify these problems.

With improvement in the health care system, particularly in the control of communicable diseases, the incidence of infective diseases such as tuberculosis, pneumonia, gastro-enteritis and other diarrhoeal diseases has decreased considerably over the years. However, diseases characterized by degenerative disorders are becoming more important.

Background and Objectives of the Study

This study is an attempt to examine the socio-economic correlates of mortality in Malaysia. While mortality rates at the national level appears relatively low by the standard of developing countries, the decline has not been uniform among the various segments of the population. Because of the lack of reliable data and research in this area, very little is known about the mortality differentials in the country.

Recognizing the dearth of research in this area, researchers are now beginning to direct their attention to mortality study so as to better understand the dynamics of mortality decline. Findings of these studies will help provide information to planners regarding the factors influencing mortality. Such information could be fed into public health policies.

Specifically the aims of this project are as follows:

(1) Studying the regional trends and differentials in mortality in Peninsular Malaysia;

(2) Identifying the socio-economic correlates of mortality;

(3) Ascertaining the role of health services and extent of use by different social groups.

Related Research

There are not many studies on mortality in Malaysia. Among the few research papers on mortality in Malaysia may be mentioned the work of Hirschman and Tan (1971) on the analysis of death registration statistics. Another study focused on examination of the socio-economic and medical aspects of rural-urban mortality differentials (Zainal A. Yusof and Khairuddin Yusof 1974). Using the vital statistics and data collected from a special project in a maternity hospital in Kuala Lumpur, Kader (1983) also examined the differentials in neo-natal mortality focusing on birth weight, maternal age, ethnicity and place of residence. Recently, using results from the Health and Family Planning Survey in Johore and Perak, Ang and Tey (1984) also show that foetal wastage and early childhood mortality were inversely related to education and urban residence. In addition, the National Population and Family Development Board with the co-operation of the Department of Statistics and the Ministry of Health have produced the following papers on mortality trends and patterns and the impact of programme inputs:

(1) Health Administration District Level Differences in Maternal, Infant and Toddler Mortality Rates as Related to Mother and Child and Family Planning Programme Inputs and Socio-economic Conditions (1982);

(2) The Changing Fertility and Mortality Rates in the Administrative Districts of Peninsular Malaysia (1983);

(3) The Changing Ethnic Patterns of Mortality in Malaysia 1957-1979 (1983).

The findings reported in these papers suggest that Mother and Child inputs and socio-economic conditions are important determinants of mortality differentials at the district level.

Sources of Data

Studies on mortality differentials at the individual level are limited due to the inavailability of information on socio-economic characteristics of the deceased in the death certificates. In this study, we have resorted to areal analysis using the districts as the unit of analysis. Mortality rates are related to socio-economic indicators in the districts.

The vital registration system provides the basic data for the computation of the various mortality rates used in this study. While vital registration in Peninsular Malaysia is notable for its completeness, the same cannot be said of Sabah and Sarawak. Therefore, this study restricts the analysis of the district level differences in mortality to Peninsular Malaysia.

Prior to 1982, mortality rates for the administrative districts were based on deaths reported at place of occurrence rather than at place of residence of the deceased. To the extent that some significant number of deaths occur in hospitals which are located in the urban areas, mortality rates by place of occurrence would distort the true distribution of deaths by place of residence. In order to relate the actual mortality conditions with other socio-economic indicators, mortality rates for the year 1982 for each of the 78 districts reported by place of residence were used in the analysis.

The 1980 Population Census provides much information on the characteristics of the districts, that is, urbanization, educational attainment, ethnic distribution, ownership of TV and radio, availability of electricity, piped water and modern toilet facilities as well as data on economic activities. Data on health facilities and utilization of health services were mainly obtained from the evaluation studies of the Population and Family Health Project.

Data collected from the Malaysian Fertility and Family Survey (1974) were used in the analysis of mortality differentials at the individual level to supplement the areal analysis.

Trends and Differentials in Ethnic Mortality:
An Analysis of Vital Statistics

Mortality rates in Malaysia are amongst the lowest for developing countries. The crude death rate of 19.4 per 1,000 population in 1947 had declined steadily to 5.2 by 1982. This compares favourably with crude death rates recorded in many developed countries. However, it must be mentioned that the low crude death rate is partly attributed to the youthfulness of the population. Hence, standardizing on the age distribution of the Coale-Demeny "West" female population with $e_0 = 65$ and $r = 0.01$, the crude death rates in 1980 would have been 10.2 for the Malays, 9.5 for the Chinese and 24.9 for the Indians respectively. With the impending ageing of the population, further reduction in the age-specific death rates is necessary in order to maintain the crude death rate at this low level.

Although the Malays started out at a much higher mortality level than the other ethnic groups, they have, however, experienced a more rapid decline in mortality such that by 1980 they had the lowest crude death rate among the three major ethnic groups in the country (see Table 1). On the other hand, the crude death rate among the Indians, particularly the males, remains significantly higher than the Malays and the Chinese.

An examination of the age specific death rates in Table 2 shows that at ages under 15, the Malays and Indians of both sexes have substantially higher mortality rates than the Chinese. At aged 15 and above, mortality rates for the Malay males are generally lower than that of the Chinese males. In contrast, Chinese females had considerably lower mortality rates than Malay females at all ages except aged 80 and above. In most of the age groups, Indians of both sexes have substantially higher mortality rates than the Malays and the Chinese. With the exception of aged 80 and above, the age specific mortality rates of the Indians were one and a half times or twice as high as that of the Chinese.

Analysing the changing ethnic patterns of mortality in Peninsular Malaysia for the period 1957-79, Noor Laily et al.

108

TABLE 1
Trends in Crude Death Rates, Infant Mortality Rate,
Neo-natal Mortality Rate and Toddler Mortality Rate
by Ethnic Group, Peninsular Malaysia, 1957-80

Year	Total	Malay	Chinese	Indians
			Crude Death Rate	
1947	19.4	24.3	14.3	15.8
1957	12.4	14.9	9.8	11.1
1960	9.5	11.1	7.7	8.9
1966	7.6	8.3	6.5	8.5
1970	7.0	7.3	6.2	8.1
1975	6.2	6.3	5.7	7.7
1980	5.5	5.3	5.4	7.0
1982	5.2	5.0	5.1	6.6
			Infant Mortality Rate	
1957	75.5	95.6	46.9	75.7
1960	68.9	87.4	42.5	65.1
1966	48.0	57.6	30.9	51.1
1970	40.8	47.6	28.5	46.0
1975	33.2	37.2	24.0	38.3
1980	24.0	26.9	16.0	28.7
1982	19.3	21.9	12.1	21.2
			Neo-natal Mortality Rate	
1957	29.6	34.6	22.2	30.6
1966	24.9	27.2	20.0	28.3
1970	22.9	24.1	19.7	28.0
1975	20.6	22.1	17.3	22.6
1980	15.6	16.6	12.0	16.6
1982	12.1	13.5	9.0	12.0
			Toddler Mortality Rate	
1957	10.7	14.1	6.6	9.0
1966	5.1	6.8	2.6	5.1
1970	4.2	5.6	2.1	3.8
1975	3.1	4.0	1.4	3.4
1980	2.0	2.5	1.0	2.3
1982	1.7	2.1	0.8	1.9

SOURCES: Report of Registrar General on Population, Births,
Deaths, Marriages and Adoption (1947-62) and Vital
Statistics, Statistics Department, Kuala Lumpur,
Malaysia.

TABLE 2

Age-specific Death Rates by Ethnicity and Sex, Peninsular Malaysia, 1980

Age	Malays			Chinese			Indians		
	Both Sexes	Male	Female	Both Sexes	Male	Female	Both Sexes	Male	Female
0	27.5	30.8	24.1	17.1	19.3	14.8	30.8	32.6	28.0
1	2.6	2.7	2.6	1.1	1.1	1.2	2.5	2.4	2.7
5	1.0	1.1	0.9	0.5	0.6	0.4	0.8	0.8	0.8
10	0.7	0.8	0.6	0.5	0.6	0.3	0.8	1.1	0.6
15	0.9	1.2	0.7	0.9	1.3	0.5	1.5	1.5	1.5
20	1.2	1.7	0.8	1.3	2.0	0.6	2.1	2.6	1.5
25	1.5	1.9	1.2	1.3	1.9	0.7	2.5	3.1	1.8
30	1.9	1.8	2.0	1.6	2.0	1.2	2.5	3.1	2.0
35	2.3	2.5	2.2	2.0	2.5	1.5	3.4	3.8	3.0
40	3.4	3.7	3.0	3.0	3.8	2.1	6.1	8.1	4.1
45	5.1	5.7	4.5	5.1	6.8	3.5	9.7	12.7	6.4
50	8.7	9.8	7.6	8.0	10.9	5.4	14.9	18.9	9.4
55	14.5	17.0	12.0	12.2	16.7	8.5	24.5	30.2	16.7
60	23.7	26.3	21.3	21.3	28.3	15.8	39.1	44.1	30.8
65	38.3	40.9	35.6	34.8	45.4	25.5	57.8	65.7	44.9
70	60.8	63.3	58.2	53.0	64.4	42.3	83.6	90.2	71.4
75	83.5	99.3	76.4	81.5	97.4	66.5	126.8	131.3	114.6
80	114.4	116.7	105.2	123.1	144.3	105.8	146.1	150.7	134.7
85+	132.6	141.3	124.2	198.1	200.1	193.8	160.4	174.8	130.0

SOURCE: 1980 Vital Statistics (p. 187), Statistics Department, Kuala Lumpur, Malaysia, 1983.

(1983) have shown that improvement in life chances in Peninsular Malaysia since independence (1957) has been remarkable, with a gain in life expectancies of 11.4 years and 14.3 years respectively for males and females (see Table 3). Further, their analysis shows that improvement among the previously disadvantaged Malays has been especially remarkable. In 1957, the Malays had the lowest expectation of life at birth for both sexes (males 50.2 years, females 53.4 years); but by 1967 they overtook the Indians and the Malay males appeared to have equalled the Chinese by 1972. In contrast, the Indians have gained the least, if at all, since 1957, reversing their earlier advantage over the Malays. After aged 20, there was an increase in mortality rate among the Indian males in an otherwise improving mortality condition. To the extent that majority of the Indian population is concentrated in the estates, a study looking into the living conditions in these areas is warranted.

Infant mortality rate has often been used as a development indicator since it is most responsive to changes in socio-economic conditions. This is borne out by the fact that the infant mortality rate for Peninsular Malaysia as a whole had declined by 74.4 per cent from 75.5 in 1957 to 19.3 per 1,000 live births in 1982. Interestingly, infant mortality decline has accelerated in the more recent years, falling at an average of about 6 per cent per annum during the period 1957-82 as compared to an average of 3.7 per cent per annum during the period 1970-75.

In 1957 the infant mortality rate was highest among the Malays (95.6), followed by the Indians (75.7) and the Chinese (46.9). However, as a result of a more rapid decline in infant mortality among the Malays, they overtook the Indians by 1975 and have been occupying the intermediate position since then. The trend indicates a covergence of infant mortality rates among the three ethnic groups, indicating that the benefits of the rapid socio-economic development which has taken place in the last two decades have benefited all groups.

Between 1957-82, the neo-natal mortality rate had declined by 59 per cent from 29.6 to 12.1 per 1,000 births. Although again starting at a disadvantage, the more rapid decline in neo-natal mortality rate among the Malays and to a certain extent the Indians as compared to the Chinese has brought about a gradual convergence of the neo-natal mortality rates among the ethnic groups.

In 1957 neo-natal deaths made up about 39 per cent of infant deaths, but by 1982 they constituted some 63 per cent of infant deaths. A more detailed breakdown shows that 53.2 per cent of infant death had occurred during the early neo-natal period (under one week). This indicates that decline in mortality during the

111

TABLE 3

Expectation of Life at Birth, e_0, for Peninsular Malaysia by Sex and Ethnic Group, 1957-79

Year	Peninsular Malaysia		Malay		Chinese		Indian		Others	
	Male	Female	Male	Female	Male	Female	Male	Female	Male	Female
1957	55.8	58.2	50.2	53.7	59.5	66.7	57.1	54.6	n.a.	n.a.
1967	63.5	66.3	61.7	63.0	66.6	71.9	62.2	62.1	69.5	73.9
1968	63.3	66.1	61.7	62.9	66.2	71.7	61.4	60.2	n.a.	n.a.
1969	63.8	66.7	62.4	63.8	66.6	72.0	61.6	61.2	n.a.	n.a.
1970	63.5	68.2	63.7	65.5	65.1	73.4	60.2	63.9	63.6	69.3
1971	64.0	69.1	64.5	66.8	65.7	73.9	59.9	63.5	64.1	69.9
1972	64.6	69.8	65.9	68.2	65.6	73.3	60.7	64.5	65.1	70.9
1973	64.5	69.7	65.4	67.9	65.6	73.5	60.1	62.9	65.1	69.8
1974	65.0	70.3	66.1	68.4	66.0	74.3	60.0	63.9	67.1	70.0
1975	65.4	70.8	66.1	69.0	66.7	74.8	60.7	65.1	68.3	73.9
1976	66.2	71.4	67.2	69.7	67.1	75.0	61.9	67.4	69.9	73.3
1977	66.1	71.4	66.8	69.8	67.3	75.2	61.9	66.9	71.0	72.0
1978	67.1	72.7	68.0	71.1	67.9	76.3	63.4	67.5	71.5	74.5
1979	67.2	72.5	67.9	71.0	68.1	75.8	63.2	68.0	71.3	73.9

n.a. = Not available and/or not ascertained.

SOURCE: 1957 and 1970 values are from abridged Life Tables: Malaysia 1970, Department of Statistics, 1974, Tables 23-30, pp. 43-50 and Tables 13-22, pp. 33-42. All other values are from the annual series of Vital Statistics Peninsular Malaysia, Department of Statistics.

TABLE 4

Still Birth Rate by Ethnicity, Place of Residence and Age of Mother,
Peninsular Malaysia, 1982

| | All Age Groups | Age of Mother | | | | | | | |
		15-19	20-24	25-29	30-34	35-39	40-44	45-49
Total	15.8	16.4	13.2	12.8	16.2	23.5	35.9	57.2
Malays	18.0	19.0	14.5	14.5	18.3	25.3	38.3	61.2
Chinese	8.7	8.2	7.5	7.2	9.6	13.7	19.7	40.4
Indians	22.4	17.6	19.4	20.3	26.1	44.3	58.2	74.1
Urban Areas	12.1	11.2	10.5	10.0	13.1	19.0	28.2	39.0
Malays	14.1	13.0	12.5	11.4	16.1	20.6	26.2	38.8
Chinese	8.7	8.5	6.6	7.2	10.1	14.4	27.0	46.5
Indians	19.4	14.2	18.0	17.9	17.8	38.5	51.3	-
Rural Areas	17.4	17.9	14.4	14.2	17.7	25.0	37.8	61.9
Malays	19.0	19.9	15.0	15.5	18.8	26.2	40.2	64.9
Chinese	8.6	7.9	8.5	7.1	9.1	13.1	13.3	36.0
Indians	24.0	19.1	20.1	21.6	31.1	48.1	61.3	100.0

SOURCE: 1982 Vital Statistics, Statistics Department, Kuala Lumpur, Malaysia, April 1984.

early neo-natal period has not been as rapid as during the post neo-natal period.

For all ethnic groups, decline in toddler mortality rate during the same period has been even more spectacular, falling from 10.7 in 1957 to 1.7 in 1982. The period 1957-66 witnessed the most rapid decline in toddler mortality rate, dropping from 14.1 to 6.8 for the Malays, 6.6 to 2.6 for the Chinese and 9.0 to 3.8 for the Indians. However, the latest available data show that toddler mortality rates for the Malays and the Indians were still twice as high as for the Chinese.

Data from vital registration show that out of every 1,000 births in 1982, 15.8 were still births. The data also clearly reveals that there is an increase in the risk of having a still birth with growing age. Within each age group and stratum, still birth rate was generally highest among the Indians and lowest among the Chinese, while the Malays were in between.

From all age groups, still birth rate was substantially higher in the rural areas as compared to the urban areas. Further ethnic differentials were found to be larger in the rural areas than in the urban areas, indicating that differentials in still birth rates could be reduced with improvement in socio-economic conditions and the provision of better facilities such as those found in the urban areas.

Causes of Deaths

Although there is a growing concern and interest on the causes of deaths, such information remains deficient. In 1980, out of the 64,212 deaths registered in Peninsular Malaysia, only 24,075 (37.5 per cent) were medically certified. Of the uncertified deaths, 62 per cent were classified under the broad category of "other known causes of deaths".

Table 5 shows that the principal causes of deaths are characteristically that of a developed rather than a developing country. It shows a growing importance of diseases of the circulatory system and accidents on the one hand and a steady decline in communicable diseases such as tuberculosis, malaria infections and parasitic diseases on the other. Although diseases of early infancy continue to be the major cause of death, it has declined from 3,422 in 1972 to 2,865 in 1980.

TABLE 5

Major Causes of Deaths in Government Hospitals in Peninsular Malaysia by Rank Order and Percentage, 1970, 1977 and 1980

Major Cause	Deaths 1970		Deaths 1977		Deaths 1980	
	Rank*	Per cent	Rank*	Per cent	Rank*	Per cent
Accidents	3	8.06	3	11.36	3	13.14
Gastro-enteritis	8	4.06	8	2.71	8	1.87
Heart Disease	2	13.94	2	15.68	1	16.44
Diseases of Early Infancy	1	18.86	1	18.65	2	14.90
Cardio-Vascular Disease	6	6.71	4	7.69	4	7.93
Neoplasm	4	7.21	5	7.07	5	7.78
Pneumonia	5	6.55	6	5.17	6	4.05
Malaria	-	-	-	-	-	-
Skin Disease	-	-	-	-	-	-
Tuberculosis	7	5.88	7	3.16	7	3.12
Pyrexis of Unknown Origin	-	-	-	-	-	-
Disease of Liver	-	-	9	2.12	-	-
Total	16,509		17,423		17,014	

NOTE: * Refer to the rank order of the major causes of deaths in Government Hospitals in Peninsular Malaysia.

SOURCES: (1) Ministry of Finance, Malaysia 1981/1982, Economic Report, Table 1, 158.

(2) Ministry of Health (MCH), Malaysia.

Indirect Methods for Estimating Mortality

The probability of dying between birth and selected ages can be approximated by the proportion dead among children ever born to women in a particular age group regardless of marital status or marital duration. Several variations of the method used to derive indirect estimates of mortality exist, differing only in their choice of a fertility model.

Brass has shown that the proportion dead of children born to women 20-24 is roughly equivalent to the probability of dying between birth and aged 2 and the proportion dead for children of women 25-29 and 30-34 are equivalent to the probabilities of dying before ages 3 and 5 respectively. The assumption of this method is that children of women 20-24 were born on the average two years earlier and children of women 25-29 were born on average, three years earlier.

We will now consider Trussell's variant of the Brass method in estimating the probabilities of dying before a selected age for the various sub-groups of the sample population (United Nations 1983), using data obtained in the Malaysia Fertility and Family Survey, 1974. First, it must be noted that this method of estimation is based on the assumption that fertility and childhood mortality have remained constant in the recent past. In deriving the estimates of the probability of dying between births and various childhood ages, the proportions of dead children can be tabulated by women grouped either into standard age categories or duration of marriage. The estimates presented in Table 6 are based on data classified by duration and marriage, with the assumption that women marry and stay married until aged 50.

Before examining socio-economic differentials in mortality, it is important to note that the reliability of the estimates derived from marriage duration depends largely on the accuracy of measuring the duration of marriage and marital stability. It should also be noted that the data are somewhat abnormal in that the proportions dead decrease with age of mother in some instances, contrary to expectation, since children of older mothers have had a longer period of exposure to the risk of dying. This is probably due to sampling variation or biases in reporting.

Higher child mortality among the Malays and the Indians as compared to the Chinese is manifested by the higher probabilities of dying in the early stages of life. The probability of dying between birth and aged 2 was about 0.055 for the Malays, 0.033 for the Chinese and 0.052 for the Indians. By aged 5, some 7.3 per cent of the children of Malays and 9.2 per cent of the children of Indians would have died in contrast to 3.6 per cent of the Chinese

116

TABLE 6
Mortality Estimates Derived by Applying Trussell's Method to Data
from Malaysia's Fertility and Family Survey (1974)
on Proportion of Children Dead by Marital Duration
and Selected Socio-economic Characteristics

	qx			
	q2	q3	q5	q10
Ethnic Group				
Malays	0.05474	0.06551	0.07327	0.09162
Chinese	0.03334	0.02712	0.03625	0.04983
Indian	0.05185	0.08909	0.09150	0.06922
Place of Residence				
Metropolitan Towns	0.04033	0.03175	0.04783	0.04605
Small Towns	0.02603	0.03516	0.05615	0.05105
Rural Areas	0.05254	0.05963	0.11734	0.08647
Years of Education				
No Schooling	0.05054	0.05937	0.07949	0.08341
1-6 years	0.05220	0.05247	0.05577	0.07221
7 years	0.02993	0.03057	0.02833	0.01158
Average Monthly Income				
$125	0.07546	0.06804	0.08003	0.10069
$125 - $249	0.05323	0.04758	0.05919	0.07341
$250 - $374	0.03583	0.04719	0.06756	0.06217
$375 - $624	0.02401	0.03952	0.04124	0.06774
$625+	0.02747	0.04795	0.02957	0.05433
Father's Occupation				
White Collar	0.02862	0.03645	0.04722	0.04474
Farm	0.06951	0.07507	0.06908	0.08748
Blue Collar	0.03500	0.04217	0.06283	0.07395

117

children. Although some of these differentials could be attributed to misreporting or marital instability, particularly among the Malays, we believe that substantial ethnic mortality differentials exist.

The probability of dying by aged 2 in the rural areas was about twice as high as in the small towns. Surprisingly, mortality risks in the metropolitan towns were substantially higher than in the smaller towns during the first two years of life. However, the pattern reversed itself by aged 3.

The threshold by which education seemed to have some significant effect in lowering mortality risk is observed between children of women with primary education and those of women with at least some secondary education.

The inverse relationship between income and probabilities of dying shows that those who are better off tend to provide better care for their children and therefore enhance their survivorship.

Father's occupation also provides sharp differentials in child mortality in favour of children of white collar and blue collar workers over farm workers.

PRELIMINARY EXAMINATIONS OF AREAL DIFFERENCES IN MORTALITY

The following sections will be directed to identifying and evaluating the factors that account for the inter-district variability in mortality in 1982. Our approach is to test the relationship between levels of mortality and the various socio-economic-demographic and health-related programme variables at the district level through multivariate areal analyses. In the multivariate areal analysis, districts are the units of analysis and the focus is on aggregate levels of mortality. Rather than analysing individual correlations which are often not available, areal analysis has the decided advantage of identifying high mortality areas so that programmes can be developed to reduce it. It must be recognized, however, that results obtained by this type of analysis cannot be presumed to hold true among individuals (Hermalin 1975).

The Variables

The following mortality indices available at the district level constituted the dependent variables for the study:

1.	Crude death rate	CDR
2.	Infant mortality rate	IMR
3.	Toddler mortality rate	TMR
4.	Still birth rate	SBR

The numerator for all these rates were based on deaths in 1982 tallied by place of residence of the deceased. The denominators for crude death rate and toddler mortality rate in 1982 were estimated by extrapolating the 1980 population based on the intercensal growth rates for the districts. The denominators for infant mortality rate and still birth rate were the births in 1982 registered by place of residence (of the mother).

The independent variables were classified under:

I.   Demographic and Background Characteristics

1.	Total fertility rate	TFR
2.	Per cent population living in urban areas	URBAN
3.	Per cent population Malays	MALAY
4.	Per cent population Chinese	CHINESE
5.	Per cent population Indians	INDIAN
6.	Ageing Index	AGEING

The total fertility rates (TFR) were calculated based on births in 1982 tallied by place of residence over the extrapolated population, as in the case of the mortality measures. Degree or urbanization (URBAN), ethnic composition and the ageing index (AGEING) were obtained from unpublished data of the 1980 Population and Housing Census. Urban areas were defined as gazetted areas with a population of 10,000 or more. The ageing index was obtained by dividing the number of persons aged 65 and over with the number of persons aged below 15.

II. Socio-economic Variables

1.	Per cent of total population completed at least lower secondary education	LOWSEC
2.	Secondary school enrolment ratio	ENROL
3.	Per cent households owning TV	TV
4.	Per cent households supplied with piped water	PIPE
5.	Per cent labour force engaged in non-agricultural activities	NON-AGRI

III. Health Programme and Sanitation Variables

| 1. | Per cent live births completed 3 doses of triple antigen | TA |

2. Per cent home deliveries among all
   deliveries 1977-79   HOME-DEL
3. Post-natal nursing care for newborn
   per 100 live births   POST-NATAL
4. Government hospital beds per 10,000
   population   BED
5. Nursing personnel per 10,000 married
   women 15-49   NURSE
6. Per cent households with modern
   sanitation (flush/pour toilets)   TOILET
7. Family planning acceptors per 1,000
   eligible women in 1978-82   FP

Several summary measures of central tendency, dispersion, maximum value and minimum value for each of the study variables across all 78 districts are displayed in Table 7.

Areal Differences in Mortality

Substantial deviations in mortality rates exist among the districts. The infant mortality rate in Ulu Kelantan, for instance, is almost 4½ times as high as in the federal territory (Kuala Lumpur).

Figure 1 illustrates the departure of infant mortality rate for each of the 78 districts in terms of standard deviation units from the rates for Peninsular Malaysia as a whole. It shows that infant mortality rate tends to be higher in the less developed states of the Peninsular, particularly in the north-east region and in the more rural districts in the central and west coast states. Within each state, pronounced differences in the infant mortality rate (IMR) between the more developed and the less developed districts can also be observed.

Differentials in the crude death rate is to some extent influenced by the age structure of the population. This is shown by the extremely low crude death rates in Selangor and the federal Territory (Table 8) among the Malays where in-migration, biased in favour of the younger population, had played an important role in affecting the population structure. In Pahang the effect of the land resettlement scheme on the crude death rate among the Malays through changing the age structure can also be observed. In contrast, crude death rates in the less developed states where there had been an exodus in the young population were considerably higher than the national average.

The infant mortality rate, for instance, was considerably higher in the east coast states, particularly as compared to the

120

TABLE 7

Summary Statistics of Study Variations

Year	Variable	Mean	Std. Error	Std. Deviation	Kurtosis	Skewness	Min.	Max.
1982	CDR	5.7	0.11	1.0	0.00	0.03	3.8	8.7
1982	IMR	21.7	0.75	6.7	0.27	0.59	8.9	39.6
1982	TMR	2.0	0.12	1.0	1.50	1.20	0.6	5.8
1982	SBR	15.3	0.55	4.8	-0.03	0.35	5.2	29.1
1982	TFR	463.0	122.5	108.2	2.50	1.00	232.4	899.2
1980	MALAY	65.3	2.5	22.3	-1.17	-0.12	18.8	98.4
1980	CHINESE	25.3	1.9	16.9	-0.90	0.24	1.3	67.7
1980	INDIAN	8.7	0.9	7.9	-0.12	0.82	0.0	31.6
1980	URBAN	19.4	2.9	25.5	0.98	1.36	0.0	100.0
1980	AGEING	9.5	0.3	2.4	1.90	0.68	4.3	17.4
1980	LOW SEC	17.1	0.6	5.5	2.71	1.50	8.3	37.6
1980	ENROL	67.3	0.96	8.5	3.94	-1.6	35.0	82.5
1980	TV	45.0	1.93	17.0	-0.81	-0.24	6.9	75.0
1980	PIPE	62.2	3.0	26.7	-0.73	-0.63	4.2	100.0
1980	NON-AGRI	50.0	2.4	21.0	-0.18	0.82	18.0	99.0
1977-79	TA	75.5	1.7	15.1	0.74	-1.1	28.1	96.5
1977-79	POSTNATAL	441.0	18.3	161.8	-0.58	0.26	122.6	785.0
1977-79	HOME-DEL	54.6	2.8	25.1	-1.3	0.04	11.2	93.5
1977-79	NURSE	42.2	2.2	19.9	0.44	0.97	15.0	97.1
1980	BED	17.7	1.8	16.1	7.6	2.2	0.0	91.4
1980	TOILET	57.4	1.9	16.7	-1.1	-0.04	21.0	91.0
1978-82	FP	115	4.3	38.3	0.04	0.17	29	225

FIGURE 1

Infant Mortality Rate Shown in Standard Deviation Units Above and Below the Average for Peninsular Malaysia, 1982 for All Districts

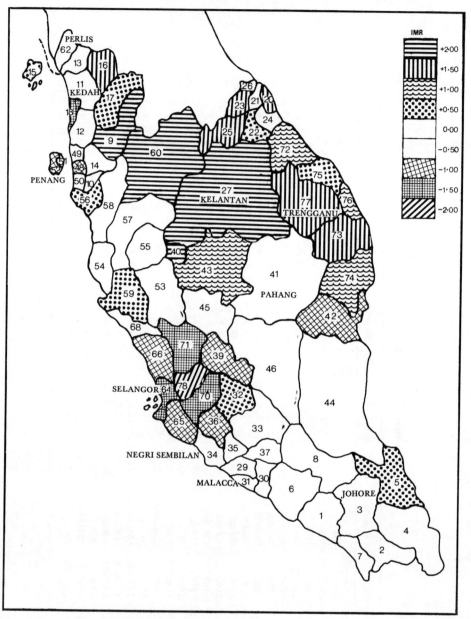

SOURCES: (a) Map: <u>Atlas Kebangsaan Malaysia</u> (Kuala Lumpur: Dewan Bahasa dan Pustaka, 1977).

(b) Statistics: 1980 Population and Housing Census of Malaysia; State Population Reports, Department of Statistics, Kuala Lumpur, pp. 580 and 600.

FIGURE 1 (continued)

**Infant Mortality Rate Shown in Standard Deviation Units Above and Below
the Average for Peninsular Malaysia, 1982 for All Districts**

Johor

1 Batu Pahat
2 Johor Bahru
3 Kluang
4 Kota Tinggi
5 Mersing
6 Muar
7 Pontian
8 Segamat

Kedah

9 Baling
10 Bandar Bharu
11 Kota Setar
12 Kuala Muda
13 Kubang Pasu
14 Kulim
15 Pulau Langkawi
16 Padang Terap
17 Sik
18 Yen
19 Pendang

Kelantan

20 Bachok
21 Kota Bharu
22 Machang
23 Pasir Mas
24 Pasir Puteh
25 Tanah Merah
26 Tumpat
27 Ulu Kelantan
28 Kuala Krai

Malacca

29 Alor Gajah (Utara)
30 Jasin (Selatan)
31 Melaka Tengah

Negeri Sembilan

32 Jelebu
33 Kuala Pilah
34 Port Dickson
35 Rembau
36 Seremban
37 Tampin
38 Jempol

Pahang

39 Bentong
40 Cameron Highlands
41 Jerantut
42 Kuantan
43 Lipis
44 Pekan
45 Raub
46 Temerloh
47 Rompin

Penang

48 S.P. Tengah (B. Mertajam)
49 S.P. Utara (Butterworth)
50 S.P. Selatan (N. Tebal)
51 Timor Laut (Georgetown)
52 Barat Daya

Perak

53 Batang Padang
54 Manjung (Dinding)
55 Kinta
56 Kerian
57 Kuala Kangsar
58 Larut dan Matang
59 Hilir Perak
60 Ulu Perak
61 Perak Tengah

Perlis

62 Perlis

Selangor

63 Gombak
64 Klang
65 Kuala Langat
66 Kuala Selangor
67 Petaling
68 Sabak Bernam
69 Sepang
70 Ulu Langat
71 Ulu Selangor

Trengganu

72 Besut
73 Dungun
74 Kemaman
75 Kuala Trengganu
76 Marang
77 Ulu Trengganu

W. Persekutuan

78 Wilayah Persekutuan

TABLE 8
Crude Death Rate and Infant Mortality Rate by States and Ethnicity, 1982

State	Crude Death Rate per 1,000 population				Infant Mortality Rate per 1,000 population			
	Total	Malays	Chinese	Indians	Total	Malays	Chinese	Indians
Johore	4.9	4.5	5.2	6.7	18.9	20.8	14.7	23.3
Kedah	6.0	5.9	5.6	7.7	22.2	23.3	13.9	25.5
Kelantan	6.7	6.8	6.1	7.0	27.1	27.5	17.0	23.8
Malacca	5.9	6.1	5.5	6.5	17.9	20.1	13.8	14.9
Negeri Sembilan	5.8	5.3	5.8	7.4	19.8	21.8	13.3	25.4
Pahang	4.9	4.4	5.4	7.5	21.2	22.5	10.6	34.0
Penang	6.1	5.8	6.0	7.7	15.9	20.1	12.8	14.7
Perak	6.2	5.9	6.0	8.0	21.5	24.3	13.6	30.0
Perlis	6.4	6.2	6.0	9.0	18.5	18.9	11.3	38.8
Selangor	4.7	3.9	4.9	6.6	12.2	14.1	8.8	13.3
Trengganu	6.3	6.3	5.9	12.2	27.5	27.8	19.9	-
Federal Territory (Kuala Lumpur)	4.0	2.3	4.6	5.7	8.9	9.1	8.0	11.7

SOURCE: 1982 Vital Statistics, Statistics Department, Kuala Lumpur, Malaysia, April 1984.

federal territory and Selangor. Within each state the infant mortality rate for the Chinese is lowest. This is partly due to their tendency to live in urban areas where sanitation facilities are better and piped water and health services more readily available.

Table 9 is presented to assess the effects of development and health programme inputs on mortality levels by comparing the socio-economic characteristics of the districts with highest infant mortality rates against those with the lowest infant mortality rates. Several observations can be made:

(1) Districts with high infant mortality rates also have high still birth rates and districts with low infant mortality rates tend to have lower still birth rates.

(2) Infant mortality rate is highly positively correlated with total fertility rate.

(3) Infant mortality rate is generally higher in districts with higher concentration of Malays (with the exception of Cameron Highlands), and which are less urbanized and by contrast tends to be lowest in districts with lower Malay concentration and which are more urbanized.

(4) Socio-economic and health programme variables have strong influence on infant mortality. The most striking fact is that more than 80 per cent of the births in three of the five districts with the highest level of infant mortality were delivered at home.

Inter-correlations between Variables

In mortality analyses, the dependent variables and a host of socio-economic demographic and programme variables are intricately inter-related. It is useful to begin the analysis by looking at the bivariate relationships among the study variables, taking one pair at a time. As the variables are all measured in interval scales, the personian product moment correlations (r) provides an appropriate measure of the strength and direction of the bivariate relationships of the study variables.

Table 10 presents the correlation coefficients between each pair of the study variables. The correlation coefficients in Table 10 show the various mortality rates are positively and significantly related to one another (r value from about 0.4 to 0.7). This is probably due to some common underlying factors which affect mortality and will be the focus of this report.

125

TABLE 9
Comparison of Socio-economic Background of Districts with the Five Highest and Five Lowest Infant Mortality Rate, 1982

District	Infant Mortality Rate	Still Birth Rate	Total Fertility Rate	Urban (%)	Urban (%)	Population with at least lower secondary education (%)	Secondary Enrolment Ratio
5 Highest IMR							
Ulu Kelantan	39.6	30.0	8992	0.0	82.3	8.3	35.0
Cameron Highlands	38.9	14.6	3342	0.0	21.4	14.9	57.5
Baling	36.4	21.8	4821	0.0	82.0	11.1	59.6
Hulu Perak	35.0	20.4	4641	0.0	70.3	12.1	60.8
K. Kerai	33.7	24.4	5916	18.1	91.7	12.5	61.0
Average (Unweighted)			5542	3.6	69.5	11.8	54.8
5 Lowest IMR							
Wilayah Persekutuan	8.9	7.9	3044	100.0	33.2	33.5	75.0
Petaling	9.1	9.0	3028	67.4	33.3	37.6	71.7
Gombak	10.6	6.5	3856	0.0	54.4	31.1	74.3
Yen	11.1	16.4	3931	0.0	87.2	15.6	73.0
Klang	11.4	5.2	4145	68.8	37.7	24.8	72.7
Average (Unweighted)			3601	47.2	49.2	28.6	73.3

TABLE 9 (continued)
Comparison of Socio-economic Background of Districts with the
Five Highest and Five Lowest Infant Mortality Rate, 1982

Households with TV (%)	Households with piped water (%)	Non-agri-cultural activities (%)	Household with modern sanitation (%)	Births delivered at home (%)
		5 Highest IMR		
6.9	39.2	24.0	28.5	87.2
48.5	83.2	30.0	71.0	59.5
19.4	23.3	24.0	33.0	83.7
24.3	62.8	40.0	50.0	40.6
22.8	60.8	29.0	37.2	87.2
24.4	53.9	29.4	43.9	
		5 Lowest IMR		
66.2	94.1	99.0	76.0 ⎤	
75.0	97.5	95.0	88.4 ⎬	17.7
74.2	98.8	94.0	91.0 ⎦	
31.8	78.8	28.0	37.6	37.5
71.8	100.0	90.2	77.2	25.8
63.8	93.8	81.2	74.4	

SOURCE: <u>1982 Vital Statistics</u>, Statistics Department, Kuala Lumpur, Malaysia.   April 1982.

TABLE 10
Zero-order Correlations between Mortality Rates and Socio-economic, Demographic
and Programme Variables at the District Level

	CDR	IMR	TMR	SBR	TFR	AGEING	URBAN	MALAY	CHINESE	INDIAN
CDR	1.0									
IMR	0.39	1.0								
TMR	0.47	0.65	1.0							
SBR	0.32	0.68	0.52	1.0						
TFR	0.42	0.64	0.75	0.52	1.0					
AGEING	0.46	-0.26	-0.25	-0.29	-0.34	1.0				
URBAN	-0.23	-0.38	-0.35	-0.24	-0.36	0.10	1.0			
MALAY	0.32	0.53	0.65	0.54	0.72	-0.19	-0.40	1.0		
CHINESE	-0.30	-0.54	-0.66	-0.53	-0.67	0.24	0.46	-0.96	1.0	
INDIAN	-0.25	-0.38	-0.46	-0.42	-0.58	0.02	0.15	-0.81	0.62	1.0
LOW SEC.	-0.25	-0.65	-0.49	-0.54	-0.52	0.31	0.71	-0.48	0.53	0.24
ENROL	0.24	-0.44	-0.30	-0.45	-0.26	0.60	0.40	-0.14	0.23	-0.07
TV	-0.46	-0.74	-0.72	-0.68	-0.66	0.12	0.53	-0.78	0.77	0.62
NON-AGRI	-0.25	-0.61	-0.53	-0.48	-0.60	0.19	0.73	-0.59	0.65	0.31
PIPE	-0.47	-0.64	-0.69	-0.56	-0.50	0.08	0.33	-0.82	0.80	0.68
TOILET	-0.57	-0.56	-0.64	-0.54	-0.53	0.05	0.40	-0.58	0.57	0.46
BED	-0.25	-0.37	-0.44	-0.13	-0.43	0.21	0.51	-0.42	0.47	0.21
NURSE	0.07	0.31	-0.04	0.13	0.07	0.08	-0.33	0.01	0.02	-0.04
TA	0.10	-0.06	-0.06	-0.12	-0.07	0.24	0.18	-0.09	0.13	0.01
POST-NATAL	0.48	0.24	0.26	0.08	0.34	0.15	-0.24	0.30	-0.29	-0.23
HOME-DEL	0.34	0.68	0.71	0.66	0.74	-0.34	-0.37	0.83	-0.82	-0.60
FP	-0.12	-0.31	-0.27	-0.09	-0.32	0.21	0.21	-0.28	0.35	0.04

TABLE 10 (continued)
Zero-order Correlations between Mortality Rates and Socio-economic, Demographic and Programme Variables at the District Level

LOW SEC	ENROL	TV	NON AGRI	PIPE	TOILET	BED	NURSE	TA	POST NATAL	HOME DEL	FP
1.0											
0.62	1.0										
0.70	0.36	1.0									
0.88	0.47	0.76	1.0								
0.50	0.14	0.84	0.57	1.0							
0.55	0.16	0.82	0.52	0.73	1.0						
0.53	0.26	0.51	0.56	0.42	0.42	1.0					
-0.36	-0.16	-0.09	-0.31	0.09	0.13	-0.15	1.0				
0.29	0.38	0.20	0.23	0.05	0.19	0.04	0.10	1.0			
-0.30	0.05	-0.29	-0.26	-0.33	-0.14	-0.42	0.27	0.12	1.0		
-0.60	-0.34	-0.80	-0.65	-0.81	-0.62	-0.51	0.12	-0.13	0.39	1.0	
0.16	0.06	0.28	0.25	0.30	0.20	0.23	0.06	-0.17	-0.12	-0.27	1.0

The data also clearly indicates residential segregations of the ethnic groups in the country. The zero order correlation is as high as -0.96 between MALAY and CHINESE and -0.81 between MALAY and INDIAN. The Malays are concentrated in the less urbanized districts, and in districts where socio-economic conditions are poorer, as reflected by the large negative correlations between MALAY and TV, PIPE, TOILET and NON-AGRI. The reverse is true in districts where there are more CHINESE or more INDIANS. The correlation ratio between MALAY and LOW SEC is -0.48 as compared to -0.15 between MALAY and ENROL (secondary enrolment ratio), indicating that the ethnic differentials in education have been reduced substantially in the recent years.

The more urbanized districts also tend to have a higher education level, higher ownership of TV, better water supply and a heavier dependence on non-agricultural activities.

Both the educational variables (LOWSEC and ENROL) are positively correlated with ownership of TV, modern sanitation and supply of piped water, all of which are indicative of the relative affluence or a better living condition in the district. These variables are in turn highly intercorrelated, as reflected by the large positive correlation coefficients.

The data also show a positive association between the non-agricultural activities and the standard of living as measured by the set of socio-economic variables.

The more urbanized districts tend to have more hospital beds per 10,000 population but less nursing personnel per 10,000 married women, as compared to the less urbanized districts. This suggests that the more sparsely populated rural districts may be better covered in terms of rural health services. These results, however, must not be taken to mean that accessibility of MCH facilities is less adequate in urban areas since fewer facilities could presumably cover a more densely settled population than a sparsely populated one.

In terms of utilization of health facilities, the coefficients show that the Malays, the rural women and the "less well to do" women were much more likely to deliver their births at home, while the reverse is true for the Chinese and the Indians as well as the "better off" segments of the population. Other MCH services such as immunization (as measured by completion of 3 doses of Triple Antigen) and post-natal care for the newborn do not seem to correlate strongly with other socio-economic variables or with mortality rates in the district.

Factors Affecting Mortality

An examination of the correlation coefficients in Table 10 reveals that the mortality rates are significanlty related to most of the socio-economic demographic and programme variables, and are generally in the expected direction.

Mortality rates are clearly higher in districts where there are more Malays (r values ranging from 0.36 for CDR to 0.60 for TMR) and lower in districts where there are more Chinese or Indians. Because of the extremely high negative correlations between MALAY and CHINESE, the magnitude of the association between these two ethnic variables and the mortality rates are identical but different in direction. However, it should be noted that the ethnic variables are also closely related to other socio-economic demographic variables, which are in turn significantly correlated with mortality.

The degree of urbanization is negatively correlated with the various mortality rates. However, the magnitude of the relationship is small.

The two education variables are generally negatively correlated with mortality. The only exception is the positive correlation observed between secondary enrolment ratio and crude death rate. This could be explained by the fact that secondary education is now very well spread, with high enrolment ratio even in the less developed districts where adult mortality remains relatively high.

Districts where a higher proportion of the labour force is engaged in non-agricultural activities and which are relatively better off as measured by percentage of households with TV sets, piped water supply and modern sanitation have significantly lower mortality rates. In contrast, mortality rates are higher in districts where social amenities and socio-economic conditions are poorer. Almost all the correlation coefficients between mortality rates and socio-economic factors have values of not less than 0.40.

Of the variables on health facilities and utilization of health services, HOME-DEL appears to be the very important variable in affecting mortality differentials. The availability of hospital beds is also associated with lower mortality rates. The nurse-married women ratio is associated only with lower infant mortality rate but is unrelated to other mortality rates.

Post-natal home visits for the newborn and immunization surprisingly do not seem to be highly associated with childhood mortality.

The correlation coefficients indicate that higher mortality is significantly associated with higher fertility. However, it is difficult to posit any casual relationships at this juncture of the analysis.

MULTIVARIATE AREAL ANALYSIS OF SOCIO-ECONOMIC CORRELATIONS OF MORTALITY

The simple bivariate analyses in the foregoing section serve to identify the inter-relationships among the factors affecting mortality. However, differentials in mortality by socio-economic characteristics are often attributed to the compositional effects of other variables. To assess the net effect of each of the factors, it is therefore necessary to partial out the confounding effects of other variables affecting mortality. The multiple regression technique provides a useful means for disentangling the intercorrelated relationships and determining the effects of the independent variables individually and jointly on the dependent variable. It is also used to explain the variance of the dependent variable and to determine the predictive power of the model.

Before proceeding further in our analysis, the basic assumptions of the regression equation have to be considered. These are:

(1) Normal distribution

(2) Linear relationships of the study variables

(3) Additivity (that is, absence of interaction effects between the independent variables)

(4) Homoscedasticity (that is, zero means and constant variance for the random error term)

(5) Errors terms e_i and e_j are uncorrelated so that their covariance is zero for all pairs of different observations i, j

(6) Absence of multicollinearity and

(7) Absence of measurement error

The linearity and homoscedasticity assumptions were tested by means of analysis of the residuals. Generally, no serious violations of these assumptions were detected. The plotting of

the standardized residuals (error terms) of the dependent
variables (mortality rates) against the predicted standardized
dependent variable shows that the residuals do not deviate
systematically from zero or with the predicted dependent
variables.

While it is desirable to partial out the effects of all other
variables, the inclusion of too many of them could lead to severe
shrinkage of the adjusted R^2. Moreover, the bivariate analysis
shows that many of the study variables are themselves highly
intercorrelated. Hence, for the sake of parsimony and to avoid
problems of multicollinearity, only a few variables need to be
considered in the multiple regressions.

Hierarchical Regression Analysis

The main focus of this section is to examine the socio-economic
correlates of mortality, net of the influence of other variables
through multiple regression. The introduction of an hierarchical
ordering enables the effects of each study variable to be assessed
in terms of increment in R^2 after controlling for other variables
in the model. The order of inclusion of variables and results
from the regression analyses are shown in Tables 11-14.

The results of the hierarchical analysis show that the full
regression models explain about 70 per cent of the variance in
Crude Death Rate (CDR), about two-thirds of the variance in Infant
Mortality Rate (IMR) and Toddler Mortality Rate (TMR) and some 55
per cent of the variance in Still Birth Rate (SBR). We now
examine the gross and net effects of each of the study variables.

Ethnic Variables

The bivariate relationships examined previously indicate that the
ethnic variables are highly correlated with almost all other
variables in this study, including the various mortality rates.
Besides, the ethnic variables also subsume many of the cultural
norms and practices which are difficult to measure but
nevertheless may have a significant influence on mortality.

Results from bivariate regressions show that MALAY or CHINESE
explains about 9-10 per cent of the variance in CDR, 29 per cent
in IMR and SBR and up to 42 per cent in TMR. Because of the
smaller proportionate share in the population, INDIAN accounts for

133

TABLE 11
Hierarchical Regression Analysis in Crude Death Rate
on Socio-economic Variables

Variables in Equation	Multiple R^2	Increment[a] in R^2	Beta[a]
		MALAY	
1. MALAY	0.101	0.101	0.318*
TFR, AGEING, MALAY	0.578	0.001	-0.038
TFR, AGEING, BED, TOILET, MALAY	0.694	0.020	-0.216*
TFR, AGEING, BED, TOILET, TV, ENROL, MALAY	0.699	0.011	-0.215
		CHINESE	
2. CHINESE	0.089	0.089	-0.298*
TFR, AGEING, CHINESE	0.578	0.001	-0.050
TFR, AGEING, BED, TOILET, CHINESE	0.682	0.007	0.125
TFR, AGEING, BED, TOILET, TV, ENROL, CHINESE	0.689	0.001	0.058
		INDIAN	
3. INDIAN	0.064	0.064	-0.253+
TFR, AGEING, INDIAN	0.596	0.019	0.174
TFR, AGEING, BED, TOILET, INDIAN	0.713	0.039	0.255*
TFR, AGEING, BED, TOILET, TV, ENROL, INDIAN	0.724	0.036	0.297*
		URBAN	
4. URBAN	0.053	0.053	-0.229+
TFR, AGEING, URBAN	0.582	0.005	-0.074
TFR, AGEING, BED, TOILET, URBAN	0.675	0.001	0.039
TFR, AGEING, BED, TOILET, TV, ENROL, URBAN	0.688	0.000	-0.003

TABLE 11 (continued)
Hierarchical Regression Analysis in Crude Death Rate
on Socio-economic Variables

Variables in Equation	Multiple R^2	Increment[a] in R^2	Beta[a]
		LOWSEC	
5. LOWSEC	0.062	0.062	-0.249+
TFR, AGEING, LOWSEC	0.598	0.021	-0.171
TFR, AGEING, BED, TOILET, LOWSEC	0.674	0.000	-0.006
TFR, AGEING, BED, TOILET, TV,			
ENROL, LOWSEC	0.692	0.004	-0.092
		ENROL	
6. ENROL	0.058	0.058	0.241+
TFR, AGEING, ENROL	0.577	0.000	0.007
TFR, AGEING, BED, TOILET, ENROL	0.677	0.003	0.070
TFR, AGEING, BED, TOILET, TV, ENROL	0.688	0.000	0.004
		TV	
7. TV	0.214	0.214	-0.462**
TFR, AGEING, TV	0.602	0.024	-0.210+
TFR, AGEING, BED, TOILET, TV	0.688	0.014	0.237
TFR, AGEING, BED, TOILET, ENROL, TV	0.688	0.011	0.234
		NON-AGRI	
8. NON-AGRI	0.061	0.061	-0.247+
TFR, AGEING, NON-AGRI	0.582	0.004	-0.075
TFR, AGEING, BED, TOILET, NON-AGRI	0.680	0.005	0.095
TFR, AGEING, BED, TOILET, TV,			
ENROL, NON-AGRI	0.688	0.000	-0.003

TABLE 11 (continued)
**Hierarchical Regression Analysis in Crude Death Rate
on Socio-economic Variables**

Variables in Equation	Multiple R^2	Increment[a] in	
		R^2	Beta[a]
		TOILET	
9. TOILET	0.321	0.321	-0.566**
TFR, AGEING, TOILET	0.672	0.095	-0.367**
TFR, AGEING, BED, TOILET	0.674	0.080	-0.352**
TFR, AGEING, BED, TV, ENROL, TOILET	0.688	0.074	-0.494**
		PIPE	
10. PIPE	0.223	0.223	-0.472**
TFR, AGEING, PIPE	0.591	0.014	-0.166
TFR, AGEING, BED, TOILET, PIPE	0.681	0.007	0.146
TFR, AGEING, BED, TOILET, TV, ENROL, PIPE	0.689	0.001	0.068
		BED	
11. BED	0.063	0.063	-0.251+
TFR, AGEING, BED	0.594	0.017	-0.143
TFR, AGEING, TOILET, BED	0.674	0.002	-0.052
TFR, AGEING, TOILET, TV, ENROL, BED	0.688	0.005	-0.084

NOTE: [a] The increments in R^2 and the beta coefficients are attributed to the variable in brackets.

   ** $p < 0.001$
   * $p < 0.01$
   + $p < 0.05$

TABLE 12
Hierarchical Regression Analysis of Infant Mortality Rate
on Socio-economic Variables

Variables in Equation	Multiple R^2	Increment[a] in R^2	Beta[a]
		MALAY	
1. MALAY	0.286	0.286	0.535**
TFR, MALAY	0.422	0.011	0.153
TFR, TOILET, HOME-DEL, MALAY	0.551	0.019	-0.257
TFR, TOILET, HOME-DEL, TV, ENROL, MALAY	0.664	0.036	-0.412*
		CHINESE	
2. CHINESE	0.293	0.293	-0.541**
TFR, CHINESE	0.433	0.022	-0.201
TFR, TOILET, HOME-DEL, CHINESE	0.541	0.009	0.173
TFR, TOILET, HOME-DEL, TV, ENROL, CHINESE	0.652	0.024	0.298+
		INDIAN	
3. INDIAN	0.141	0.141	-0.376**
TFR, INDIAN	0.411	0.000	0.005
TFR, TOILET, HOME-DEL, INDIAN	0.547	0.014	0.156
TFR, TOILET, HOME-DEL, TV, ENROL, INDIAN	0.645	0.016	0.197
		URBAN	
4. URBAN	0.145	0.145	-0.381**
TFR, URBAN	0.436	0.025	-0.171
TFR, TOILET, HOME-DEL, URBAN	0.538	0.006	-0.086
TFR, TOILET, HOME-DEL, TV, ENROL, URBAN	0.633	0.004	0.081

TABLE 12 (continued)
Hierarchical Regression Analysis of Infant Mortality Rate
on Socio-economic Variables

Variables in Equation	Multiple R²	Increment[a] in R²	Beta[a]
		LOWSEC	
5. LOWSEC	0.425	0.425	-0.652**
TFR, LOWSEC	0.550	0.139	-0.437**
TFR, TOILET, HOME-DEL, LOWSEC	0.591	0.059	-0.318*
TFR, TOILET, HOME-DEL, TV, LOWSEC	0.623	0.025	-0.222+
		ENROL	
6. ENROL	0.196	0.196	-0.443**
TFR, ENROL	0.491	0.080	-0.294**
TFR, TOILET, HOME-DEL, ENROL	0.586	0.054	-0.247*
TFR, TOILET, HOME-DEL, TV, ENROL	0.629	0.028	-0.185+
		TV	
7. TV	0.552	0.552	-0.743**
TFR, TV	0.592	0.181	-0.568**
TFR, TOILET, HOME-DEL, TV	0.601	0.069	-0.609**
TFR, TOILET, HOME-DEL, ENROL, TV	0.629	0.043	-0.500*
		NON-AGRI	
8. NON-AGRI	0.373	0.373	-0.611**
TFR, NON-AGRI	0.524	0.113	-0.388**
TFR, TOILET, HOME-DEL, NON-AGRI	0.567	0.034	-0.248+
TFR, TOILET, HOME-DEL, TV, ENROL, NON-AGRI	0.628	0.000	-0.008

TABLE 12 (continued)
Hierarchical Regression Analysis of Infant Mortality Rate
on Socio-economic Variables

Variables in Equation	Multiple R^2	Increment[a] in	
		R^2	Beta[a]
		TOILET	
9. TOILET	0.314	0.314	-0.561**
TFR, TOILET	0.480	0.069	-0.309*
TFR, HOME-DEL, TOILET	0.532	0.023	-0.193
TFR, HOME-DEL, TV, ENROL, TOILET	0.629	0.001	0.048
		PIPE	
10. PIPE	0.410	0.410	-0.640**
TFR, PIPE	0.486	0.075	-0.378*
TFR, TOILET, HOME-DEL, PIPE	0.533	0.001	-0.066
TFR, TOILET, HOME-DEL, TV, ENROL, PIPE	0.629	0.000	-0.027
		HOME-DEL	
11. HOME-DEL	0.469	0.469	0.685**
TFR, HOME-DEL	0.510	0.099	0.465**
TFR, TOILET, HOME-DEL	0.532	0.052	0.369
TFR, TOILET, TV, ENROL, HOME-DEL	0.629	0.002	0.090
		FP	
12. FP	0.095	0.095	-0.308*
TFR, FP	0.423	0.124	-0.117
TFR, TOILET, HOME-DEL, FP	0.540	0.008	-0.094
TFR, TOILET, HOME-DEL, TV, ENROL, FP	0.634	0.006	-0.079

NOTE: [a] The increments in R^2 and the beta coefficients are attributed to the variable in brackets.

** $p < 0.001$
* $p < 0.01$
+ $p < 0.05$

139

TABLE 13
Hierarchical Regression Analysis of Toddler Mortality Rate
on Socio-economic Variables

Variables in Equation	Multiple R^2	Increment[a] in R^2	Beta[a]
		MALAY	
1. MALAY	0.419	0.419	0.647**
TFR, MALAY	0.584	0.025	0.227+
TFR, TOILET, HOME-DEL, MALAY	0.657	0.000	-0.020+
TFR, TOILET, HOME-DEL, TV, ENROL, MALAY	0.667	0.000	-0.041
		CHINESE	
2. CHINESE	0.432	0.432	-0.657**
TFR, CHINESE	0.602	0.043	-0.281*
TFR, TOILET, HOME-DEL, CHINESE	0.659	0.002	-0.089
TFR, TOILET, HOME-DEL, TV, ENROL, CHINESE	0.668	0.001	-0.074
		INDIAN	
3. INDIAN	0.214	0.214	-0.463**
TFR, INDIAN	0.560	0.001	-0.042
TFR, TOILET, HOME-DEL, INDIAN	0.661	0.004	0.085
TFR, TOILET, HOME-DEL, TV, ENROL, INDIAN	0.671	0.005	0.109
		URBAN	
4. URBAN	0.119	0.119	-0.346*
TFR, URBAN	0.565	0.006	-0.086
TFR, TOILET, HOME-DEL, URBAN	0.657	0.000	-0.005
TFR, TOILET, HOME-DEL, TV, ENROL, URBAN	0.669	0.003	0.065

TABLE 13 (continued)
Hierarchical Regression Analysis of Toddler Mortality Rate
on Socio-economic Variables

Variables in Equation	Multiple R^2	Increment[a] in	
		R^2	Beta[a]
		LOWSEC	
5. LOWSEC	0.239	0.239	-0.489**
TFR, LOWSEC	0.573	0.014	-0.138
TFR, TOILET, HOME-DEL, LOWSEC	0.657	0.001	0.033
TFR, TOILET, HOME-DEL, TV, LOWSEC	0.666	0.003	0.083
		ENROL	
6. ENROL	0.092	0.092	-0.303*
TFR, ENROL	0.571	0.012	-0.113
TFR, TOILET, HOME-DEL, ENROL	0.662	0.006	-0.081
TFR, TOILET, HOME-DEL, TV, ENROL	0.666	0.003	-0.062
		TV	
7. TV	0.520	0.520	-0.721**
TFR, TV	0.650	0.091	-0.403**
TFR, TOILET, HOME-DEL, TV	0.663	0.006	-0.186
TFR, TOILET, HOME-DEL, ENROL, TV	0.666	0.004	-0.149
		NON-AGRI	
8. NON-AGRI	0.276	0.276	-0.525**
TFR, NON-AGRI	0.590	0.031	-0.203+
TFR, TOILET, HOME-DEL, NON-AGRI	0.658	0.001	-0.045
TFR, TOILET, HOME-DEL, TV, ENROL, NON-AGRI	0.667	0.001	0.048

TABLE 13 (continued)
**Hierarchical Regression Analysis of Toddler Mortality Rate
on Socio-economic Variables**

Variables in Equation	Multiple R^2	Increment[a] in R^2	Beta[a]
			TOILET
9. TOILET	0.403	0.403	-0.635**
TFR, TOILET	0.640	0.081	-0.335**
TFR, HOME-DEL, TOILET	0.657	0.044	-0.268*
TFR, HOME-DEL, TV, ENROL, TOILET	0.666	0.012	-0.197
			PIPE
10. PIPE	0.481	0.481	-0.693**
TFR, PIPE	0.619	0.061	-0.339**
TFR, TOILET, HOME-DEL, PIPE	0.658	0.001	-0.063
TFR, TOILET, HOME-DEL, TV, ENROL, PIPE	0.667	0.001	-0.068
			HOME-DEL
11. HOME-DEL	0.501	0.501	0.708**
TFR, HOME-DEL	0.613	0.054	0.343*
TFR, TOILET, HOME-DEL	0.657	0.017	0.209
TFR, TOILET, TV, ENROL, HOME-DEL	0.666	0.004	0.123
			FP
12. FP	0.072	0.072	-0.268+
TFR, FP	0.560	0.001	-0.036
TFR, TOILET, HOME-DEL, FP	0.657	0.000	-0.017
TFR, TOILET, HOME-DEL, TV, ENROL, FP	0.666	0.000	-0.012

NOTE: [a] The increments in R^2 and the beta coefficients are attributed to the
variable in brackets.

** $p < 0.001$
* $p < 0.01$
+ $p < 0.05$

TABLE 14
Hierarchical Regression Analysis of Still Birth Rate
on Socio-economic Variables

Variables in Equation	Multiple R^2	Increment[a] in	
		R^2	Beta[a]
		MALAY	
1. MALAY	0.292	0.292	0.540**
TFR, MALAY	0.328	0.056	0.341+
TFR, TOILET, HOME-DEL, MALAY	0.472	0.002	−0.092
TFR, TOILET, HOME-DEL, TV, ENROL, MALAY	0.547	0.001	−0.066
		CHINESE	
2. CHINESE	0.280	0.280	−0.529**
TFR, CHINESE	0.330	0.058	−0.326+
TFR, TOILET, HOME-DEL, CHINESE	0.473	0.004	0.107
TFR, TOILET, HOME-DEL, TV, ENROL, CHINESE	0.553	0.006	0.151
		INDIAN	
3. INDIAN	0.174	0.174	−0.417**
TFR, INDIAN	0.292	0.020	−0.172
TFR, TOILET, HOME-DEL, INDIAN	0.470	0.000	0.012
TFR, TOILET, HOME-DEL, TV, ENROL, INDIAN	0.550	0.003	−0.084
		URBAN	
4. URBAN	0.056	0.056	−0.237+
TFR, URBAN	0.275	0.003	−0.056
TFR, TOILET, HOME-DEL, URBAN	0.473	0.003	0.062
TFR, TOILET, HOME-DEL, TV, ENROL, URBAN	0.584	0.037	0.239+

TABLE 14 (continued)
Hierarchical Regression Analysis of Still Birth Rate
on Socio-economic Variables

Variables in Equation	Multiple R^2	Increment[a] in	
		R^2	Beta[a]
		LOWSEC	
5. LOWSEC	0.293	0.293	-0.541**
TFR, LOWSEC	0.372	0.100	-0.370
TFR, TOILET, HOME-DEL, LOWSEC	0.487	0.017	-0.172
TFR, TOILET, HOME-DEL, TV, LOWSEC	0.506	0.005	-0.101
		ENROL	
6. ENROL	0.204	0.204	-0.452**
TFR, ENROL	0.378	0.106	-0.337**
TFR, TOILET, HOME-DEL, ENROL	0.534	0.064	-0.270*
TFR, TOILET, HOME-DEL, TV, ENROL	0.547	0.041	-0.237*
		TV	
7. TV	0.461	0.461	-0.679**
TFR, TV	0.471	0.198	-0.594**
TFR, TOILET, HOME-DEL, TV	0.501	0.031	-0.410+
TFR, TOILET, HOME-DEL, ENROL, TV	0.547	0.012	-0.269
		NON-AGRI	
8. NON-AGRI	0.234	0.234	-0.484**
TFR, NON-AGRI	0.339	0.067	-0.298*
TFR, TOILET, HOME-DEL, NON-AGRI	0.471	0.001	-0.048
TFR, TOILET, HOME-DEL, TV, ENROL, NON-AGRI	0.565	0.019	0.228

TABLE 14 (continued)
**Hierarchical Regression Analysis of Still Birth Rate
on Socio-economic Variables**

Variables in Equation	Multiple R^2	Increment[a] in	
		R^2	Beta[a]
		TOILET	
9. TOILET	0.295	0.295	-0.544**
TFR, TOILET	0.372	0.100	-0.372**
TFR, HOME-DEL, TOILET	0.470	0.028	-0.214
TFR, HOME-DEL, TV, ENROL, TOILET	0.547	0.003	-0.096
		PIPE	
10. PIPE	0.311	0.311	-0.558**
TFR, PIPE	0.347	0.075	-0.378*
TFR, TOILET, HOME-DEL, PIPE	0.474	0.004	0.130
TFR, TOILET, HOME-DEL, TV, ENROL, PIPE	0.549	0.002	0.113
		HOME-DEL	
11. HOME-DEL	0.440	0.440	0.663**
TFR, HOME-DEL	0.442	0.170	0.610**
TFR, TOILET, HOME-DEL	0.470	0.098	0.503**
TFR, TOILET, TV, ENROL, HOME-DEL	0.547	0.026	0.304+
		FP	
12. FP	0.008	0.008	-0.088
TFR, FP	0.279	0.006	0.085
TFR, TOILET, HOME-DEL, FP	0.482	0.012	0.115
TFR, TOILET, HOME-DEL, TV, ENROL, FP	0.560	0.013	0.121

NOTE: [a] The increments in R^2 and the beta coefficients are attributed to the variable in brackets.

    ** $p < 0.001$
     * $p < 0.01$
    + $p < 0.05$

a much smaller fraction of the variance in the areal mortality rates.

The bivariate regression coefficients in Table 10 show that mortality rates tend to be higher in districts where there are more Malays. However, data from the vital registration show that the crude death rate for the Malays (in 1982) was not higher than the other ethnic groups. In fact, higher mortality rates in these districts could be due to higher fertility rate, an older population, poorer socio-economic conditions and infrequent utilization of the health facilities.

Controlling for differences in TFR and ageing index among the districts, the partial regression coefficients (beta weights) and the increment in R^2 for all three ethnic variables become insignificant in explaining CDR. This suggests that higher mortality in districts where Malays predominate is largely due to higher fertility and an older age structure of the population.

IMR, TMR and SBR remain lower in districts where there are more Chinese and higher in districts where there are more Malays even after controlling for TFR. The p values for the partial regression coefficients for MALAY and CHINESE are less than 0.05 in the case of TMR and SBR.

The addition of the health programme and sanitation variables attenuates and changes the direction of the "ethnic" effects on IMR, TMR and SBR, albeit statistically insignificant. This could be explained by the fact that districts where there are more Malays tend to have poorer sanitation and lower utilization of health facilities for deliveries which are in turn associated with higher mortality levels. Controlling for the demographic and health variables, INDIAN would have significantly higher CDR than MALAY.

With a further adjustment in the areal differences in socio-economic conditions, IMR becomes significantly lower for MALAY and higher for CHINESE. It is worth noting that INDIAN adds as much as 3.6 percentage points to the explained variance in CDR, while Malay adds 3.6 percentage points to the explained variance in IMR accounted by all other variables in the model.

The above analyses suggest that higher mortality in districts where there are relatively more Malays and lower mortality in districts where there are relatively more Chinese and Indians is largely attributed to differences in fertility rates, health programme and sanitation variables, as well as socio-economic conditions. Hence removing such differences will improve the mortality condition in districts where Malays predominate.

Urbanization

Although mortality rates are significantly lower in districts where a larger proportion of population are living in the urban areas, the URBAN factor explains a much smaller fraction of the variance as compared to the other socio-economic and health variables. Moreover, URBAN mortality differentials are largely due to areal differences in fertility (and in the case of CDR the age structure as well). None of the partial regression coefficients is significantly different from zero once fertility is held constant. Controlling further for differences in health and socio-economic variables URBAN mortality differentials disappear. This suggests that with improvement in socio-economic conditions and better utilization of health services, mortality rates in the rural areas could be as low, or even lower than in the urban areas.

Education Variables

The section on indirect mortality estimates shows that mortality rates are lower among individuals with higher educational attainment. In areal analysis, districts where a higher proportion of the population had completed at least lower secondary education were also found to have significantly lower mortality rates. By itself, this factor explains up to 43 per cent of the variance in IMR, 29 per cent in SBR, 24 per cent in TMR, but only about 6 per cent in CDR. Adjusting for areal differences in fertility attenuates the educational effects somewhat. This is due to the fact that better educated couples tend to have fewer children and hence lower mortality rates. Therefore holding constant the fertility rates removes part of the educational effects on mortality. Nevertheless, it remains a significant factor in IMR and SBR.

Since districts with better educational attainment are also better off in terms of other socio-economic and health conditions, controlling for differences in these variables further dampens the LOWSEC effects on areal mortality differentials; but it remains significant in explaining the variance in infant mortality rate.

As secondary school enrolment ratio is significantly and positively related to an older population ($r = 0.60$) crude death rate is higher in districts with better enrolment ratio. Controlling for the age structure and fertility, however, areal differences in CDR decreases.

The IMR, TMR and SBR are significantly lower in districts

with better enrolment ratio. Holding constant all other variables in the models, IMR and SBR remain significantly lower in these districts. The effect of secondary school enrolment ratio on TMR diminishes to insignificance when any set of the other variables in the models are controlled.

Percentage of Households Owning TV

Ownership of TV is a very powerful predictor of mortality differentials. By itself, this factor accounts for over half of the variance in IMR and TMR and 46 per cent of the variance in SBR.

Nutritional status and health care are presumably better in districts where ownership of TV is more common. Moreover, accessibility to mass media could have promoted the adoption of modern health practices, contributing towards the lowering of mortality rates. This factor remains significant after controlling for areal differences in fertility (and ageing index in the case of CDR). Holding constant health programme and sanitation variables as well as socio-economic variables, the CDR would have been higher (albeit, statistically insignificant) in districts where ownership of TV is more common. In contrast, IMR remains significantly lower in the districts with higher ownership of TV, after controlling for all other variables in the model, adding 4.3 percentage points to the explained variance.

To the extent that ownership of TV set is a good indicator of the relative affluence of the districts, it appears that childhood mortality and late foetal loss are much more sensitive than CDR to changes in economic conditions. In other words, an improvement in economic conditions will bring about greater decline in childhood and mortality foetal loss than in all other ages.

Percentage of Labour Force Engaged in Non-Agricultural Activities

In this study, the percentage of labour force engaged in non-agricultural activities is used as a socio-economic indicator of the development processes.

Bivariate regression analyses show that mortality rates are significantly lower in districts where a higher proportion of the labour force is engaged in non-agricultural activities. Districts characterized by a higher proportion of the labour force in non-agricultural activities tend to have lower fertility, better health/sanitation facilities and better socio-economic conditions. After adjusting for areal differences in these variables effects NON-AGRI are substantially reduced.

Percentage of Households Having Flush Toilet Facilities (Sanitation Variables)

The bivariate analyses show that districts with better sanitation facilities have significantly lower mortality rates. By itself, this factor explains 30-40 per cent of the variances in the mortality rates.

The effect of this variable on CDR remains highly significant even when all other variables in the model are held constant, and contributes an additional 7.4 percentage points to the explained variance on CDR. It also remains significant in explaining TMR after controlling for demographic and health variables. However, due to the close association with other socio-economic variables, its effects on the other mortality rates, with the single exception of CDR, become insignificant when these variables are held constant.

Supply of Piped Water

Piped water supply is a powerful predictor of mortality differentials. It explains 22 per cent of the variance in CDR, 41 per cent of the variance in IMR, 48 per cent of the variance in TMR and 31 per cent of the variance in SBR within the bivariate context.

Districts where a higher proportion of households are supplied with piped water tend to have a much lower mortality rate. Controlling for TFR and AGEING, however, reduces the effect of this factor on CDR adding only 1.4 percentage point to the explained variance in CDR. Although PIPE remains significant in explaining IMR, TMR and SBR after controlling for TFR, it becomes insignificant with further adjustment for health and socio-economic variables.

Percentage of Births Delivered at Home

Regression coefficients show that the IMR, TMR and SBR are significantly higher in districts where home delivery of births is more prevalent, and remain so after controlling for areal differences in total fertility rate. The importance of HOME-DEL on mortality differentials can be assessed by examining the increment in R^2 after controlling for TFR; it adds 10 percentage points to the explained variance in IMR, 5.4 percentage points in TMR and 7.5 percentage points in SBR.

While the effect of this variable on IMR and TMR becomes insignificant after controlling for TOILET, and other socio-economic variables, it remains significant in explaining SBR.

The analysis suggests that the utilization of health facilities which is reflective of some underlying cultural norms and practices, is an important determinant in mortality differentials. Therefore, while endeavouring to improve the health facilities, proper health education should be provided to promote effective utilization of these facilities and services so as to reduce the mortality rates further among those segments of the population where mortality rates are still high.

Availability of Hospital Beds

The number of government hospital beds per 10,000 population is a relatively weak predictor of CDR as compared to the other study variables. It explains only 6.3 per cent of the variance in CDR. Nevertheless, the bivariate regression coefficient shows that districts with more hospital beds tend to have lower crude death rates. After adjusting for TFR and AGEING, this factor accounts for an additional 1.7 percentage points of the variance in CDR. The effects practically disappear with further adjustment of health and other socio-economic variables.

Family Planning

Studies have shown that children born to multiparity mothers, or to mothers who are too young or too old encounter greater risks than others (Wray 1971; Omran and Standley 1976; Omran 1974; Nortman 1974; Lyle et al. 1978). Moreover, research evidence from several studies in India, Hawaii and Britain show that childhood mortality and foetal wastage were extremely high for pregnancy intervals of less than one year, and decreases steadily with the length of the intervals. It has also been postulated that family planning acceptance tends to be low where infant mortality rate is high.

Our study also shows that childhood mortality is significantly lower in districts where family planning acceptance is high suggesting that proper spacing of births can result in the lowering of childhood mortality. The analysis shows that even after controlling for areal differentials in fertility, the FP factor adds 12.4 percentage points to the explained variance of IMR. However, because family planning is highly correlated with other socio-economic and health variables, its effects on mortality become insignificant once these variables are held constant.

By contrast, family planning acceptance does not provide significant differentials in SBR.

To the extent that a significant proportion of couples practising family planning obtain their supplies through non-programme sources, the effects of family planning on mortality and late foetal wastage reported above must be held as tentative.

CONCLUSIONS AND RECOMMENDATIONS

Although the mortality level in the country is relatively low by the standard of developing countries, there is still a wide variation in mortality among the various sub-groups of the population. Both at the individual as well as at the aggregate levels, mortality rates are 3-4 times higher in the "lower" socio-economic strata as compared to the "higher" strata of the population.

This report highlights the sub-groups of the population among whom mortality rates are still much higher than the national average, so that special programme efforts can be directed to reduce such imbalances.

An examination of the data reveals that mortality rates are higher in the less developed districts of Peninsular Malaysia, particularly in the north-east region and in the more rural parts in the central and west coast states.

Results from the multivariate areal anlayses show that socio-economic factors, sanitation, piped water supply, utilization of health facilities and services as well as family size have

151

significant effects on mortality. Education and ownership of TV, in particular, have a strong impact on differentials in mortality rates as they reflect both the socio-economic well-being effect and exposure to modernity effect on the various sub-groups of the population.

Districts where supply of piped water is lacking and where a smaller proportion of the households use flush toilets exhibit considerably higher mortality rates than in districts where these facilities are more readily available. Further, a much higher mortality is recorded in districts where majority of the births are delivered at home.

Acceptance of family planning for purpose of spacing and preventing excess fertility has also been shown to facilitate further reduction in mortality rates.

The analyses show that higher mortality in the less urbanized districts and in districts where the overwhelming majority of the population are Malays could be reduced substantially with improvement in socio-economic conditions, environmental hygiene, proper spacing of births and greater use of health services.

Because high mortality is largely due to poor socio-economic conditions, policies and programmes aiming at a more equitable distribution of wealth and services will bring about a further reduction in the level of mortality.

In spite of the excellent health infrastructure, certain groups of the population have not made full use of such facilities and services. Family life and family health education should therefore be given special emphasis. It should be provided through formal and non-formal educational channels. Dialogues and talks covering the various aspects on pregnancies, delivery, nutrition, home economics, spacing of births and child care and so forth should be further intensified.

Since a large number of infant deaths are related to home delivery, and since infant deaths are disproportionately concentrated during the early neo-natal period, special programmes should be directed to ensure that home deliveries are attended to and followed up by trained personnel.

In view of the importance of sanitation and clean water supply, the relevant authorities should take the necessary measures to improve environmental hygiene and to expand and purify the water supply.

Although the vital registration has been virtually complete in Peninsular Malaysia, efforts should be made to improve the coverage and quality of vital registration in Sabah and Sarawak. Special attention should also be given to collect information on morbidity and causes of death so that appropriate programmes can be formulated and implemented to tackle these problem areas.

Due to the lack of information on the socio-economic characteristics of the deceased, this report has focused on the examination of socio-economic correlates of mortality at the district level. The inclusion of more basic socio-economic background information about the deceased on the death certificate should prove useful for detailed analysis of mortality differentials at the individual level.

Many studies have shown that maternal age, parity and birth interval are important determinants of mortality. These aspects have not been adequately covered in this report and it would be an important subject for further investigation.

References

Ang, E.S. and N.P. Tey. Health and Family Planning Survey in Johore and Perak. Kuala Lumpur: National Population and Family Development Board, 1984.

Hermalin, A.I. "Regression Analysis of Areal Data". In Measuring the Effect of Family Planning Programmes on Fertility, ed. C. Chandrasekaran and A.I. Hermalin. Paris: OECD Development Centre, International Union for the Scientific Study of Population, 1975.

Hirschman, C. and E.K.J. Tan. Evaluation of Mortality Data in the Vital Statistics of West Malaysia, Research Paper No. 5. Kuala Lumpur: Department of Statistics Malaysia, 1971.

Kader, H.A. "Neo-natal Morbidity and Mortality in Peninsular Malaysia". Malaysian Journal of Reproductive Health, Vol. 1, No. 2 (1983).

Khoo Teik Huat. Population and Housing Census of Malaysia, 1980 -- General Report of the Population Census. Kuala Lumpur: Department of Statistics, Malaysia, 1983.

Lyle, K.C., S.J. Segal, and L. Chien. "Perinatal Study in Tientsin: 1978". International Journal of Gynaecology and Obstetrics, 18, No. 4 (1980).

Malaysia. Vital Statistics, Peninsular Malaysia. Kuala Lumpur: Department of Statistics. (Various Years).

_____. Health Administration and District Level Differences in Maternal, Infant and Toddler Mortality Rates as Related to MCH and Family Planning

Program Inputs and Socio-Economic Conditions.   Kuala Lumpur: National
Population and Family Development Board, 1982.

_____. The Changing Fertility and Mortality Rates in the Administrative
Districts of Peninsular Malaysia. Kuala Lumpur, 1983.

Noor Laily, A.B., Y. Takeshita, P. Majumdar, and B. A. Tan. "The Changing Ethnic
Patterns of Mortality". In Peninsular Malaysia. Research Series 6. Kuala
Lumpur: National Family Planning Board (NFPB), 1983.

Nortman, D. "Parental Age as a Factor in Pregnancy Outcome and Child
Development". In Reports on Population/Family Planning. New York:
Population Council, 1974.

Omran, A.R. The Health Theme in Family Planning. Monograph 16. Chapel Hill:
Carolina Population Center, 1971.

Omran, A.R. and C.C. Standley, eds. Family Formation Patterns Health: An
International Collaborative Study in India, Iran, Lebanon, Philippines and
Turkey. Geneva: World Health Organization, 1976.

United Nations. Indirect Techniques for Demographic Estimation, Manual X,
Population Studies No. 81 ST/ESA/SER.A/81. New York: Department of
International Economic & Social Affairs, 1983.

Wray, J.D. "Population Pressure on Family Size and Child Spacing". In Rapid
Population Growth. Baltimore: John Hopkins Press, 1971.

Zainal A. Yusof and Khairuddin Yusof. Some Socio-Economic and Medical Aspects of
Malay Mortality in Urban and Rural Areas. Kuala Lumpur: Malaysian Centre
for Development Studies, Prime Minister's Department, 1974.

Gabriel C. Alvarez

Introduction

Studies of differential mortality levels within the Philippines and an assessment of factors thereof have not received much attention. Only a limited number of studies have made inter-regional and/or inter-provincial comparisons. Flieger et al. (1981) have carried out this type of analysis. Mortality estimates were calculated with the help of provincial life tables. In an earlier paper, Flieger (1980) discussed the lack of consistency of mortality patterns when doing national, regional and provincial comparisons. More specifically, mortality improvement does not prevail at the sub-national level. From the findings one can readily conclude that sub-national mortality analysis is demonstrably plausible and admittedly crucial in better comprehending the mortality situation of the Philippines.

This type of analysis, however, is impeded by a number of drawbacks, some of which are: (1) varying state of completeness in the collection of vital registration statistics; (2) the long delay in issuing these statistics for public use; (3) the lack of comparability if a diachronic analysis is to be conducted; and, (4) death registration is still mainly based on place of occurrence rather than place of residence. The fourth limitation can explain why mortality levels are somewhat high in highly urbanized areas like Metro Manila, Cebu, and Davao del Sur. Understandably, these provinces have better hospital and health care facilities. People from other provinces go to these areas to avail of better hospital care. Besides, vital registration is better supervised in urbanized areas. With respect to the first limitation mentioned, the problem of under-reporting or under-enumeration still prevails in a considerable number of provinces, more specifically the less urbanized and those directly affected by political conflicts claimed to be instigated by the Muslim secessionist movement and the National People's Army. As mentioned above, long delays in issuance are characteristic of vital registration statistics mainly on account of persistent inefficiencies, like delayed submission of provincial yearly reports, duplicating of collection efforts and so on. Consequently, the latest published vital statistics report is that of 1978.

However, it is the contention of this study that the problems enumerated above should not be used as arguments to vindicate the study of mortality as a futile attempt. It must also be pointed out that data inadequacy has been an overused excuse in not venturing into mortality analysis. The vital importance of this type of demographic study, as was pointed out by Flieger et al. (1981) as useful inputs to population policy and development planning cannot be underemphasized. The present study is not a mere replication of Flieger and his associates' effort. It aims to accomplish the following objectives:

(1) to examine national and regional mortality trends at least within the last three decades as depicted by selected mortality indices made available from published sources;

(2) to assess mortality differentials on the national scale in terms of age, sex, cause of death, occupation, and longevity;

(3) to compare regional mortality patterns as based on recent vital registration data; and

(4) to assess the importance of socio-economic factors in affecting mortality levels on the sub-national (provincial) level.

Data Sources

The data used for this study are drawn from varied sources. Statistical publications of the National Census and Statistics Office (NCSO) were among the major data sources. Mortality data and measures as well as selected demographic factors were obtained from the following:

NCSO. Philippine Yearbook. Manila: National Economic and Development Authority -- National Census and Statistics Office (1975, 1976, 1978, 1980 and 1983).

NCSO. Vital Statistics Report. Manila: National Economic and Development Authority -- National Census and Statistics Office (1975, 1976, 1977 and 1978).

NEDA. Philippine Statistical Yearbook. Manila: National Economic and Development Authority -- National Census and Statistics Office (1979 and 1983).

United Nations. Demographic Yearbook. Special Issue: Historical Supplement. New York, 1979.

NCSO. Age and Sex Population Projections for the Philippines by Province. 1970-2000. UNFPA-NCSO Population Research Project. Monograph No. 2. Manila, 1976.

NEDA, POPCOM, NCSO. Population Dimension of Planning, Vol. II, Population Projections for the Philippines by Province, 1970-2000. Manila, March 1975.

NCSO. 1978 Integrated Census of the Population and its Economic Activities. Vol. II, Phase 1. Manila, 1978.

NCSO. Journal of Philippine Statistics (Quarterly publication). Manila (1975 through 1981).

It must be noted that discrepancies exist between mortality estimates provided by the NCSO and those made by the local demographers. The latter, however, have not come up with more recent estimates. The most recent provincial-level mortality estimates based on vital registration data were made for 1970. Mortality levels for six regions (Central Luzon, Bicol, Western Visayas, Northern Mindanao, Southern Mindanao and Metro Manila) and their respective provinces were determined by way of survey data (Area Fertility Study) gathered in 1980. The findings of this study is not comprehensive enough to represent inter-provincial variations. Moreover, mortality levels assessed by way of direct estimates made from the survey data were noted to be inconclusive. More promise was shown by indirect estimates using the Brass technique but these results were not comprehensive enough to account for those provinces with low living standards. Recent vital registration data, although deficient in some respects, should be able to provide fairly reasonable estimates given the limitations mentioned earlier.

The data used in estimating the measures representing the socio-economic factors reflect a time period which extends from 1970 to 1976. Except for data on housing, the other factors are characterized by data for the mid-1970s.

The Mortality Experience

Philippine mortality on the national level can be shown to have declined when depicted by the adjusted crude rates estimated for two distinctive periods, namely, pre-World War II and post-World War II. From these adjusted rates, one notes fluctuating mortality levels during the first time period exhibiting peak levels during the years 1903, 1918 and 1919. These high death rates were attributable to the cholera, smallpox and influenza epidemics which caused a large loss of lives. Mortality levels during the other years fluctuated from 20 to 30 deaths per 1,000 population. From these observations, we can deduce a high and stable trend. After World War II, mortality level showed a more drastic decline. In a matter of 14 years (from 1946 to 1960), the death rate was reduced by one-half and further reduction is shown during the subsequent decade (see Table 1). A more vigorous implementation of public health measures coupled with the promotion of sanitation and medical aid programmes in the rural areas are believed to be among the major factors contributing to mortality decline during the recent decades.

An almost identical pattern of age-specific death rates is observed when comparing profiles for 1960 and 1978 in Figure 1.* A decline in death rates for the youngest age groups is noted during the 28-year period. This can account for improvements in infant and child mortality and, thus, a tendency towards increasing survival of the young sector of the population. Deaths in the oldest age groups, on the contrary, are shown to have slightly increased in 1978.

The age-specific death rates for males and females for 1978 are depicted in Figure 2. Lower mortality schedules are noted for females starting from aged 15. The gap increases in later ages only to close around aged 75. Low mortality rates for females does not simply mean higher survivorship but it also signifies a greater propensity to remain exposed to reproductive behaviour.

Infant mortality has likewise shown dramatic changes in the early 1950s when it started its downtrend from a high of 125.5 infant deaths per 1,000 births in 1946. The 32-year trend depicted in Figure 3 shows a steady decline. The lowest levels of infant mortality are observed in the late 1970s. The present rate of 49.1 is based on registered infant deaths. Some sources hold

---

* These estimated rates are based on statistical data provided by the United Nations, Demographic Yearbook, Special Issue: Historical Supplement and the NCSO, Philippine Yearbook, 1981.

this figure as suspect and would estimate current levels to be between 70 to 80 infant deaths to 1,000 births. Recent trends as depicted from the 1978 Republic of the Philippines Fertility Survey estimate the level of infant mortality in 1978 to be 53. Gonzaga's (1979) estimate of infant mortality for the same year is 62.0 Despite the discrepancies, these assessments can be seen as indicative of gradual mortality improvement.

Mortality improvement is likewise evidenced by increased longevity of the Philippines population as measured by life expectancy at birth (see Figure 4). During the 80-year period,

TABLE 1
**Estimated Adjusted Annual Crude Death Rates,
Philippines, 1903-71**

Year	CDR	Year	CDR	Year	CDR	Year	CDR
1903	58.0	1923	25.2	1946	25.7	1964	9.9
1904	25.4	1924	26.6	1947	21.6	1965	10.7
1905	28.2	1925	23.5	1948	22.0	1966	10.3
1906	23.8	1926	26.7	1949	20.3	1967	10.0
1907	22.6	1927	26.1	1950	19.3	1968	10.1
1908	30.5	1928	24.3	1951	19.7	1969	9.9
1909	28.2	1929	25.9	1952	19.3	1970	9.6
1910	29.5	1930	26.9	1953	18.6	1971	9.4
1911	28.5	1931	25.1	1954	16.4		
1912	27.5	1932	21.6	1955	15.5		
1913	22.4	1933	22.7	1956	15.5		
1914	23.4	1934	23.4	1957	16.5		
1915	24.7	1935	24.5	1958	14.5		
1916	26.9	1936	22.3	1959	12.7		
1917	28.6	1937	23.3	1960	13.3		
1918	49.7	1938	23.4	1961	10.6		
1919	44.3	1939	23.9	1962	10.3		
1920	26.6	1940	23.5	1963	10.0		
1921	26.7						
1922	25.8						

SOURCE: These figures were drawn from M.B. Concepcion and Peter C. Smith, "The Demographic Situation in the Philippines: An Assessment in 1977", Paper no. 44, Honolulu: East-West Population Institute, June 1977, p. 66 (Table A4).

159

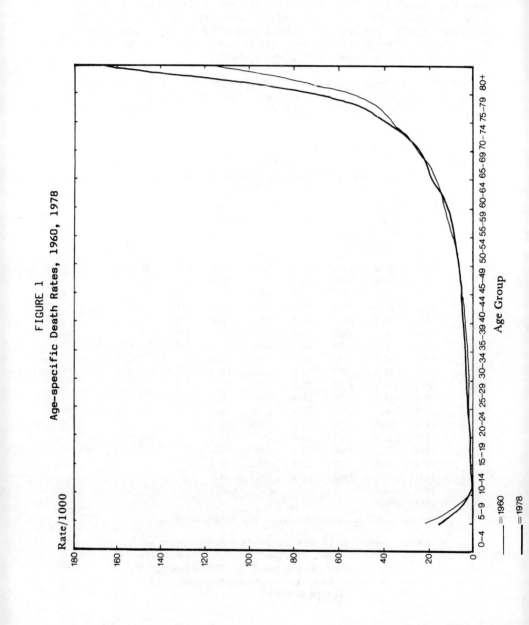

FIGURE 1

Age-specific Death Rates, 1960, 1978

Rate/1000

180

160

140

120

100

80

60

40

20

0

0-4 5-9 10-14 15-19 20-24 25-29 30-34 35-39 40-44 45-49 50-54 55-59 60-64 65-69 70-74 75-79 80+

Age Group

= 1960

= 1978

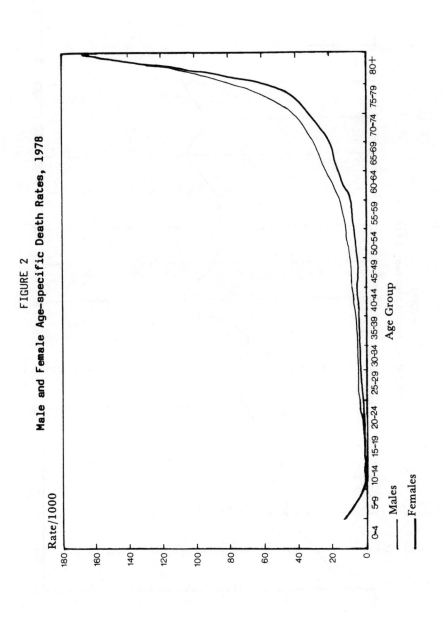

FIGURE 2

Male and Female Age-specific Death Rates, 1978

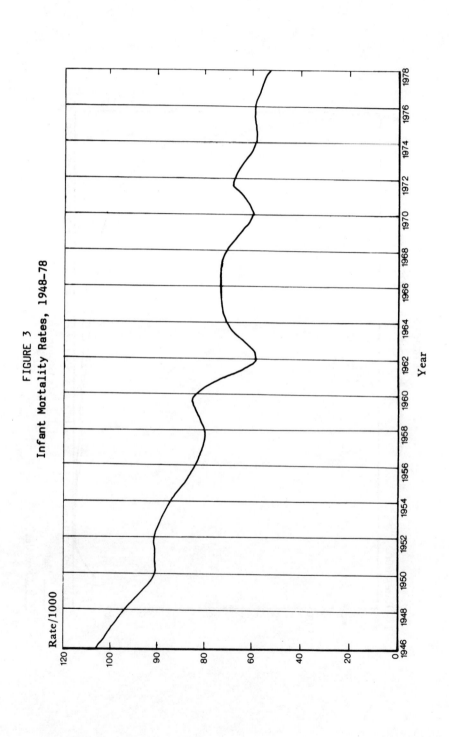

FIGURE 3

Infant Mortality Rates, 1948-78

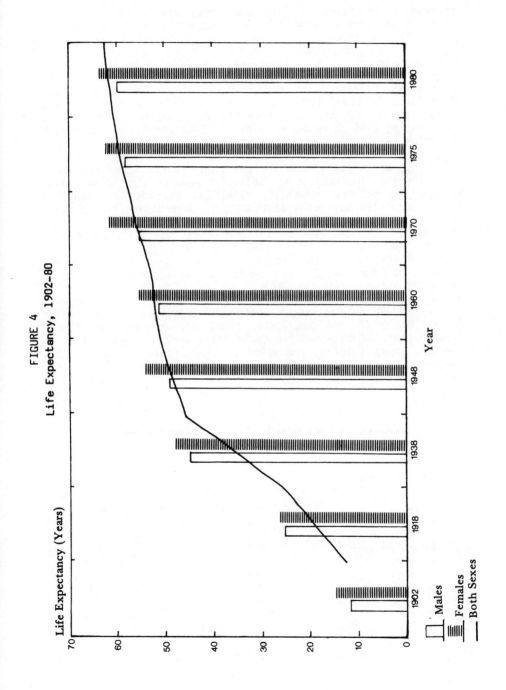

FIGURE 4
Life Expectancy, 1902–80

progressive increases of life expectancy are noted. Dramatic increases are particularly shown prior to World War II, especially during the late 1930s. Life expectancy almost doubled during this period. Sex differentials have begun to be more visible. In later assessments, female longevity superseded male longevity by about 5 years. It is also noted that the Philippine population reached an average life expectancy of 60 years during the mid-1970s. In 1980, life expectancy was estimated by the United Nations to be 62 years, a level to be achieved by developing countries by 1985 as recommended by the 1974 World Population Plan of Action (Salas 1983).

Other mortality trends are shown in Figures 5 and 6. These reflect deaths incurred as a result of pregnancy and childbirth as measured by maternal mortality rates and the loss of potential life as depicted by foetal death rates. Once again, the downward trend of these rates are quite evident. Within the 30-year time span extending from 1948 to 1978, maternal mortality rates have dropped from a high of 4.1 in 1948 to 1.2 in 1978. In the case of foetal death rates, the decline has not been as pronounced. However, during the 20-year period of assessment, decline is primarily noted during the 1970s.

As based on registered deaths in 1978, among the leading causes of death are pneumonia, heart disease and respiratory tuberculosis. Cause-specific death rates were also estimated for specific years starting from 1960 to 1978 (Table 2). Within the 18-year period, the ten listed causes were singled out as the leading causes of deaths in the Philippines. It is further noted

TABLE 2
Cause-specific Death Rates for Ten Leading Causes of Death,
Philippines, 1960-78

Causes of Death	1960	1965	1970	1975	1978
Pneumonia	100.40	121.20	118.20	102.08	98.53
Heart Diseases	27.60	33.60	34.00	54.31	71.78
TB, all forms	92.10	83.40	77.00	69.31	61.27
Gastric diseases	60.50	46.00	35.00	27.83	33.91
M Neoplas	18.20	22.20	25.60	29.42	31.63
Accidents	20.60	23.20	24.80	19.15	26.48
Vascular diseases	20.60	27.90	35.80	34.22	24.33
Nutritional deficiencies	54.40	49.90	25.50	26.00	18.89
Bronchitis, asthma	57.20	43.10	27.90	15.20	12.79
Measles	3.70	8.70	4.50	8.55	12.09

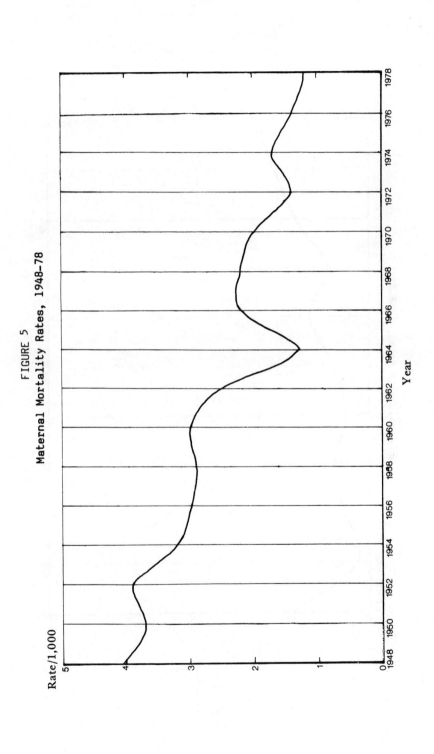

FIGURE 5
Maternal Mortality Rates, 1948–78

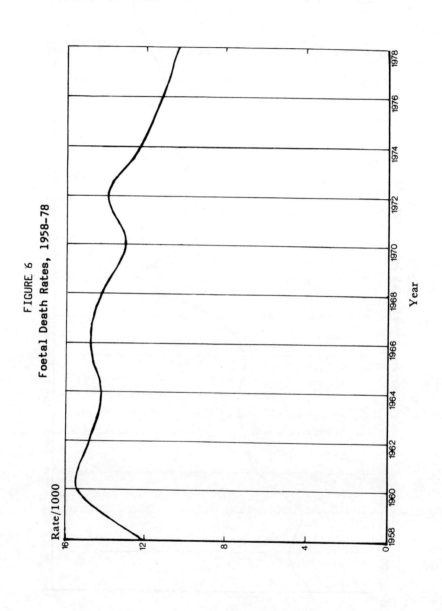

FIGURE 6

Foetal Death Rates, 1958-78

that heart diseases and malignant neoplasms have increased in prominence, as demonstrated by substantial per cent increases during this period (Table 3). Pneumonia, tuberculosis, vascular diseases, and bronchitis can be said to show some signs of decline. From these observations we can say that infectious and parasitic diseases are gradually being replaced by degenerative diseases as the major causes of death in the Philippines. This is most likely due to increasingly effective public health and sanitation measures and the influx of modern medical technology in the rural areas.

Cause-specific infant mortality rates have been estimated from 1972 to 1978 and are presented in Table 4. In 1978, the highest rates are observed for pneumonia, immaturity, diarrhoeal diseases, asphyxia and atelectases and malnutrition. It is also interesting to note that pneumonia is seen to be the leading cause of death for infants as well as for the other age groups.

The second major concern of the study is to assess mortality differentials when comparing geographical areas. The Philippines is divided into 12 development regions and these are: (I) Ilocos; (II) Cagayan Valley; (III) Central Luzon; (IV) Southern Tagalog; (V) Bicol; (VI) Western Visayas; (VII) Central Visayas; (VIII) Eastern Visayas; (IX) Western Mindanao; (X) Northern Mindanao; (XI) Southern Mindanao; and (XII) Central Mindanao. The regional division scheme has been incorporated in the country's development plan to ensure a more effective implementation in meeting development needs of various geographical settings. Mortality levels are assessed for the 12 regions during a 30-year period, that is, from 1950 to 1979. Table 5 depicts the crude death rates (based on vital registration statistics) which reveal interesting trends for the different regions. Keeping in mind the deficiency of the registration statistics, the following observations can be made: (a) the regions exhibiting the highest death rates are regions II (Cagayan Valley), III (Central Luzon), VII (Central Visayas), and I (Ilocos) at the start of the 30-year period while regions XII (Central Mindanao) and IX (Western Mindanao) show the lowest death rates in the same year (1950); (b) recent regional mortality levels reveal a considerable reduction when compared to those observed at the start of the time period; (c) death rates of the 12 regions in 1979 ranged from 2.7 (per 1,000) to 7.6, the highest (7.0 and above) rates being observed for regions I, II, V, VI, VII and VIII. These regions' death rates are slightly higher than the national rate of 6.5 per 1,000 population; (d) although slight fluctuations are noted, a downward trend is unanimous for all regions; and (e) in most regions, present mortality levels were attained in the late 1960s or early 1970s.

Looking now at the yearly infant mortality rates estimated for the 30-year period as shown in Table 6, the following

167

TABLE 3
Percentage Change of Cause-specific Death Rates for Ten Leading Causes of Death, Philippines, 1960-78

Causes of Death	1960-65	1965-70	1970-75	1975-78
Pneumonia	20.72	-2.48	-13.64	-3.48
Heart Diseases	21.74	1.19	59.74	32.17
TB, all forms	-9.45	-7.67	-9.98	-11.61
Gastric diseases	-23.97	-23.91	-20.49	21.85
M Neoplas	21.98	15.32	14.91	7.51
Accidents	12.62	6.90	-22.77	38.23
Vascular diseases	35.44	28.32	-4.40	-28.90
Nutritional deficiencies	-8.27	-48.90	1.97	-27.35
Bronchitis, asthma	-24.65	-35.27	-45.53	-15.83
Measles	135.14	-48.28	90.05	41.39

TABLE 4
Infant Cause-specific Mortality Rates for Leading Causes of Death, Philippines, 1972-78

Causes of Death	1972	1973	1974	1975	1976	1977	1978
Diarrhoeal diseases	NA	1.18	1.46	2.66	4.83	5.89	4.93
Tetanus	2.77	2.50	2.61	2.66	2.39	2.06	1.76
Septicaemia	0.33	1.64	2.01	1.65	2.22	2.70	2.49
Measles	0.51	1.02	0.78	0.70	0.98	1.13	1.14
Beri-beri	3.24	2.40	2.01	1.55	1.32	1.16	1.06
Malnutrition	2.48	1.82	1.26	4.90	4.80	4.14	3.39
Meningitis	0.65	0.64	0.66	0.54	0.63	0.74	0.72
Bronchitis	3.94	4.24	3.73	2.91	3.10	2.56	2.54
Pneumonia	19.17	17.09	15.31	12.84	12.86	13.46	13.45
Gastro-enteritis and coliti	6.11	5.13	3.33	0.12	0.02	0.01	0.01
Congenital anomalies	1.03	4.83	1.49	1.31	1.97	1.97	1.69
Birth injury	0.72	0.33	0.31	0.22	0.26	0.21	0.15
Asphyxia and atelectases of newborn	NA	3.38	4.31	3.30	3.70	3.65	3.81
Immaturity	7.83	6.98	7.14	6.33	6.37	6.77	5.93
Other conditions of newborn	NA	2.97	4.87	0.66	3.46	2.10	1.72

TABLE 5

Crude Death Rates Estimated for the Twelve Philippine Regions, 1950-79

Year	Region											
	I	II	III	IV	V	VI	VII	VIII	IX	X	XI	XII
1950	12.5	14.9	13.3	11.7	11.3	10.4	12.5	11.4	5	11.9	7	3.4
1951	13.4	15.5	13.8	12	10.7	10.8	12.7	12	4.7	11.8	6.6	3.2
1952	12.1	14.8	13.1	11.6	11.3	11.5	13	11.2	5	11.3	7.1	3.7
1953	12	15.9	12.4	11.3	11	10.4	12.1	11.3	5.1	11.1	8	3.2
1954	10.1	14.6	10.2	9.7	10.3	8.9	11.7	10	4.5	10.4	6.5	3
1955	9.6	13	9.6	9.1	9.1	8.9	11.1	10.4	4.4	10	5.6	3
1956	9.8	13.3	9.1	9	9.4	8.9	11.7	10.3	4.5	10.2	5.5	3.2
1957	9.9	13.9	9.7	9.6	10.2	10	12.7	10.9	4.6	11.1	5.8	3.2
1958	9.4	11.8	9.3	8.6	8.4	7.9	10.7	9.3	4.3	9.8	5.9	3.1
1959	8.3	10.5	7.5	7.6	8.3	7	8.9	9	3.8	8.5	5.4	2.1
1960	8.5	10	7.8	8.5	7.7	6.4	8	6.6	2.9	7.6	4	3
1961	8.9	8.7	8.2	8.2	7.4	6.9	8.8	7.6	3.5	6.8	5.1	3.1
1962	6.9	6.8	6.1	6.6	6	4.9	7.5	6.2	2.6	6	4.3	2.5
1963	8	8.1	7	8	7.8	6.3	9.4	8	3.7	7.3	4.6	3.2
1964	8.1	8.8	7.5	8.3	7.6	6.1	9	7.3	3.7	7.1	5.3	3.4
1965	8.8	8.9	7.5	8.2	7.9	6.6	9.6	7.9	3.7	7	4.5	3.4
1966	9.1	8.7	7.2	8.2	7.4	6.7	9.2	8.1	3.5	7.1	3.6	3.1
1967	8.9	7.8	7.6	8.2	7.5	6.8	8.4	7.6	3.3	6.5	4.2	3.2

TABLE 5 (continued)

Crude Death Rates Estimated for the Twelve Philippine Regions, 1950–79

Year	I	II	III	IV	V	VI	VII	VIII	IX	X	XI	XII
1968	8.4	8.2	7.3	8.6	7.9	8	10	7.8	3.8	6.8	5.2	2.8
1969	7.5	7.7	6.5	7.7	6.8	7	8.8	7.3	3.6	6.2	5.1	2.5
1970	7.5	6.6	6.2	7.3	6.5	6.4	7.7	6.6	3.6	6	5	2.4
1971	7.9	7.2	6.2	7.7	7.4	6.9	7.6	7.4	3.3	5.7	4.7	2.2
1972	8.8	8.2	7.1	8.5	7.8	7.8	8.9	7.8	3.7	6.6	5.5	2.1
1973	8.3	8.6	6.5	7.3	9	7.5	9.1	8	3.9	6.3	4.8	3.1
1974	8.1	8.2	6.3	7.4	7.8	7.7	8.5	7.9	3.8	6	5.6	2.6
1975	7.6	7.4	6.1	6.8	7.3	6.7	7.7	7.2	4.7	5.7	4.8	2.6
1976	7.5	7.3	6.2	7.6	7.9	7.4	7.9	7.3	5	6.5	5.3	3.2
1977	7.6	7	6.3	7	8.1	7.1	8.3	7.7	4.2	5.8	5.1	2.9
1978	7.4	7.2	6	6.7	7.8	6.9	7.6	7.3	4.4	5.9	5.1	3
1979	7.6	7.2	6.1	6.7	7.5	7.1	7.5	7.3	4	5.4	5	2.7

SOURCE: National Economic and Development Authority, 1981 Philippine Statistical Yearbook and 1983 Philippine Statistical Yearbook. Manila, 1981 and 1983.

TABLE 6

Infant Mortality Rate Estimated for the Twelve Philippine Regions, 1950–79

Year	I	II	III	IV	V	VI	VII	VIII	IX	X	XI	XII
						Region						
1950	94.29	121.9	123.84	97.23	70.47	129.82	100.78	86.54	113.5	128.47	63.81	97.83
1951	98.3	127.24	126.96	100.61	73.19	133.2	108.25	100.55	100.42	122.76	67.3	89.17
1952	90.22	116.97	115.24	94.82	84.51	133.2	101.95	91.76	107.25	126.29	66.87	89.21
1953	102.2	132.86	115.34	100.98	65.08	126.27	109.81	102.17	117.67	131.64	81	88.26
1954	84.54	124.33	101.73	84.35	82.72	111.2	105.6	85.48	101.83	115.59	69.3	75.51
1955	74.72	100.13	84.15	76.75	72.3	101.58	100.81	86.99	85.75	104.58	53.74	73.32
1956	77.37	107.27	80.5	75.2	72.14	103.81	99.46	83.73	99.66	96.19	53.97	79.3
1957	83.48	118.18	90.97	82.75	84.69	120.28	114.2	91.48	100.76	104.78	55.32	77.13
1958	72.18	96.89	81.75	73.72	67.65	91.35	93.9	76.74	95.3	95.73	61.38	78.92
1959	69	95.53	68.99	61.33	69.31	86.71	82.85	76.51	92.45	91.04	57.82	55.46
1960	70.5	117.92	75.4	72.02	82.36	149.59	92.55	135.64	85.67	108.57	51.44	73.54
1961	73.34	102.83	79.72	76.54	81.57	137.03	108.65	149.07	123.82	101.14	63.89	74.24
1962	47.2	55.86	46.72	56.63	45.5	85.61	69.98	102.28	72.55	72.56	53.85	61.24
1963	58.25	101.87	64	60.88	79.31	109.75	79.77	129.13	83.64	85.27	54.83	61.88
1964	57.32	88.6	63.48	63.3	74.32	91.13	75.32	105.01	84.87	79.05	58.09	64.01
1965	65.82	95.08	64.51	62.32	70.83	105.12	79.87	111.88	90.14	83.08	58.42	69.19
1966	62.68	85.75	61.53	65.75	69.33	109.23	76.13	111.08	88.57	88.35	50.47	56.18
1967	66.68	84.86	65.21	66.62	67.89	102.07	75.63	100.31	86.28	90.32	50.96	61.34

TABLE 6 (continued)

Infant Mortality Rate Estimated for the Twelve Philippine Regions, 1950-79

Year						Region						
	I	II	III	IV	V	VI	VII	VIII	IX	X	XI	XII
1968	61.7	76.65	60.71	65.2	70.72	107.76	76.61	96.3	92.62	88.72	50.16	63.04
1969	57.37	71.54	54.93	66.88	63.26	103.45	68.12	88.21	81.74	79.45	49.33	65.67
1970	53.92	63.78	52.37	58.49	58.15	95.72	58.58	76.49	76.01	67.91	43.63	50.31
1971	55.52	73.96	52.85	61.44	67.31	98.92	54.65	86.45	65.59	62.78	40.87	48.8
1972	62.46	78.84	59.03	67.15	64.6	109.21	63.63	92.67	85.6	69.62	47.91	44.78
1973	60.12	76.38	54.91	61.13	72.66	96.35	67.01	86.15	82.56	60.04	37.79	60.17
1974	54.23	72.62	51.57	59.59	58.68	79.7	59.61	76.34	59.67	52.07	41.24	44.52
1975	53.4	63.47	47.09	55.44	52.53	63.34	55.71	77.08	58.9	44.31	32.97	39.45
1976	51.68	63.32	45.89	62.6	54.64	72.84	55.38	75.46	62.76	52.86	37	42.83
1977	54	57.9	49.6	58	58.9	66.5	57.1	80.8	44.5	43	35.2	35.9
1978	48	52.1	45.9	54.8	58.9	71.4	52.3	75.8	48.3	44.6	35.1	34.8
1979	49.6	58.3	43.2	58.1	53.2	59.3	46.6	61.7	44.9	36.9	40.6	32.5

SOURCE: National Economic and Development Authority, 1981 Philippine Statistical Yearbook and 1983 Philippine Statistical Yearbook. Manila, 1981 and 1983.

observations are made: (a) regions VI (Western Visayas), X (Northern Mindanao), III (Central Luzon), and II (Cagayan Valley) exhibit the highest rates at the start of the period while regions XI (Southern Mindanao) and VIII (Eastern Visayas) have the lowest infant mortality levels; (b) at the end of the 30-year period, the 12 infant mortality rates range from 32.5 (region XII) to 59.3 (region VI); (c) although a gradual and fluctuating downward trend is commonly observed for all regions, the decline in infant mortality level is dramatic when comparing mortality levels at the start and at the end of the 30-year period; and (d) of the 12 regions, regions III, VII, IX, X, and XII exhibit infant mortality levels lower than the national level of 49.4 per 1,000 births.

The pattern of regional variation in mortality has also been discussed elsewhere. Abenoja and Lim (1979) examine provincial mortality patterns in the Visayas with the use of vital registration statistics and the 1970 Population Census. Substantial differences were noted in terms of mortality levels within the Visayan region while overall regional mortality patterns showed slight departure from national-level estimates. It is also interesting to note that mortality levels were correlated with the level of development of Visayan provinces. Concepcion and Cabigon (1979) evaluated adult mortality in two regions which resulted in inconclusive findings regarding assessments concerning orphanhood and widowhood. Assessing regional mortality differentials and its factors is an area of concern not fully explored by Philippine demographic research.

Socio-economic Correlates of Philippine Mortality

The major focus of this study is to evaluate the importance of socio-economic factors in affecting recent Philippine mortality levels. In the previous sections, national and regional mortality patterns and trends have been discussed. Yet, minimal insight is gained in attributing mortality improvement during recent years to socio-economic factors. It has been argued from the demographic transition framework that the experience of mortality decline in industrialized countries can be attributed to improved economic conditions and scientific and technological advancement, particularly in the field of medicine and major breakthroughs in public health and sanitation. All these factors cannot be regarded as conclusive in explaining drastic mortality decline in developing countries. The experience of such countries is rather unique in this respect. It is argued that the importation of medical and public health facilities rather than economic development per se has been more crucial in bringing down mortality levels in most developing countries.

173

In the case of the Philippines, mortality decline has become most evident after World War II, a demographic phenomenon resulting largely from the effective eradication of malaria and other types of infectious diseases via the proliferation of public health and sanitation facilities. In this sense, strictly socio-economic conditions cannot be considered of consequential importance in reducing mortality because the country was just recovering from the ravages of a major war. There is evidence, however, that socio-economic factors are of some significance in depicting mortality differentials under the following circumstances: (a) urban-rural residence; (b) occupational status and (c) educational attainment. Low mortality patterns as measured in terms of selected mortality indices (life expectancy, infant mortality rate, crude death rate) favour urban residents, those having professional, managerial and administrative occupations, and those who have attained higher levels of education (secondary level and above) [Zablan 1978]. Data from the 1973 National Demographic Survey was analysed to show the above observations.

Vital registration data cannot be used to evaluate socio-economic differentials in mortality for the simple reason that mortality statistics are not classified by urban-rural residence of the diseased and by educational attainment. A detailed listing of occupational characteristics of the diseased cross-classified by age and sex is presented in some tables of the registration statistics starting from 1975. Unfortunately, this is of little value because the occupational categories used do not conform with the International Standard Listing of Occupation used elsewhere.

The statistical evidence presented does not provide sufficient basis to lead one to confirm the existing relationship between socio-economic factors (as assessed in terms of socio-economic status) and mortality. To be able to investigate this particular research problem more thoroughly, it was decided in this study to do a multiple regression analysis by considering 12 socio-economic variables representing six distinct dimensions, namely: health, urbanization, education, economic, housing environment and demographic. These variables are listed in Table 7.

Two mortality measures will be used as dependent variables in the analysis and these are: (1) infant mortality rate and (2) maternal mortality rate. All 14 variables (12 independent and two dependent) are provincial-level measures. There are 73 Philippine provinces, six of which are newly formed. In some instances, data were available only for the older provinces. The two housing environment measures and one education measure (population aged 6 to 14 attending school) have only 67 and 66 data observations respectively. Data for these three variables were drawn from the

174

TABLE 7
Selected Socio-economic Measures and their Respective Dimensions, Used as Independent Variables in Multiple Regression Analysis

---

Dimensions and Variables

Housing Environment

DWLPW   Percentage of households with piped water
DWLELC   Percentage of households with electricity

Health

POPPHY   Population per physician
POPHSB   Population per hospital bed
POPAMP   Population per auxillary medical personnel

Economic

INCOME   Income per capita
EAPNAGR   Percentage of economically active population in non-agricultural activities

Education

P14ASP   Population aged 6 to 14 attending school
SECPR   Secondary school participation rate

Urbanization

URBAN   Percentage of urban population
DENSITY   Population density

Demographic

GFRATE   General fertility rate

1970 Population Census whereas those for the other nine independent variables come from more recent (1975) sources. It should also be noted that the mortality measures used as dependent variables in the analysis are derived from the 1978 vital registration statistics. The inconsistency of time periods reflected by the data should not be seen as a drawback in the study. For a better assessment of the impact of potential factors, it is more logical to select its observations from an earlier time period than that of the phenomenon under study. In this way, the assessed explanatory factors reflect conditions that have existed prior to the occurrence of the demographic event that is being evaluated.

Essentially, three multiple regression equations are being tested -- each with a common set of independent variables. Regression results based on the following three solutions will be examined, and these are: (1) standard regression results, where the explanatory capacity of the entire set of independent variables will be evaluated; (2) effects accounted by each dimension will be assessed and compared to determine its influence on mortality; and (3) stepwise regression results, a best-fitting regression technique which selects the variables that best explains mortality levels. The significance level of .05 of the T and the F statistics will be used as the criterion for significance when evaluating the zero-order, the semi-partial and the multiple correlation coefficients. However, its use will merely be a screening device to help in isolating individual or sets of socio-economic variables that best explain recent mortality levels in the Philippines. For obvious reasons, statistical testing is not adopted in this study because the data analysed are drawn from a comprehensive set of Philippine provinces rather than from a sample.

Before performing regression analysis, the data for the variables were inspected and assessed for possible sources of measurement error and unreliable estimation. Appendix Table I shows some relevant summary measures particularly to detect excessive variability in the data values. Among these measures, the most pertinent would be that of skewness which indicates that ten independent variables and the two dependent variables are highly and positively skewed. The appropriate transformations were applied on these variables. Square-root transformation was applied to seven variables and the remaining five variables were subjected to logarithmic transformation (see Appendix 1). Although skewness was greatly reduced by these transformations, two independent variables, namely, percentage of dwellings with

176

electricity (TDWLELC)* and population density (TDENSITY), continued to exhibit moderate skewness. No further transmations were applied on these two variables. The two original (untransformed) variables, namely, general fertility rate (GFRATE) and population aged 6 to 14 attending school (P14ASP) were observed to be slightly negatively skewed. No transformations were likewise applied on these variables.

Residual plots were generated and examined to confirm normality and linearity assumptions. A number of outliers were identified and were later deleted from the analysis. Provinces which obtained a standardized residual value (ZRESID) ± 2.0 and above were considered as outliers. The provinces thus identified when analysing variables affecting infant mortality rate are Northern Samar, Lanao del Sur and Quirino which obtained the following respective ZRESID scores: 3.24184, -2.36019 and 2.03109. Only one province, Siquijor (ZRESID = -2.18467), was excluded from the analysis which considered maternal mortality rate as the dependent variables.

Inter-correlation of Variables

Two tables are presented to show the strength, direction and significance of relationship among the variables used in our analysis. Table 8 exhibits the obtained zero-order correlations among the 12 socio-economic variables (original variables and transformed variables). As expected, variables belonging to specific dimensions tend to be significantly intercorrelated. Relationships are also observed to be significant among variables from different dimensions. Of the 66 correlation coefficients computed (excluding the diagonal coefficients of 1.0) only 19 or (30 per cent) were not found to be significantly different from zero. It should also be noted that extremely high correlations were observed in the following cases: (a) percentage of households with electricity (DWLELC) and percentage urban population (URBAN) (r = .889); and (b) percentage of households with electricity (DWLELC) and percentage of economically active population in the non-agricultural sector (EAPNAGR) (r = .821). The above relationships should be treated cautiously particularly in later analysis for fear that these may contribute to problems of multicollinearity and singularity. At this point, we can simply say that one particular variable, namely, percentage of

---

*   The letter "T" in front of the variable label denotes that the variable(s) has been subjected to transformation.

TABLE 8

Zero-order Correlation Matrices of the Socio-economic Variables

A. Original Variables

	DWLPW	DWLELC	POPPHY	POPHSB	POPAMP	INCOME	EAPNAGR	P14ASP	SECPR	URBAN	DENSITY	GFRATE
DWLPW	1.000											
DWLELC	.428***	1.000										
POPPHY	-.183	-.484***	1.000									
POPHSB	-.375***	-.262*	.550***	1.000								
POPAMP	-.193	-.307**	.552***	.512***	1.000							
INCOME	.256*	.450***	-.177	-.151	-.214	1.000						
EAPNAGR	.292**	.821***	-.464***	-.206	-.319**	.413***	1.000					
P14ASP	-.381***	-.534***	-.565***	-.569***	-.558***	.204	.553***	1.000				
SECPR	.213	.193	-.218	-.255*	-.212	.120	.195	.437***	1.000			
URBAN	.393***	.889***	-.482***	-.276*	-.318**	.498***	.783***	.471***	.177	1.000		
DENSITY	.371***	.566***	-.222	-.180	-.147	.628***	.459***	.267*	.118	.596***	1.000	
GFRATE	-.024	.120	-.219	-.056	.009	.156	.121	.119	.134	.175	.272*	1.000

TABLE 8 (continued)

Zero-order Correlation Matrices of the Socio-economic Variables

B. Transformed Variables

	TDWLPW	TDWLELC	TPOPPHY	TPOPHSB	TPOPAMP	TINCOME	TEAPNAGR	P14ASP	TSECPR	TURBAN	TDENSITY	GFRATE
TDWLPW	1.000											
TDWLELC	.371***	1.000										
TPOPPHY	-.235*	-.632***	1.000									
TPOPHSB	-.444***	-.295**	.487***	1.000								
TPOPAMP	-.386***	-.575***	.586***	.578***	1.000							
TINCOME	.158	.361**	-.185	-.183	-.335**	1.000						
TEAPNAGR	.295**	.771***	-.566***	-.187	-.491***	.336**	1.000					
P14ASP	.367***	.554***	-.586***	-.540***	-.726***	.169	.540***	1.000				
TSECPR	.177	.296**	-.281*	-.311**	-.414***	.122	.290**	.543***	1.000			
TURBAN	.235*	.769***	-.558***	-.224*	-.418***	.314**	.692***	.411***	.217	1.000		
TDENSITY	.343**	.628***	-.489***	-.133	-.383***	.285**	.756***	.435***	.206	.526***	1.000	
GFRATE	-.059	.199	-.248*	-.046	.013	.124	.145	.119	.154	.219	.239*	1.000

NOTE: Correlation coefficients marked with an asterisk sign (*) are found to be significantly different from zero in the following
levels of significance: (a) r* = .05 level; (b) r** = .01 level; (c) r*** = .001 level.

households with electricity, can be a possible source of collinear problems. Table 9 shows the zero-order correlations between the socio-economic variables and the two mortality measures by inspecting these correlations, we can say that a high occurrence of significant relationships are observed more specifically between one mortality measure (maternal mortality rate) and the 12 factors. Strong positive relationships were shown between maternal mortality with the following variables: (1) population per auxiliary medical personnel (POPAMP) (r = .543), and (2) population per physician (POPPHY) (r = .393). Significant inverse correlations were exhibited with the following factors: (1) population aged 6 to 14 attending school (P14ASP) (r = -.359); (2) dwellings with electricity (DWLELC) (r = -.357); (3) percentage urban population (URBAN) (r = -.295); (4) income per capita (INCOME) (r = -.281); and (5) economically active population engaged in non-agricultural activities (EAPNAGR) (r = -.253). Only one factor was significantly related with infant mortality rate and this was general fertility rate (GFRATE) (r = -.246).

Analysing the Multiple Regression Results

As mentioned above, three kinds of multiple regression results will be presented and analysed. The main aim is to attempt at gaining some insights on the following matters: (a) the importance of socio-economic variables in explaining recent Philippine mortality; (b) assessing the explanatory capability of each of the six socio-economic dimensions, namely, housing environment health, education, economic, urbanization, and demographic; and (c) determining the explanatory model containing the most important (statistically significant) socio-economic variables in terms of providing explanation on Philippine mortality.

Impact of Socio-economic Dimensions

The 12 socio-economic variables were assessed with respect to their dimensional capacity in explaining infant and maternal mortality. In our discussion, we will particularly take note of a number of measures included in the regression results and these are: (a) the coefficient of multiple determination (R^2) which indicates the explanatory value of the dimension (or variables) under consideration; (b) the squared semi-partial correlation (SSPC) which indicates the unique contribution of the particular dimension (or variables) to the total variance; and (c) the

TABLE 9

Inter-correlation of the Twelve Socio-economic Variables with the Three Mortality Measures
(Zero-order Correlation Coefficients)

A. Original Variables

	DWLPW	DWLELC	POPPHY	POPHSB	POPAMP	INCOME	EAPNAGR	P14ASP	SECPR	URBAN	DENSITY	GFRATE
IMR	-.045	-.111	.040	.026	-.153	-.062	.037	.057	-.091	-.099	.014	-.246*
MMR	.040	-.357**	.393***	.142	.543***	-.281*	-.253*	-.359**	-.210	-.295**	-.160	-.057

B. Transformed Variables

	TDWLPW	TDWLELC	TPOPPHY	TPOPHSB	TPOPAMP	TINCOME	TEAPNAGR	P14ASP	TSECPR	TURBAN	TDENSITY	GFRATE
TIMR	-.023	-.158	.013	.042	-.092	-.086	.072	.144	-.018	-.092	.071	-.207
TMMR	.034	-.447***	.387***	.103	.480***	-.279*	-.278*	-.416***	-.251*	-.286**	-.258*	-.067

NOTE: Correlation coefficients marked with an asterisk sign (*) are found to be significantly different from zero in the following
levels of significance: (a) r* = .05 level; (b) r** = .01 level; (c) r*** = .001 level.

standardized regression coefficient (beta) and its obtained level of significance which measures the individual weight or impact of an individual variable per unit change of the dependent variable.

Upon examining the importance of the housing dimension in explaining infant mortality, we note that the two variables representing this dimension merely explain slightly over 3 per cent of total variation with dwellings with electricity (TDWLELC) showing higher importance and a negative effect. The betas for both variables and the R^2 were found to be not significant (see Table 10). The obtained R^2s for the other dimensions are as follows: (a) the health dimension ($R^2 = .08845$); (b) the economic dimension ($R^2 = .0289$); (c) the education dimension ($R^2 = .021$) (d) the urbanization dimension ($R^2 = .07031$); and (e) the demographic dimension ($R^2 = .01948$) (see Tables 11 to 20). Clearly, the most important dimensions are health and education. However, their explanatory capacity are only 8 per cent and 7 per cent respectively. None of the these regression results obtained a significant R^2. It is interesting to note, however, the population per hospital bed (TPOPHSB) has the most dominant, significant and positive impact among the health variables. The two variables representing the urbanization dimension show equal importance and significance but different effects on infant mortality. A negative effect is shown by per cent urban population while a positive effect is shown by population density. (See Table 10.)

The six socio-economic dimensions exhibit higher explanatory values when explaining the second dependent variable, maternal mortality. From the results presented in Table 11, we note that the obtained R^2s for the six dimensions and these are as follows: (1) the housing environment dimension ($R^2 = .29716$); (2) the health dimension ($R^2 = .33719$); (3) the economic dimension ($R^2 = .15322$); (4) the education dimension ($R^2 = .18454$); (5) the urbanization dimension ($R^2 = .12001$); and (6) the demographic dimension ($R^2 = .00788$). The highest R^2s are particularly noted for two dimensions, namely, health and housing. Both coefficients were found to be highly significant. Among the three health variables, population per auxiliary medical personnel (TPOPAMP) exhibited the highest contribution to total variance and a high positive beta indicating a strong positive influence on maternal mortality. This finding is surprising as the reverse situation is thought to be more plausible since an increase in health manpower resources can mean better health care and treatment leading to improvements in mortality levels. Of the three variables representing this dimension, only population per hospital bed (TPOPHSB), the next dominant variable, exhibits a significant negative effect, one which conforms to expectation.

Both variables of the housing dimension show opposing

182

TABLE 10
Standard Multiple Regression Results Assessing the Various Socio-economic
Dimensions Affecting Infant Mortality Rate

Housing Environment Variables	BETA	SSPC	T	Significance of T
TDWLELC	-.18962	.0307797	-1.46	.149
TDWLPW	.0299	7.639E-4	.23	.8187

Analysis of Variance

	DF	SS	MS	F	Signifiance Level
Regression	2	4.0657	2.03285	1.12638	.3301
Residual	67	120.8658	1.80397		

R^2 .03254

Health Variables	BETA	SSPC	T	Significance of T
TPOPAMP	-.25829	.0413838	-1.731	.0882
TPOPPHY	.14804	.0154599	1.058	.2937
TPOPHSB	.28466	.0566912	2.026	.0469

Analysis of Variance

	DF	SS	MS	F	Signifiance Level
Regression	3	11.05066	3.68355	2.13432	.1042
Residual	66	113.8808	1.72547		

R^2 .08845

Economic Variables	BETA	SSPC	T	Significance of T
TEAPNGR	-.17562	.0274826	1.377	.173
TINCOME	-.0954	.0081095	-.748	.457

Analysis of Variance

	DF	SS	MS	F	Signifiance Level
Regression	2	3.61003	1.80502	.99682	.3745
Residual	67	121.3215	1.81077		

R^2 .0289

Education

Variables	BETA	SSPC	T	Significance of T
TSECPR	-.09017	.0058548	-.633	.5291
P14ASP	.17088	.0210061	1.199	.2348

Analysis of Variance

	DF	SS	MS	F	Significance Level
Regression	2	2.62359	1.3118	.7186	.4912
Residual	67	122.3079	1.82549		

R^2 .021

Urbanization

Variables	BETA	SSPC	T	Significance of T
TDENSITY	.27726	.0547847	1.987	.051
TURBAN	.27334	.0353008	-1.959	.0543

Analysis of Variance

	DF	SS	MS	F	Significance Level
Regression	2	8.78385	4.39192	2.53349	.087
Residual	67	116.1477	1.73355		

R^2 .07031

Demographic

Variables	BETA	SSPC	T	Significance of T
GFRATE	-.13958	.0194826	1.162	.2492

Analysis of Variance

	DF	SS	MS	F	Significance Level
Regression	1	3.43385	2.43385	1.35106	.2492
Residual	68	122.4977	1.80144		

R^2 .01948

TABLE 11
Standard Multiple Regression Results Assessing the Various Socio-economic
Dimensions Affecting Maternal Mortality Rate

Housing Environment Variables	BETA	SSPC	T	Significance of T
TDWLELC	-.58568	.2959272	-5.39	0
TDWLPW	.25306	.0552518	2.329	.0228

Analysis of Variance

	DF	SS	MS	F	Signifiance Level
Regression	2	1.03227	.51614	14.58669	0
Residual	69	2.4415	.03538		
R^2	.29716				

Health Variables	BETA	SSPC	T	Significance of T
TPOPAMP	.54487	.1616996	4.073	.0001
TPOPHSB	-.31503	.0628356	-2.539	.0134
TPOPPHY	.24254	.0367224	1.941	.0564

Analysis of Variance

	DF	SS	MS	F	Signifiance Level
Regression	3	1.17131	.39044	11.53096	0
Residual	68	2.30246	.03366		
R^2	.33719				

Economic Variables	BETA	SSPC	T	Significance of T
TEAPNGR	-.22579	.0454761	-1.925	.0583
TINCOME	-.25406	.0575756	-2.166	.0338

Analysis of Variance

	DF	SS	MS	F	Signifiance Level
Regression	2	.53226	.26613	4.2427	.0032
Residual	69	2.94151	.04263		
R^2	.15322				

TABLE 11 (continued)
Standard Multiple Regression Results Assessing the Various Socio-economic Dimensions Affecting Maternal Mortality Rate

Education Variables	BETA	SSPC	T	Significance of T
TSECPR	-.03609	9.199E-4	-.279	.7812
P14ASP	-.40893	.1179377	-3.159	.0023

Analysis of Variance

	DF	SS	MS	F	Significance Level
Regression	2	.54106	.32053	7.8076	.0009
Residual	69	2.8327	.04105		

R^2 .18454

Urbanization Variables	BETA	SSPC	T	Significance of T
TDENSITY	-.09783	.0067406	-.727	.4694
TURBAN	-.23801	.0566722	-2.108	.0387

Analysis of Variance

	DF	SS	MS	F	Significance Level
Regression	2	.41688	.20844	.0121	.087
Residual	69	3.05689	.0443		

R^2 .12001

Demographic Variables	BETA	SSPC	T	Significance of T
GFRATE	-.08874	.0078664	-.745	.4585

Analysis of Variance

	DF	SS	MS	F	Significance Level
Regression	1	.02736	.02736	.55567	.4585
Residual	70	3.44641	.04923		

R^2 .00788

influences on maternal mortality. The more dominant influence is observed for dwellings with electricity (TDWLELC) which is, at the same time, a negative and highly significant one. Its unique contribution to total variance is about 30 per cent. The other variable, namely, dwellings with piped water (TDWLPW), is comparatively weak. Strangely enough, it exhibits a positive influence on maternal mortality. This finding does not seem to conform to the expectation that improvements of living conditions tend to be inversely related to mortality.

A common feature of the two multiple regression solutions is that the health dimension predominates in influencing recent Philippine mortality. It would be interesting if this observation persists after examining the results of other regression strategies. In the discussion above, the individual impact of the selected dimensions was assessed. This should be regarded as a preliminary evaluation. More meaningful insights can be gained when these dimensions (or variables) are analysed jointly.

Hierarchical Regression Analysis

A more refined mode of assessment of the unique impact of each of the six dimensions is by estimating the net effect of the variables representing the socio-economic dimensions from the results derived from the hierarchical regression solution. When estimating the net effect of the particular socio-economic dimension on mortality levels, the following regression estimates are evaluated; (a) the obtained R^{2*} for the standard multiple regression which includes all the socio-economic dimensions except the one being assessed; (b) the obtained R^2 based on the standard regression results which includes the assessed socio-economic dimension as well as the rest; (c) the R^2 change which accounts for the added contribution of the assessed dimension; (d) the F statistics estimated for the R^2 change; and (e) the significance level of the F statistic. The R^2 change will be used as a measure to ascertain the net influence of a specific socio-economic dimension on mortality. Its statistical significance, as being tested by the F statistic, will simply be interpreted as a screening criteria in reporting and discriminating dimensions with the highest net effects. Two sets of results will be presented. One set will contain estimates reflecting the full representation of variables per dimension. (Originally, 12 variables represented the six socio-economic dimensions; three variables were later discarded in the analysis because these were causing problems of multicollinearity.) The second set of results will show estimates based on the remaining variables. A comparison of these two sets of results can show more clearly the individual performance of the six socio-economic dimensions in trying to explain Philippine mortality levels.

Let us first examine the hierarchical regression results based on the entire set of socio-economic variables. The only dimension that showed the pronounced net impact on infant mortality is the "housing environment" factor as represented by two variables (TDWLPW and TDWLELC). It registered an R^2 change of 10.2 per cent which is found to be significant at the .05 level (Table 12). The other five factors have relatively minimal impact. Looking now at the results evaluating the differential impact of the same factors on maternal mortality, two factors are observed to have considerable influence on the total explained variation of maternal mortality. These are: the "housing environment" factor and the "economic factor". The former's contribution is 11.4 per cent in the R^2 change, while the latter's about 6 per cent (see Table 13).

The revised hierarchical regression results based on a selected set of socio-economic variables are presented in Tables 14 and 15. In this analysis only nine variables (instead of all twelve) representing the six socio-economic factors were assessed as predictors of infant mortality. None of the six factors showed considerable net effects on infant mortality. Among these factors, only the "demographic" factor represented by a single indicator (general fertility rate) exhibits an R^2 change of 4 per cent. This is assessed to be significant at the .10 (Table 14) level. This finding seems to indicate that socio-economic factors, when taken singly, do not have much influence on infant mortality.

Maternal mortality, however, is influenced by at least one socio-economic factor, namely, the "health" factor. Its added impact on total variation is found to be significant at the .05 level. A somewhat lower net effect is observed for the "housing environment" factor which indicates an R^2 of 3 per cent and found to be significant at the .08 level (Table 15).

The first set of results are unreliable on account of the inclusion of variables that are highly intercorrelated with some of the remaining ones. In fact, the factors that consistently showed significant impact were the "housing environment" factor and the "economic" factor, both depicted by variables causing multicollinearity problems. The second set of results proved to be not very promising either in terms of highlighting the importance of any of the socio-economic factors. However, these results show that the "health" factor has an effect on maternal mortality while the "demographic" factor registers the strongest net effect on infant mortality. From these results, one can readily see the weak impact the six socio-economic factors have on

188

TABLE 12

Net Effect of the Six Socio-economic Factors on Infant Mortality Rate,
as Measured by the R Square Change as Derived from
Hierarchical Regression Results

Factor: Housing Environment	R^{2*}	.1337
(TDWLELC TDWLPW)	R^2	.2357
	R^2 Change	.102
	F Change	4.00378
	Significance of F	.0233
Factor: Health	R^{2*}	.21836
(TPOPAMP TPOPPHY TPOPHSB)	R^2	.2357
	R^2 Change	.01734
	F Change	.45385
	Significance of F	.7155
Factor: Economic	R^{2*}	.21714
(TEAPNGR TINCOME)	R^2	.2357
	R^2 Change	.01856
	F Change	.72839
	Significance of F	.4869
Factor: Education	R^{2*}	.0313
(TSECPR P14AS)	R^2	.2357
	R^2 Change	.03257
	F Change	1.27842
	Significance of F	.286
Factor: Urbanization	R^{2*}	.2285
(TDENSITY TURBAN)	R^2	.2357
	R^2 Change	.0072
	F Change	.28253
	Significance of F	.7549
Factor: Demographic	R^{2*}	.20964
(GFRATE)	R^2	.2357
	R^2 Change	.02606
	F Change	2.04573
	Significance of F	.1578

NOTE: The results presented are drawn from the standard multiple
regression results where the variables belonging to the six
dimensions were entered last in the multiple regression
solutions. The first R Square (R^{2*}) presented corresponds to
all the socio-economic variables excluding the specific factor
while the second R Square (R^2) reflects the explanatory value
of all the socio-economic factors including the particular
factor being assessed.

TABLE 13

Net Effect of the Six Socio-economic Factors on Maternal Mortality Rate, as Measured by the R Square Change as Derived from Hierarchical Regression Results

Factor: Housing Environment (TDWLELC TDWLPW)	R^{2*}	.36505
	R^2	.47903
	R^2 Change	.11398
	F Change	6.56355
	Significance of F	.0026
Factor: Health (TPOPAMP TPOPPHY TPOPHSB)	R^{2*}	.41913
	R^2	.47093
	R^2 Change	.0599
	F Change	2.29969
	Significance of F	.0864
Factor: Economic (TEAPNGR TINCOME)	R^{2*}	.42039
	R^2	.47093
	R^2 Change	.05865
	F Change	3.37726
	Significance of F	.0407
Factor: Education (TSECPR P14AS)	R^{2*}	.4544
	R^2	.47903
	R^2 Change	.02463
	F Change	1.41859
	Significance of F	.2501
Factor: Urbanization (TDENSITY TURBAN)	R^{2*}	.46767
	R^2	.47903
	R^2 Change	.01136
	F Change	.6542
	Significance of F	.5235
Factor: Demographic (GFRATE)	R^{2*}	.47429
	R^2	.47903
	R^2 Change	.00474
	F Change	.54643
	Significance of F	.4627

NOTE: The results presented are drawn from the standard multiple regression results where the variables belonging to the six dimensions were entered last in the multiple regression solutions. The first R Square (R^{2*}) presented corresponds to all the socio-economic variables excluding the specific factor while the second R Square (R^2) reflects the explanatory value of all the socio-economic factors including the particular factor being assessed.

mortality when taken singly. A combination of some of them may improve their explanatory capacity.

Assessing Combined Effects of Socio-economic Factors

Before performing statistical analysis to generate the results needed for this section, the 12 independent variables were assessed for possible multicollinearity and singularity problems. The procedure adopted in detecting these problems is by examining the squared multiple correlation coefficients (SMC) of each independent variable with all other variables included in the regression solution (Tabachnick and Fidell 1983). In effect, two sets of SMCs were assessed, as based on two distinct regression solutions (our analysis involves two dependent variables). From the results shown in Table 16, the highest SMCs were noted for three variables, namely: percentage urban population (TURBAN), dwellings with electricity (TDWLELC), and economically active population engaged in non-agricultural activities (TEAPNGR). All these variables exhibited SMCs greater than or equal to 0.8. An obtained SMC estimate of this magnitude clearly indicates a near perfect correlation between the particular variable with other variable(s). The decision adopted was to delete these variables from the analysis to avoid unstable matrix inversions implemented during multivariate analysis. In effect, only nine variables will be assessed when analysing the first dependent variable, infant mortality rate. A somewhat similar situation is observed in the second set of SMCs (see Table 16). Two variables exhibited SMCs as high as 0.8 and these are: dwellings with electricty (TDWLELC) and economically active population engaged in non-agricultural activities (TEAPNGR). Thus, these variables will be eliminated when carrying out this facet of the analysis.

Let us first look at the standard regression results obtained using infant mortality as the dependent variable (see Table 17). The obtained R^2 when the nine independent variables were assessed jointly is .183, that is, about 18 per cent of the total variance is explained by all the considered socio-economic variables. Among the highest contributors (above .03) to the total variance are: (1) population per hospital bed (TPOPHSB); (2) population per physician (TPOPPHY), and (3) population aged 6 to 14 who are attending school (P14ASP). It would likewise be interesting to note that the three socio-economic variables have a positive influence on infant mortality, as measured by their obtained betas. These coefficients, however, are statistically not significant. It should also be noted that this standard regression results failed to obtain a significant F. Clearly, the most important factors tend to be health and education factors.

191

TABLE 14
**Net Effect of the Six Socio-economic Factors on Infant Mortality Rate,
as Measured by the R Square Change as Derived from
the Revised Hierarchical Regression Results**

Factor: Housing Environment (TDWLELC TDWLPW)	R^{2*}	.11398
	R^2	.12247
	R^2 Change	.0085
	F Change	.61001
	Significance of F	.4377

Factor: Health (TPOPAMP TPOPPHY TPOPHSB)	R^{2*}	.1072
	R^2	.12247
	R^2 Change	.01527
	F Change	.36548
	Significance of F	.7781

Factor: Economic (TEAPNGR TINCOME)	R^{2*}	.11415
	R^2	.12247
	R^2 Change	.00832
	F Change	.59728
	Significance of F	.4425

Factor: Education (TSECPR P14ASP)	R^{2*}	.09182
	R^2	.12247
	R^2 Change	.03065
	F Change	1.10035
	Significance of F	.3391

Factor: Urbanization (TDENSITY TURBAN)	R^{2*}	.1139
	R^2	.12247
	R^2 Change	.00857
	F Change	.61522
	Significance of F	.4358

Factor: Demographic (GFRATE)	R^{2*}	.083
	R^2	.12247
	R^2 Change	.03947
	F Change	2.83366
	Significance of F	.0973

NOTE: The results presented are drawn from the standard multiple
regression results based on the remaining set of socio-economic
variables. The variables representing a particular dimension
were entered last in the hierarchical regression strategy in
order to evaluate its net contribution to total explained
variation. the first R Square (R^{2*}) presented corresponds to
all the socio-economic variables excluding the specific factor
while the second R Square (R^2) reflects the explanatory value
of all the socio-economic factors including the particular
factor being assessed.

TABLE 15

Net Effect of the Six Socio-economic Factors on Maternal Mortality Rate, as Measured by the R Square Change as Derived from the Revised Hierarchical Regression Results

Factor: Housing Environment		
(TDWLPW)	R^{2*}	.34614
	R^2	.37767
	R^2 Change	.03113
	F Change	3.14115
	Significance of F	.0813

Factor: Health		
(TPOPAMP TPOPPHY TPOPHSB)	R^{2*}	.28278
	R^2	.37767
	R^2 Change	.09489
	F Change	3.15106
	Significance of F	.0311

Factor: Economic		
(TINCOME)	R^{2*}	.35605
	R^2	.37767
	R^2 Change	.02162
	F Change	2.15412
	Significance of F	.1472

Factor: Education		
(TSECPR P14ASP)	R^{2*}	.35733
	R^2	.37767
	R^2 Change	.02034
	F Change	1.01302
	Significance of F	.3691

Factor: Urbanization		
(TDENSITY TURBAN)	R^{2*}	.37755
	R^2	.37767
	R^2 Change	.00012
	F Change	.00593
	Significance of F	.9941

Factor: Demographic		
(GFRATE)	R^{2*}	.37678
	R^2	.37767
	R^2 Change	.00088
	F Change	.088
	Significance of F	.7677

NOTE: The results presented are drawn from the standard multiple
        regression results based on the remaining set of socio-economic
        variables. The variables representing a particular dimension
        were entered last in the hierarchical regression strategy in
        order to evaluate its net contribution to total explained
        variation. The first R Square (R^{2*}) presented corresponds to all
        the socio-economic variables excluding the specific factor while
        the second R Square (R^2) reflects the explanatory value of all
        the socio-economic factors including the particular factor being
        assessed.

We now proceed to determine the best-fitting regression model with the use of a second regression strategy, namely, the stepwise regression solution. This particular strategy is a model-building procedure where variable selection and inclusion is statistically determined. This would help us select the "best" variable(s) in our explanatory model whose aim it is to evaluate and eventually extract the most important ones affecting Philippine mortality. The stepwise regression results for infant mortality are presented in Table 18. Two variables were selected and these are population per hospital bed (TPOPHSB) and population aged 6 to 14 who are attending school (P14ASP). The health and education variables have a combined explanatory value of 10.9 per cent and show a positive relationship with infant mortality. Health has the most relevant impact on infant mortality. The positive relationship shown by the health variable with infant mortality is suggestive that health facilities are still adequate in the Philippines such that an increase in the population per hospital bed ratio does not automatically have any beneficial impact on the level of infant mortality. The positive relationship between the education variable with infant mortality offers some difficulty in providing some explanation. One would expect that an educated population would be more conscious of health care needs and this, in turn,

TABLE 16

Squared Multiple Correlations of the Independent Variables
Used in the Multiple Regression Analysis

Variable	Dependent Variable Infant Mortality Rate SMC	Dependent Variable Maternal Mortality Rate SMC
TDWLPW	.34986	.64013
TDWLELC	.78447	.78895
TPOPPHY	.58526	.59019
TPOPHSB	.53135	.55202
TPOPAMP	.65395	.67155
TINCOME	.22371	.24382
TEAPNGR	.75797	.76819
P14ASP	.68729	.68564
TSECPR	.31386	.30327
TURBAN	.83349	.63891
TDENSITY	.61109	.61038
GFRATE	.21418	.19472

194

could lead to mortality improvements. In this sense, the education variable should exhibit a negative relationship with infant mortality. This particular finding leads one to suspect that the positive relationship of this variable may be due to a more intensive effort in improving levels of school participation by channelling financial resources to improve educational facilities rather than health facilities.

The standard multiple regression results for maternal mortality are presented in Table 19. Slightly over 42 per cent is explained by the ten socio-economic variables considered in the regression equation. On the whole, the standard multiple regression results obtained a highly significant F. Among the highest contributors are: (1) population per physician (TPOPPHY); (2) population per hospital bed (TPOPHSB); (3) income per capita (TINCOME); and (4) dwellings with piped water (TDWLPW). (Each of the variables obtained an SSPC of .03 and above.) Curiously, the two health variables show different influences, as portrayed by their obtained betas. Population per hospital bed has a negative relationship while population per physician has a positive one. Income per capita negatively influences maternal mortality while dwellings with piped water shows a positive relationship with the dependent variable. Of the four mentioned, only the two health variables obtained significant betas (significant at the .05 level and below).

Looking now at the stepwise regression results displayed in Table 20, five socio-economic variables qualified for inclusion in the best-fitting regression model. Together these variables provide a joint explanatory capacity of 40.3 per cent of total variation. The five variables are: (1) population per hospital bed (TPOPHSB); (2) income per capita (TINCOME); (3) dwellings with piped water (TDWLPW); (4) population per auxiliary medical personnel (TPOPAMP); and (5) population per physician (TPOPPHY). The health dimension becomes a more prominent explanatory factor in the sense that the three representative variables are assessed to be statistically significant. At the same time, an economic variable and a housing variable were also found to be similarly significant. Of the three health variables, two show a positive relationship with maternal mortality. This finding reinforces the contention made earlier that a deteriorated health situation, as depicted by increments in these ratios may, in turn, bring about increasing levels of maternal mortality.

The third health variables, namely, population per hospital bed (TPOPHSB), shows a negative relationship with maternal mortality, when comparing it to its performance in explaining infant mortality. It is difficult to find a plausible explanation for the contrasting role of this particular health variable. One is led to suspect that improvements in health resources with

195

TABLE 17
Standard Multiple Regression Results Assessing Socio-economic Variables Affecting Infant Mortality Rate

Variable	Beta	SSPC	T	SIG
TDENSITY	.22856	.0286801	1.451	.1521
TPOPHSB	.26377	.0392292	1.697	.0948
GFRATE	-.14548	.0170267	-1.118	.268
TINCOME	-.03723	.0011299	-.288	.7745
TSECPR	-.05696	.0022676	-.408	.6849
TDW1PW	-.06798	.0029708	-.467	.6422
TPOPPHY	.25086	.0334918	1.568	.1222
TPOPAMP	-.06636	.0017851	-.362	.7185
TP14ASP	.30066	.0348727	1.6	.1148

Analysis of Variance of Standard Multiple Regression Results

Variable	DF	SS	MS	F	SIG
REGRESSION	9	22.82113	2.53568	1.48996	.1725
RESIDUAL	60	102.1104	1.70184		

R SQUARE .18267

TABLE 18
Stepwise Multiple Regression Results Assessing Socio-economic Variables Affecting Infant Mortality Rate

Variable	Beta	SSPC	T	SIG
TPOPHSB	.34676	.0933654	2.649	.01
P14ASP	.28695	.0639298	2.192	.0318

Analysis of Variance of Stepwise Multiple Regression Results

Variable	DF	SS	MS	F	SIG
REGRESSION	2	13.56098	6.78049	4.07911	.0213
RESIDUAL	67	111.3705	1.66225		

R SQUARE .10855

TABLE 19

Standard Multiple Regression Results Assessing Socio-economic
Variables Affecting Maternal Mortality Rate

Variable	Beta	SSPC	T	SIG
TDENSITY	.07655	.0030719	.571	.5701
TPOPHSB	-.27486	.0375366	-1.996	.0505
TGFRATE	.0039973	8.325E-5	.094	.9254
TINCOME	-.20828	.0345158	-1.914	.0603
TSECPR	-.02433	4.076E-4	-.208	.8363
TDW1PW	.21998	.0327009	1.863	.0673
TURBAN	-.05945	.0020023	-.461	.6462
TPOPPHY	.4095	.0588392	2.499	.0152
TPOPAMP	.19475	.0160702	1.306	.1966
TP14ASP	-.20734	.0144870	-1.24	.2197

Analysis of Variance of Standard Multiple Regression Results

Variable	DF	SS	MS	F	SIG
REGRESSION	10	1.4773	.14773	4.51374	.0001
RESIDUAL	61	1.99647	.03273		

R SQUARE .42527

TABLE 20

Stepwise Multiple Regression Results Assessing Socio-economic
Variables Affecting Maternal Mortality Rate

Variable	Beta	SSPC	T	SIG
TPOPHSB	-.23561	.0319767	-1.88	.0645
TINCOME	-.18733	.0311319	-1.855	.0681
TDW1PW	.21974	.0373196	2.031	.0463
TPOPAMP	.52787	.1370450	3.892	.0002
TPOPPHY	.23167	.0333866	1.921	.059

Analysis of Variance of Stepwise Multiple Regression Results

Variable	DF	SS	MS	F	SIG
REGRESSION	5	1.39951	.2799	8.90607	0
RESIDUAL	66	2.07426	.03143		

R SQUARE .40288

regard to increased hospital bed capacity, although conducive in arresting or controlling maternal mortality, may in some sense enhance the capability of monitoring and reporting maternal deaths. Income per capita, as expected, has a negative relationship with maternal mortality. As economic conditions improve, better affordability in terms of pre-natal care is expected. The positive relationship observed for the lone housing variable fails to give an obvious explanation. One would expect that better health and sanitation go hand in hand with better housing conditions. This is not supported by the results. One contention which can be made from these particular findings is that health care, as provided by health personnel, and the capability of obtaining this essential service through better earnings, are the main factors conducive to improving conditions of maternal mortality.

Summary and Conclusions

The study provides a recent assessment of Philippine mortality trends and patterns. It attempts at evaluating the importance of socio-economic factors in explaining this demographic phenomenon. When explaining mortality trends during previous decades till the present, a dramatic decline particularly after World War II has been noted. Further reduction was observed during the subsequent decades.

Upon scrutinizing the mortality experiences of different age groups during the past three decades, it was observed that the incidence of death from the youngest age group (0-4 years) to the 55-59 age group showed an identical pattern, during the past three decades. Increasing mortality levels are noted for the oldest age groups as evidenced in the 1979 mortality schedule while a large proportion of those belonging to the younger age groups tend to survive. The latter has definitely contributed to sustained high fertility levels as well as providing a conducive scenario for a continued high performance in fertility. Infant mortality has likewise shown dramatic changes in the early 1950s and its lowest levels were evidenced in the late 1970s. Mortality improvement is likewise portrayed by increased longevity of the Philippine population.

Life expectancy at birth for males and females during the 80-year period showed dramatic increase starting during the late 1930s. In later decades, female longevity superceded male longevity by about five years. Other mortality trends showing the downward trend of maternal mortality rates and foetal death rates serve as further evidence in support of Philippine mortality decline.

Communicable and infectious diseases like pneumonia, tuberculosis, vascular diseases, and bronchitis declined in prominence as leading causes of death. Degenerative diseases like heart disease and malignant neoplasms have increased in prominence, as demonstrated by substantial percentage increases.

Regional crude death rates and infant mortality rates reflecting three decades (1950 to 1979) were observed. The yearly rates reveal a gradual and fluctuating downtrend for all regions. Drastic declines were noted for specific Luzon and Visayan regions. Low mortality levels were particularly observed in the Mindanao regions. These mortality measures are, however, suspected not to reflect the real situation due to under-enumeration.

The dramatic decline in Philippine mortality is believed to be due to the effective eradication of malaria and other types of infectious diseases via the proliferation of public health and sanitation facilities. The impact of socio-economic factors in reducing further mortality levels is argued to have taken effect much later. In earlier studies low mortality rates were observed for those residing in urban areas, for those belonging to white-collar occupational groups, and for those with higher educational attainment. However, these findings do not provide sound basis to empirically justify the importance of socio-economic factors in affecting recent mortality levels. To further investigate this research problem, a multivariate analysis was adopted by the present study. Twelve socio-economic variables representing six distinct dimensions, namely: health, urbanization, education, socio-economic, housing environment and demographic, were evaluated. Two mortality measures were to be used as dependent variables in the analysis, namely: (1) infant mortality rate and (2) maternal mortality rate. All 14 variables are provincial-level measures. Three multiple regression strategies were implemented to enlighten us on the following matters: (a) the joint capacity of socio-economic factors in explaining recent Philippine mortality; (b) the influence of each specific socio-economic dimension in affecting mortality level as assessed in terms of its exclusive as well as its net effects on the dependent variables; (c) the selection of a best-fitting explanatory model based on the selected socio-economic factors.

When assessing the net effects of each socio-economic factor on infant mortality, it was noted that none of the factors had a significant (.05 level or less) singular influence on mortality. The only factor which showed promising results was the demographic factor represented by a lone variable, general fertility rate. In itself, this finding is not a surprising one. The inter-relationship between fertility and mortality, although not clearly defined in the causal sense, has also been observed in other studies.

199

When jointly assessing the socio-economic variables, the health and education factors provided 18 per cent explanation, an indication that other unconsidered factors may provide a more adequate explanation for infant mortality in the Philippines. Among the socio-economic variables that contributed substantially to explained variables are: (1) population per hospital bed (TPOPHSB); (2) population per physician (TPOPPHY), and (3) population aged 6 to 14 who are attending school (P14ASP). All these variables show a positive relationship with infant mortality. The above results failed to attain statistical significance.

Stepwise regression strategy was applied to determine the best-fitting regression model. Two variables were selected and included in the model, namely, population per hospital bed (TPOPHSB) and population aged 6 to 14 who are attending school (P14ASP). The health and education variables have a combined explanatory value of 10.9 per cent and show a positive relationship with infant mortality, with the latter variable exhibiting a more dominant impact on infant mortality. The positive relationship of the education variable with infant mortality is somewhat peculiar in nature and poses some difficulty in interpretation. Although confounding at the outset, this result should be regarded more as contributive or linked with the impact of the health factor.

When assessing the individual and collective impact of the six socio-economic dimensions on maternal mortality, the health and housing dimensions turned out to be the more dominant ones. When taken collectively, the set of socio-economic variables explain slightly over 42 per cent of total variation. This result indicates that the selected socio-economic variables are better explanatory factors of maternal mortality. The specific variables that contributed substantially to total variation are: (1) population per physician (TPOPPHY); (2) population per hospital bed (TPOPHSB); (3) income per capita (TINCOME); and (4) dwellings with piped water (TDWLPW).

Five socio-economic variables qualified for inclusion in the best-fitting regression model. Together these variables provide a joint explanatory capacity of 40.3 per cent of total variation. The five variables are: (1) population per hospital bed (TPOPHSB); (2) income per capita (TINCOME); (3) dwellings with piped water (TDWLPW); (4) population per auxiliary medical personnel (TPOPAMP); and (5) population per physician (TPOPPHY). The health dimension gains more prominence as an explanatory factor. Its three representative variables were included among the statistically significant variables. Two other variables were included in the best-fitting model, an economic variable and a housing variable. The positive relationship of the latter and the

200

negative relationship of one health indicator (population per hospital bed) with maternal mortality for the moment defy a rational and plausible interpretation.

These oddities in our results can also be due to measurement error. One source of error is the underestimation of the mortality indices particularly in the southern and more remote provinces on account of under-reporting. Despite problems of data inadequacy, the study concludes by summing up its major findings: (1) an assessment of socio-economic factors affecting recent Philippine mortality has demonstrated that a select number of these can provide some explanation to the demographic phenomenon under consideration; (2) the health dimension is the most dominant factor affecting mortality; (3) different factors come into play in influencing mortality -- health and education play a dominant role in affecting infant mortality while health, income and housing are prime factors in influencing maternal mortality; and (4) socio-economic variables show a more substantial impact on maternal mortality than on infant mortality. Future studies of this nature can improve upon the approach taken and the techniques adopted by the present study. Further enlightenment concerning mortality determinants can be achieved if the following points can be accommodated in future studies: (a) a more meaningful characterization of socio-economic factors with the use of more representative measures of socio-economic conditions; (b) the inclusion of other plausible factors which can improve upon the results of the present study; (c) other mortality indices can be utilized to characterize the demographic phenomenon under study; and (d) the assessment can employ a longtitudinal or diachronic perspective in the sense that data for both the factors and mortality should reflect different time periods.

The study can provide guidelines to population policy with particular emphasis on further reduction in mortality levels. The following policy recommendations can be proposed for consideration: (1) mortality differentials within the country can be narrowed down by providing better channels of access to health care and resources; (2) although national mortality levels have been efficiently reduced, high mortality level still persists at the local level and for particular sectors and age groups of the population. Hence, national population policy should be translated to accommodate and be effective to local conditions; and (3) socio-economic improvement may be the key to promote mortality improvement in the local scene but the former has to incorporate programmes that are favourable to the needs of the local population. The Philippines has not completely resolved this demographic issue. This is even further compounded by the problem of mass poverty. It is this deprived sector that will be most exposed to the high risk of death.

APPENDIX 1

Summary Measures of Independent and Dependent Variables
Used in the Multiple Regression Analysis
(Based on the Original Variables)

Independent Variables	Mean	SD	Skewness	N
DW1PW	21.249	20.004	1.722	67
DWLELC	14.751	18.908	2.55	67
POPPHY	3342.247	1946.726	1.792	73
POPHSB	1205.205	744.781	1.776	73
POPAMP	1330.74	973.715	3.407	73
INCOME	1015.301	208.979	1.943	73
EAPNAGR	41.207	17.842	1.102	73
P14ASP	62.78	6.437	-.384	66
SECPR	18.071	9.506	2.073	67
URBAN	25.678	16.229	2.212	73
DENSITY	257.175	902.946	8.368	73
GFRATE	128.712	27.529	-.232	68

Dependent Variables	Mean	SD	Skewness	N
INFANT	43.305	20.541	1.375	73
MATERNAL	15.374	8.587	1.323	72

APPENDIX 2

Summary Measures of Independent and Dependent Variables
Used in the Multiple Regression Analysis
(Based on the Transformed Variables)

Independent Variables	Mean	SD	Skewness	N
TDWIPW*	4.163	1.994	.709	67
TDWLELC*	3.335	1.919	1.539	67
TPOPPHY*	55.391	16.669	.086	73
TPOPHSB*	33.225	10.135	.5	73
TPOPAMP'	3.054	.232	.654	73
TINCOME'	2.999	.083	.361	73
TEAPNAGR*	6.278	1.35	.379	73
TSECPR*	4.122	1.047	.594	67
TURBAN'	1.345	.231	.238	73
TDENSITY'	2.103	.382	1.078	73

Dependent Variables	Mean	SD	Skewness	N
TINFANT*	6.399	1.546	.137	73
TMATERNAL'	1.127	.228	.165	72

NOTE: Those variables signified with an asterisk (*) sign were subjected to
square root transformation while those with an apostrophe (') sign were
subjected to logarithmic transformation (common logarithm).

References

Abenoja, Macrina and Alice C. Lim. "Mortality in the Visayas". _Philippine Quarterly of Culture and Society_. (Special Population Issue), VII: 4 (December 1979), pp. 245-95.

Concepcion, Mercedes B. and Josefina V. Cabigon. _Adult Mortality Estimates: Central Luzon and Metro Manila_. 1979 Area Fertility Study. Special Report No. 24. Manila: Population Institute, University of the Philippines, 1979.

Flieger, Wilhelm. "Philippine Mortality: Levels, Trends and Areal Differentials". Paper presented at the WHO/ESCAP Meeting on Mortality in Asia: A Review of Changing Trends and Patterns 1950-1975. WHO/051/ESCAP/80.24. Manila, 1-5 December 1980.

Flieger, Wilhelm, Macrina K. Abenoja and Alice C. Lim. _On the Road to Longevity: 1970 National, Regional and Provincial Mortality Estimates for the Philippines_. Cebu City: Office of Population Studies, University of San Carlos, 1981.

Gonzaga, Katrina. "Estimates of Infant Mortality Rates Using Three Methods, Urban-Rural Philippines". Paper presented at the NEDA/NCSO/UNFPA Seminar on Selected Population-based Researches: Their Relevance to Development Planning. Manila, 1979.

National Census and Statistics Office (NCSO). _Age and Sex Population Projections for the Philippines by Province: 1970-2000_. UNFPA-NCSO Population Research Project. Monograph No. 2. Manila, 1976.

_____. "Vital Statistics Report". Manila: National Economic and Development Authority -- National Census and Statistics Office. 1975, 1976, 1977 and 1978.

_____. _Philippine Yearbook_. Manila: National Economic and Development Authority -- National Census and Statistics Office. 1975, 1976, 1978, 1980, 1982 and 1983.

_____. "1980 Census of Population". Special Report No. 1. Manila: National Economic and Development Authority, National Census and Statistics Office. April 1982.

_____ et al. "World Fertility Survey: Republic of the Philippines Fertility Survey, 1978". First Report. Manila: National Census and Statistics Office, University of the Philippines Population Institute, Commission on Population, National Economic and Development Authority. December, 1979.

National Economic and Development Authority (NEDA). "Five-Year Philippine Development Plan. 1978-1982". (Including the Ten-Year Development Plan 1978-1987). Manila, September 1977.

_____. _Philippine Statistical Yearbook._ Manila: National Economic and Development Authority -- National Census and Statistics Office. 1979 and 1983.

_____. Commission on Population, National Census and Statistics Office. _Population Dimension of Planning_, Vol. II, Population Projections for the Philippines by Province, 1970-2000. Manila, March 1975.

Philippines. Special Committee to Review the Philippine Population Program. Final Report. June 1978.

Salas, Rafael M. "Setting New Mortality Goals". In _POPULI_ (Journal of the United Nations Fund for Population Activities), X: 3 (1983): 3-5.

Tabachnick, Barbara G. and Linda S. Fidell. _Using Multivariate Statistics_. New York: Harper & Row Publishers, 1983.

United Nations. _Demographic Yearbook._ Special Issue: Historical Supplement. New York, 1979.

Zablan, Zelda C. "Trends and Differentials in Mortality". In _ESCAP, Population of the Philippines._ Country Monograph Series No. 5. Bangkok: United Nations, 1978.

Ng Shui Meng

Introduction

Mortality has long been a neglected aspect of population studies despite the fact that it is acknowledged as an important component of population change.   In many developing countries, population planners, concerned with rapidly growing population are beginning to realize the vital linkage between fertility and mortality and that any modification in the former may well have to be realized first through improvement of the latter.   But it is also increasingly realized that our actual understanding of the dynamics of mortality decline is very limited.   Population planners generally take mortality decline as an inevitable consequent to some vaguely defined process of development.   Yet, in many developing countries today, and even in those that are recognized as having achieved rapid strides in the development scale, there is still substantial human wastage in the form of infant and child deaths.

In the past, evidence suggested that mortality decline in Europe was linked to the general improvement of economic and social life especially in the improvement of nutrition and better housing and sanitary conditions.   But for many developing countries today, it is entirely clear to what extent mortality reduction can be attributed more to socio-economic development or to the importation of modern medicine and medical technology or both.   In many poor third world countries, post-war mortality decline appears to be more closely attributed to the latter. However, increasingly there is also evidence that shows that there is a threshold level beyond which modern medicine seem to have little incremental effect on mortality, especially in the area of neo-natal and post-natal deaths if there is no concurrent improvement in the socio-economic well-being of the populace. However, there are still very few studies on mortality which show empirically how these factors operate and the extent to which

206

mortality differentials can be attributed to certain aspects of socio-economic improvement or to environmental changes or to diffusion of modern health care and public health practices. The understanding of these linkages, it is felt, is important not only from a demographic perspective but also as a source of information for policy makers in development planning, especially in the area of reducing human wastage through infant and child deaths.

Objective and Design of the Study

Although a comprehensive approach to the study of the socio-economic correlates of mortality in Singapore at this stage is not feasible, given the limitation of the data sources, it is the objective of this study to provide some analysis of the recent pattern of mortality changes of the city state. In particular, this study attempts in a limited way to explore to what extent post-war mortality decline in Singapore could be linked to the socio-economic, environmental and health improvement of the population.

The study of socio-economic correlates of Singapore departs somewhat in analytical design from that of the other studies in this series. In the original research design, the researchers agreed to adopt areal analysis as a mode of analysis to link areal level socio-economic indicators to mortality indices in the recent period for each country in order to examine the differential impact of "development" on mortality. The assumption is that given Japan's and the ASEAN countries' (other than Singapore) population and geographical size, there would be ample heterogenity in terms of mortality experience and access to social and economic resources across regions to justify this type of analysis. But in the case of Singapore, because of its small size, compact settlement and pattern of utilization of social and health services such a mode of analysis cannot be adopted.

This does not mean that the population of Singapore is homogenous in terms of mortality experience and attainment of socio-economic status at the individual level. Singapore's population is differentiated along income, education, and class lines as well as along ethnic and religious lines, all of which would presumably have some relationship to an individual's probability of survival at every age right from the moment of conception. However, suitable individual level data for analysis to demonstrate the linkage between mortality experience and the demographic, socio-economic and environmental background characteristics of the individual are lacking. This highlights the low level of interest mortality studies feature for population planners in Singapore. Most population studies in Singapore are still largely concerned only with the fertility aspect of demographic change.

In view of the fact that the mortality data from Singapore are not amenable for areal analysis or individual level analysis, this study will focus on two aspects:

(1) analysis of the historical trend of mortality decline in Singapore especially in the post-war period, including the discussion of ethnic differentials and recent patterns of change; and

(2) multivariate analysis of socio-economic correlates of mortality by examining the relationship of mortality and selected socio-economic environmental and health related variables using time series analysis. This is where this study differs from other studies, that is, instead of studying areal differences of mortality, this study examines the mortality change in Singapore through time as it is related to changes in socio-economic development over the same period.

Data Sources

The sources of data used in the study includes vital registration data, census reports and annual demographic and social statistics put out by the Singapore Department of Statistics. The focus of study is in the post-war period although some reference is also made to earlier times.

Unlike most developing countries where vital registration leaves much to be desired, vital registration in the city state of Singapore has a high degree of validity and accuracy. Birth registration is believed to be virtually complete as the birth certificate is one of the most important documents for an individual throughout life. In most countries, birth registration is generally much more complete than death registration, but in Singapore, even death registration has a very high degree of completeness because of strict legal enforcement. The small size of the country and the widespread availability of health facilities have reduced the chance of non-registration of vital events to a minimum. Death registration in Singapore is required within three days of its occurrence, but according to the Registrar of Births and Deaths, most deaths in actual fact are registered on the same day. This is partly because a death has to be reported before a burial or cremation permit can be obtained.

In cases where the death is suspected not to be due to natural causes, a coroner's inquiry is required by law. In 1980, for example, out of 12,505 deaths only 45 (0.036 per cent) were classified as late registrations -- that is, reported after three days of occurrence (Report on the Registration of Births and Deaths 1980, p. 1).

The census data in Singapore have also improved in accuracy and validity over the years although there are still indications that some errors still exist for age misreporting especially among people in the older age groups. Among people in the younger ages, age reporting is supposedly much more accurate. Time series data, both demographic, economic and social are collected by the various departments and ministries and such data are centralized at the Singapore Department of Statistics. Annual demographic data are available dating back to the 1930s and even earlier (though more patchy). Social and economic data have shorter series with some dating back to the early 1950s. Most data, however, are much later and date back only to the late 1950s or early 1960s. The present study draws heavily upon published census data and vital registration data as well as tabulations provided by the Singapore Statistics Department.

Crude Death Rate

Although there may be some doubt about the mortality data in the pre-World War II period, it is generally accepted that mortality rates in Singapore at that time was high. Singapore by turn of the twentieth century was still very much a British colonial outpost in which the population (being largely migrant) fluctuated very dramatically in response to the fortunes of the colony. In addition to the very unstable characteristics of the population structure, health and medical services and other basic sanitation facilities in the colony were also minimal and largely accessible only to selected segments of the population. Given this, the crude death rates in Singapore then tended to be both high and unstable. The estimated crude death rates were said to range from 40 and 50 per 1,000 population (Saw Swee Hock 1970, pp. 87-90).

After 1945, mortality conditions on the island improved considerably reflecting on the one hand the global advancement of medical technology in the control of epidemic diseases such as cholera, typhoid, small-pox and malaria, and so forth; and on the other, the increasing political awareness of the public in pressuring the colonial administration to provide better health and medical services. Although many of the killer diseases were not eliminated, the small size of the island and increasing

209

awareness of the population had meant that outbreaks of epidemics could be brought under control more easily. By 1947, the recorded crude death rate had already fallen to less than 14 per 1,000. And by 1959 when Singapore achieved self rule, the mortality rate had dipped very impressively to only around 6.4 (see Table 1).

The post-war decline in mortality in Singapore has to be understood in the context of the stabilizing of the Singapore society which unlike the early days had become less prone to dramatic increases and losses of its population through out-migration and in-migration. The post-war population structure of Singapore was much more stable as a result of stricter regulation on migration. As the population took on a more stable form, natural increase became the dominant factor in the city state's population growth. Mortality too began to reflect more and more the age structure of the population. With high post-war fertility, the population became progressively younger and increasingly favourable to low crude death rates.

Hence from 1950 onwards, and especially in the more recent decades, the mortality had continued its downward trend to hover around 5 per 1,000 throughout much of the 1970s. In 1980, the crude death rate for the population as a whole stood at 5.2 per 1,000. But in the more recent years, there has been a slight increase in the crude death rate, a phenomenon which reflects the slight ageing of Singapore's population as Singapore begins to move towards replacement fertility and eventually towards zero growth.

Infant Mortality

After 1930, statistics on vital registration became systematically available. The early vital statistics were probably incomplete but nonetheless were indicative of the general level of infant mortality which prevailed during the period. The early records showed that infant mortality rates were alarmingly high. Infant mortality rates (IMR) close to 200 per 1,000 births were not uncommon and hence suggestive of the high risks of death in the first year of life. Infant mortality improved significantly only after World War II. In 1946, infant mortality rate (IMR) was recorded at 89.7 per 1,000 births, by 1955 it was halved. Between 1955 and 1975, IMR was trimmed by another 71.9 per cent (see Table 1). In 1980, the infant mortality rate of Singapore was 11.7 per 1,000 live births and comparable to that of many of the developed countries of the world.

With the prevailing infant mortality in Singapore at such a

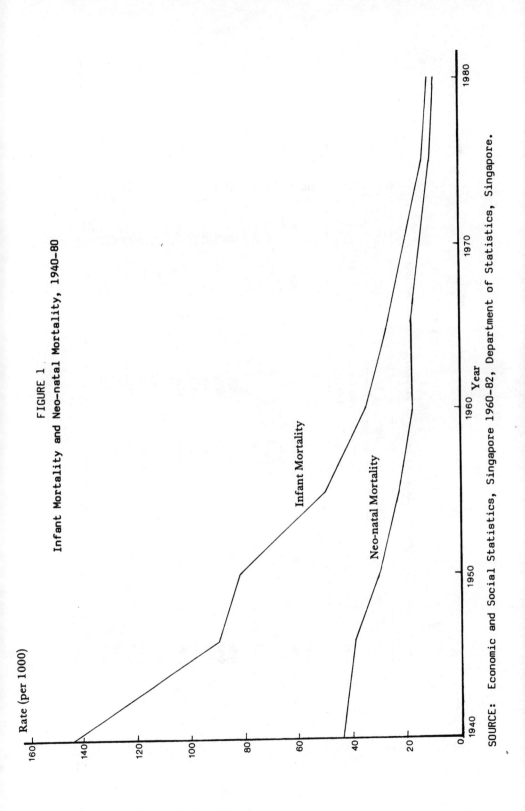

FIGURE 1

Infant Mortality and Neo-natal Mortality, 1940-80

Rate (per 1000)

Infant Mortality

Neo-natal Mortality

Year

SOURCE: Economic and Social Statistics, Singapore 1960–82, Department of Statistics, Singapore.

TABLE 1

Some Mortality Indicators of Singapore, 1931-41 and 1946-82

| Year | Per 1,000 Population | Per 1,000 Live Births | | Per 1,000 Live Births & Still Births | | |
	Deaths	Infant Mortality	Neo-natal Mortality	Peri-natal Mortality	Still Births	Maternal Mortality
1931	24.2	191.3	-	-	27.0	7.5
1932	20.4	171.6	-	-	24.8	7.5
1933	22.5	164.7	-	-	23.9	5.8
1934	24.1	166.0	-	-	25.1	4.8
1935	24.3	155.4	-	-	24.5	3.8
1936	24.2	169.0	49.2	-	24.1	3.6
1937	22.0	152.6	46.9	-	24.7	4.4
1938	21.4	158.9	44.0	-	24.0	4.7
1939	19.5	130.5	43.5	-	23.0	4.0
1940	20.9	142.6	42.8	-	20.8	4.3
1941	20.8	-	-	-	23.2	4.1
1946	-	89.7	39.0	-	16.4	3.3
1947	13.3	87.3	33.1	-	15.3	2.9
1948	12.4	80.8	32.8	35.9	16.7	2.4
1949	11.9	72.0	28.0	34.3	17.1	2.2

TABLE 1 (continued)
Some Mortality Indicators of Singapore, 1931-41 and 1946-82

| Year | Per 1,000 Population | Per 1,000 Live Births | | Per 1,000 Live Births & Still Births | | |
	Deaths	Infant Mortality	Neo-natal Mortality	Peri-natal Mortality	Still Births	Maternal Mortality
1950	12.0	82.2	29.8	35.4	17.1	1.8
1951	11.6	75.2	29.2	34.6	16.4	1.6
1952	10.7	70.0	31.7	33.9	17.3	1.7
1953	9.7	67.1	32.0	33.6	16.7	1.2
1954	8.6	56.0	26.1	31.7	16.1	1.5
1955	8.1	49.5	23.0	29.8	15.4	0.9
1956	7.5	42.5	19.1	28.4	14.7	0.7
1957	7.4	41.4	17.8	28.3	15.4	0.9
1958	7.0	43.7	19.0	29.0	15.2	0.8
1959	6.4	36.0	17.3	26.3	13.6	0.7
1960	6.2	34.9	17.7	27.9	14.1	0.4
1961	5.9	32.3	17.7	26.2	12.6	0.4
1962	5.8	31.2	19.1	26.7	12.4	0.4
1963	5.6	28.1	18.4	26.4	12.3	0.3
1964	5.7	29.9	19.6	26.1	11.8	0.4
1965	5.4	26.3	17.9	25.5	11.6	0.4
1966	5.4	25.8	16.6	24.6	11.2	0.5
1967	5.3	24.8	16.7	24.4	10.7	0.3
1968	5.5	23.4	15.9	23.2	10.5	0.4
1969	5.0	20.9	14.5	21.7	9.9	0.4

TABLE 1 (continued)

Some Mortality Indicators of Singapore, 1931-41 and 1946-82

| | Per 1,000 Population | Per 1,000 Live Births | | Per 1,000 Live Births & Still Births | | |
Year	Deaths	Infant Mortality	Neo-natal Mortality	Peri-natal Mortality	Still Births	Maternal Mortality
1970	5.2	20.5	14.6	21.5	9.7	0.3
1971	5.4	20.1	14.0	21.0	9.2	0.2
1972	5.4	19.2	14.4	20.5	8.0	0.4
1973	5.4	20.3	14.3	20.0	7.9	0.1
1974	5.2	16.8	12.1	18.1	8.2	0.2
1975	5.1	13.9	10.2	16.6	7.6	0.3
1976	5.1	11.6	8.3	14.7	7.7	0.1
1977	5.1	12.4	9.3	16.1	8.0	0.2
1978	5.1	12.6	9.7	15.2	7.0	0.2
1979	5.2	13.2	9.8	14.9	6.6	0.1
1980	5.2	11.7	8.9	13.4	6.4	-
1981	5.3	10.7	7.6	12.6	6.6	-
1982	5.2	10.7	8.2	13.0	6.4	0.1

SOURCE: Singapore Department of Statistics.

low rate, it is felt that further reduction will prove more difficult and will have to await significant breakthroughs in medical science which could deal with the endogenous causes of deaths of early infancy. This is clearly illustrated when one compares the ratio between infant mortality and neo-natal[1] and peri-natal[2] mortality over the years (see Table 1). In 1946 neo-natal mortality accounted for 43 per cent of infant mortality. In the post 1970 period, neo-natal mortality accounted for nearly three-quarters of all infant deaths. This high ratio is suggestive of the fact that most of these infants probably died from endogenous causes rather than from exogenous causes which are more amenable to medical treatment.

While the chances of survival for infants have been vastly improved, deaths of the mothers due to complications of childbirth and puerperium have also been drastically reduced. To a large measure, the decline in maternal mortality is directly the result of improved medical and maternity care made available to all mothers in the last two decades. Only about 2 per cent of all child births now do not occur in hospitals or nursing homes and only 0.1 per cent of all births are delivery without aid of doctor, nurse or midwife (Report of the Registration of Births and Deaths 1980.) Birth complication leading to maternal deaths have therefore been reduced to a minimum (see Table 1).

Life Expectancy

As the mortality conditions improved, naturally the length of life of the average person in Singapore also increased. In the pre-World World II days, life expectancy at birth was below fifty for males and females. But by the 1950s, average length of life has increased to the high fifties for males and sixties for females. The 1957 census life tables estimate for the life expectancy for the population as a whole was 62.5 years, with male life expectancy at 60.3 and female life expectancy at 65.2. In the 1970s, on an average expectation of life increased by another 5 years for males and females (65.1 for males and 70.0 for females). A decade later, life expectancy at birth for the population as a whole was 71.2 years (68.7 for males and 74.0 for

---

1   Neo-natal mortality refers to deaths of infants under 28 years of age.

2   Peri-natal mortality refers to deaths of infants under 7 days of age and still births. Still births refer to foetal deaths with gestation period of 28 weeks or more.

females).   The gap between males and females has been fairly
consistent -- about 4 to 5 years (see Table 2).   With life
expectancy for the population as a whole pushing past 70 years, it
is not expected that gains in the future could be as impressive as
in the past.

Ethnic Differentials

Any discussion of mortality for Singapore should not ignore the
fact that Singapore is a multi-ethnic and multi-religious society.
Three major ethnic groups make up the bulk of Singapore's
population.   In the 1980 census it was enumerated that the Chinese
comprise close to 77 per cent of the population; Malays make up
14.6 per cent and Indians comprise 6.4 per cent; and the rest
under the category of "Others" are made up mainly of Europeans,
Eurasians, Japanese and so on.   The Chinese and Indians were
migrants who had only come to Singapore in large numbers after the
establishment of British control in 1819.   The largest waves of
Chinese and Indian migration to Singapore occurred in the latter
part of the nineteenth century and the early half of the twentieth
century.   By the end of World War II, immigration became less
important as a factor of Singapore's demographic change (although,
it was still a major factor for the Indian population until more
recently).

Significant mortality differentials along ethnic lines were
apparent although these differences have blurred in the last one
or two decades.

An examination of the ethnic mortality differentials
indicated that these were initially related to the migration
background of the various groups and subsequently due increasingly
to the general health and welfare of the groups concerned.

In the earlier period of Sinapore's settlement history, it
can be seen that the death rates among the more settled Malay
indigenous population were more stable and its trend less
subjected to migration effects and external economic factors which
had obviously left a great impact on the mortality pattern of the
Chinese and Indian migrant groups.   For example, during the Great
Depression of the 1930s, many Chinese and Indians were
repatriated, among whom were mainly the old, the sick and the
unemployed.   The result was a marked drop in death rates for these
two ethnic groups for those years.

Other than the greater fluctuation of death rates among the
immigrant population, the difference in the population structure

of the three groups was also clearly detected. Migration was a
selective process which tended to weed out the old, the very young
and the female sex. This feature was even more prominent among
Indian migrants who until recently were predominantly male and
within the working age groups. Such a population structure
favoured low mortality. Hence the Indian ethnic group on the
whole experienced lower mortality than the other two main ethnic
groups in Singapore throughout much of the pre-war period and even
after (Saw Swee Hock 1970, p. 91).

The Chinese group, influenced by migration like the Indians,
also at times experienced lower fertility than the Malays. But
because of the increased and systematic Chinese female immigration
in the 1930s (to the exclusion of males), the sex ratio of the
Chinese population became much better balanced, unlike that of the
Indians which had remained lopsidedly dominated by males until
fairly recently. With a more balanced sex ratio, natural increase
exceeded migration as the major component of growth within the
Chinese population. As the Chinese population became more stable,
the mortality rates of the Chinese also began to approach that of
the settled population, the Malays. However, by the post-war
period, mortality among the Chinese declined rapidly and was lower
than that of the Malays, and then even the Indians.

The Malay ethnic group when compared to the Chinese and
Indian groups showed a slower decline of crude death rates after
the war. This post-war phenomenon suggested a widening of the
socio-economic gap between the migrant and indigenous population,
with the migrant populations (or at least segments of it) able to
take much more advantage of the increasing economic and social

TABLE 2
Life Expectancy for Census Years 1957, 1970, 1980

Year	Total Population			Chinese		Malay		Indian	
	All	Male	Female	Male	Female	Male	Female	Male	Female
1957	62.5	60.3	65.2	60.7	66.6	57.4	58.5	62.2	61.5
1970	67.3	75.1	70.0	65.4	70.8	64.6	65.6	63.9	65.5
1980	71.2	68.7	74.0	69.3	74.7	68.5	70.3	65.1	69.6

SOURCE: Singapore Department of Statistics.

opportunities of the post-war period to better their lot much faster than the indigenous group. On the whole the Malay ethnic group up until the last ten years tended to remain within their traditional economic and social spheres and maintained their settlement patterns of the pre-war period. Hence while the other two ethnic groups showed steep declines in mortality levels, that of the Malay group was relatively less dramatic until 1965. Since 1965, however, the mortality trend of the Malay population showed a shift. It not only caught up with the other two ethnic groups but have declined even faster than those groups. The very young age structure of the Malay population began to have a major impact in slowing the crude death rates (see Table 3).

While the Malays now have the lowest crude death rates, they in actual fact still lagged behind the other two ethnic groups in mortality decline. This is clearly illustrated when one examines the pattern of infant mortality and age-specific mortality.

Throughout the period under discussion, the Malay ethnic group more than the other ethnic groups bore the brunt of higher infant deaths. In the 1930s, the Malay IMR often exceeded 200 per 1,000 live births and its decline lagged behind that of the Indians and the Chinese very markedly. In 1955, Malay IMR was still more than 100 per 1,000 compared to 40.2 for the Chinese and 44.2 for the Indians. The gap between Malay IMR and that for the Chinese and Indians only narrowed in the 1970s and 1980s, although even today, Malay babies still have lower survival probabilities than Indian or Chinese babies.

The Chinese started with higher IMR than the Indians in the pre-war period, but the post-war era soon saw a more rapid decline of IMR among the Chinese such that the Chinese have since then experienced the lowest level of infant deaths among the three ethnic groups. However, the difference in IMR between the Chinese and Indian is not very great.

The ethnic differences and the higher mortality of the Malays, especially, can be attributed to many factors. First, Malays tend to marry much younger than the Chinese. Teenage marriages among Malay girls (and to some extent Indian girls also) were fairly common until recently. Births to teenage mothers have a greater risk of survival. This factor, in part accounts for the higher infant deaths among the Malay population. Also, until fairly recently Malay mothers still preferred to give birth in their own homes assisted only by a mid-wife. Even in 1970 nearly 40 per cent of all Malay births took place at home compared to 4 per cent among the Chinese and 6 per cent among Indians. Most Indians and Chinese give birth in the hospital or nursing homes. By 1980, about 10 per cent of the Malay births occurred at home. This difference in birth practice accounts for the higher risks of

218

TABLE 3
Crude Death Rates for the Three Main Ethnic Groups, 1886-1980

Period	Chinese	Malays	Indians
1886-90	38.4	36.8	30.4
1891-95	36.9	35.8	29.5
1896-00	42.8	35.6	31.1
1901-05	49.3	45.2	39.3
1906-10	43.3	46.1	47.7
1911-15	39.7	38.4	28.6
1916-20	36.9	36.7	28.3
1921-25	29.4	33.0	26.9
1926-30	29.8	31.4	25.5
1931-35	23.5	28.7	17.3
1936-40	22.2	25.9	15.3
1941-45	34.6	62.7	61.8
1946-50	12.6	16.7	13.4
1951-55	9.3	12.7	8.1
1956-60	6.6	9.1	5.9
1961-65	5.7	6.5	5.1
1966-70	5.3	5.0	5.8
1971-75	5.4	4.4	5.5
1976-80	5.3	4.2	4.8

SOURCE: Saw Swee Hock, 1970; and Singapore Department of Statistics.

TABLE 4
Infant Mortality Rates by Ethnic Groups
1931-40 and 1946-80

Year	Malays	Chinese	Indians
1931	261.4	183.8	163.7
1932	252.7	166.6	108.9
1933	237.2	157.8	140.3
1934	291.5	151.9	131.8
1935	225.4	150.7	116.8
1936	225.2	167.7	104.3
1937	205.8	149.9	128.0
1938	233.4	154.1	128.0
1939	184.8	127.4	94.5
1940	209.9	138.1	110.5
1946	140.5	82.3	94.7
1947	143.2	79.4	76.4
1948	155.3	71.3	76.8
1949	120.0	64.5	80.9
1950	141.7	75.1	67.6
1951	137.1	66.6	70.7
1952	120.0	62.3	66.2
1953	123.9	58.3	62.9
1954	107.0	46.7	60.2
1955	104.7	40.2	44.2
1956	94.8	33.8	34.2
1957	86.4	32.9	39.8
1958	85.5	35.3	40.3
1959	69.0	29.6	29.8
1960	65.0	28.3	33.4
1961	56.8	26.3	33.4
1962	48.0	27.2	29.7
1963	39.3	25.1	29.7
1964	42.0	26.6	30.4
1965	37.3	23.5	24.7
1966	38.9	22.3	25.3
1967	37.5	21.1	25.6
1968	35.1	20.6	23.7
1969	30.7	18.8	21.4
1970	28.7	18.5	24.5
1971	28.0	18.5	22.7
1972	25.7	17.9	17.7
1973	31.4	18.5	21.2
1974	22.2	16.2	15.2
1975	21.4	12.3	17.5
1976	18.8	10.0	19.4
1977	14.7	12.0	13.4
1978	19.9	11.3	14.6
1979	18.8	11.9	17.5
1980	15.3	11.1	12.8

SOURCE: Singapore Department of Statistics.

FIGURE 2

Infant Mortality of Major Ethnic Groups

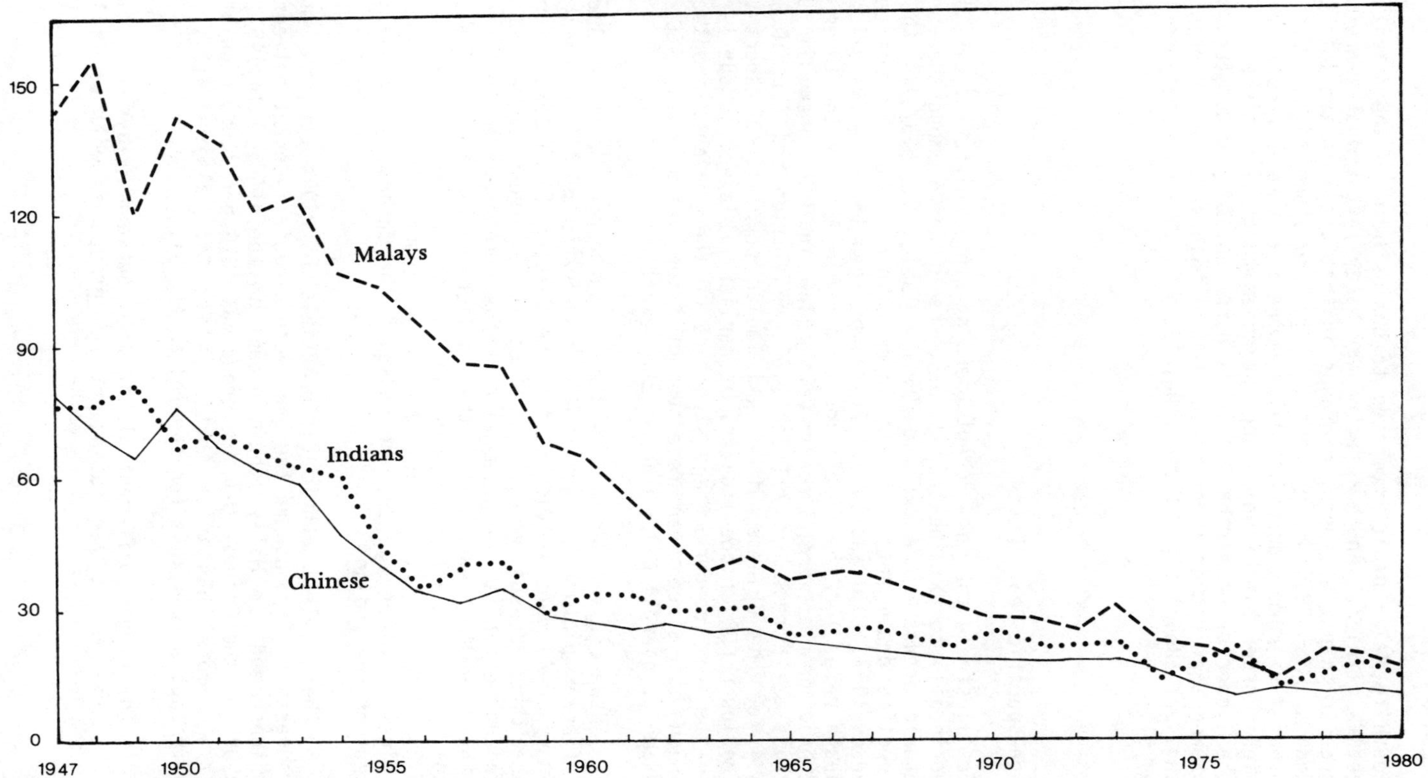

SOURCE: Singapore Department of Statistics.

death to Malay babies compared to babies born in the hospital or health clinics. Another factor why Malay infant deaths are still greater than the other two groups is that until in the late 1970s and early 1980s, Malay fertility had remained higher than the other two ethnic groups. Malay mothers are more likely to have higher order births which are subjected to greater risks of death than lower order births. This is borne out by a U.N. study which showed that higher order births tended to have a lesser chance of survival (Population Studies, No. 13, Vol. 2, United Nations 1954, p. 9).

Age-specific Death Rates

To illustrate the more recent trend of ethnic differentials, it is worthwhile to examine the age patterns of death among the various ethnic groups since the mid-1950s. Tables 5.1-5.3 show the age specific death rates for the three ethnic groups for the census years 1957, 1970 and 1980. It can be seen that the overall crude death rates for the population as a whole and for the three main ethnic groups were already fairly low in 1957 when the total crude death rate was 7.4 per 1,000 population and 7.1, 10.0 and 6.4 for the Chinese, Malay and Indian population respectively. The lower CDR of the Indians, as earlier explained is due largely to the more conducive age structure of the Indians, a situation which has since been reversed in later years. In 1980, for example, overall Malay CDR was the lowest.

However, when we examine the age pattern of deaths a slightly different picture emerges. The death rates of the youngest age group (0-4) were the lowest for the Chinese (both sexes) for all the three census years. In fact, the Chinese seemed to have faired better at every age most of the time compared to the other ethnic groups, except for the earlier period. For 1957, the age-specific death rate (ASDR) of the Indians for the age groups 5-29 seemed to be slightly better or comparable to that of the Chinese. After age 29, the ASDRs of the Chinese were lower than that of the Indians.

The greatest ethnic differentials in ASDRs occurred in the youngest age groups and the gaps were especially great between the Chinese and the Malay ethnic groups in the 1950s. In 1957, the ASDR for the Chinese 0-4 age group was 10.9 per 1,000 population. It was more than twice that rate for the Malays (24.2). The differential was less for the Indian (14.0).

The ethnic differentials in ASDR between Malays and Chinese were less marked for subsequent age groups as well as in later

TABLE 5.1
Age-specific Death Rates, 1957
(Per 1,000 Population)

Age Group (Years)	Total			Chinese			Malays			Indians			Others		
	Persons	Males	Females	Persons	Males	Females	Persons	Males	Females	Persons	Males	Females	Persons	Males	Females
Total	7.4	8.2	6.5	7.1	8.1	6.0	10.0	10.2	9.8	6.4	6.5	6.0	7.5	8.3	6.6
0-4	13.4	14.2	12.4	10.9	11.6	10.3	24.2	26.1	22.2	14.0	15.6	12.2	12.7	14.0	11.3
5-9	1.4	1.5	1.3	1.3	1.3	1.3	2.3	3.0	1.6	1.0	1.1	1.0	0.7	0.9	0.5
10-14	0.9	1.0	0.8	0.9	1.0	0.7	1.3	1.4	1.1	0.5	0.5	0.6	0.9	0.9	0.9
15-19	1.0	1.2	0.8	0.8	1.1	0.5	1.8	1.5	2.1	0.9	0.8	1.2	1.3	1.8	0.8
20-24	1.4	1.5	1.2	1.2	1.5	1.0	1.7	1.4	2.0	1.0	0.9	1.1	5.0	7.1	2.9
25-29	1.6	1.5	1.8	1.6	1.7	1.4	2.0	0.9	3.3	1.5	1.2	2.6	1.2	1.7	0.7
30-34	2.5	2.7	2.3	2.2	2.7	1.8	3.0	2.4	3.7	2.9	2.7	4.2	2.9	3.2	2.5
35-39	3.7	3.8	3.4	3.2	3.7	2.7	4.7	3.6	6.2	4.6	4.3	6.3	4.1	3.8	4.6
40-44	5.7	6.0	5.4	5.5	6.0	5.0	6.7	6.7	6.7	6.1	5.4	10.8	4.8	5.8	3.3
45-49	9.4	11.0	7.3	8.9	11.5	6.0	12.9	10.3	16.1	9.6	8.7	16.3	10.0	13.0	6.3
50-54	14.4	17.7	10.1	13.5	17.3	9.1	20.4	21.2	19.5	17.1	17.0	18.0	13.3	18.9	5.0
55-59	22.4	27.7	15.9	21.0	28.1	13.3	35.6	31.1	42.3	24.6	25.0	22.5	18.0	16.0	20.0
60-64	35.8	49.9	22.0	35.3	51.8	20.6	40.0	43.6	36.0	41.8	44.4	30.0	26.7	30.0	23.3
65-69	50.0	70.4	33.8	49.0	72.5	31.9	61.7	68.3	55.0	56.0	52.5	70.0	40.0	55.0	25.0
70 & over	92.8	116.4	79.5	94.3	124.9	79.2	86.9	104.3	73.3	14.0	62.5	120.0	90.0	85.0	93.3

SOURCE: Singapore Department of Statistics.

TABLE 5.2
Age-specific Death Rates, 1970
(Per 1,000 Population)

Age Group (Years)	Total Persons	Total Males	Total Females	Chinese Persons	Chinese Males	Chinese Females	Malays Persons	Malays Males	Malays Females	Indians Persons	Indians Males	Indians Females	Others Persons	Others Males	Others Females
Total	5.2	6.0	4.3	5.2	6.1	4.4	4.6	4.9	4.3	5.2	6.8	2.9	6.3	7.4	5.1
0-4	5.2	5.6	4.7	4.7	5.1	4.2	6.9	7.4	6.3	5.8	6.1	5.3	5.5	4.5	6.0
5-9	0.5	0.5	0.4	0.4	0.4	0.4	0.6	0.7	0.6	0.7	0.8	0.5	0.2	0.5	-
10-14	0.4	0.5	0.3	0.3	0.4	0.2	0.4	0.5	0.3	0.5	0.6	0.4	0.8	1.1	0.6
15-19	0.8	1.2	0.4	0.8	1.2	0.4	0.8	1.1	0.6	0.8	0.9	0.6	1.6	2.0	1.3
20-24	1.0	1.3	0.6	0.9	1.3	0.5	1.0	0.7	1.2	1.0	1.5	0.4	2.5	5.3	-
25-29	1.2	1.3	1.1	1.2	1.3	1.0	1.2	1.3	1.1	1.5	1.1	1.9	1.0	2.0	-
30-34	1.3	1.4	1.3	1.2	1.3	1.2	1.7	1.8	1.7	1.8	2.3	1.2	2.1	2.9	1.2
35-39	2.2	2.7	1.6	2.1	2.7	1.4	2.5	2.5	2.4	2.6	3.1	1.6	2.3	3.5	0.7
40-44	3.4	4.1	2.5	3.1	3.8	2.4	3.4	3.3	3.5	4.5	5.4	1.5	5.7	6.9	4.2
45-49	5.9	7.2	4.4	5.5	7.3	3.8	6.7	6.1	7.5	7.1	7.6	5.0	6.3	7.9	4.0
50-54	9.7	12.4	6.6	9.1	12.1	6.3	10.5	11.6	8.9	14.2	15.0	10.0	4.7	6.0	2.9
55-59	15.8	20.3	10.9	14.8	20.0	9.9	22.1	24.4	19.3	16.7	17.3	14.4	22.7	30.0	14.0
60-64	25.7	33.9	17.2	24.2	33.3	15.6	32.7	35.2	30.0	35.0	37.1	26.0	31.3	40.0	22.5
65-69	39.5	51.2	28.2	38.7	52.6	26.3	44.6	43.3	46.4	50.0	50.9	46.7	33.3	30.0	36.7
70 & over	85.7	103.4	74.2	82.7	102.6	70.8	113.5	110.0	116.9	92.0	90.0	96.7	110.0	155.0	87.5

SOURCE: Singapore Department of Statistics.

TABLE 5.3

Age-specific Death Rates, 1980

(Per 1,000 Population)

Age Group (Years)	Total			Chinese			Malays			Indians			Others		
	Persons	Males	Females	Persons	Males	Females	Persons	Males	Females	Persons	Males	Females	Persons	Males	Females
Total	5.2	5.8	4.5	5.3	5.7	4.8	4.3	4.8	3.7	6.5	8.8	3.5	4.6	5.4	3.7
0-4	3.1	3.1	3.0	2.8	2.9	2.8	3.9	4.5	3.2	4.5	3.8	5.2	2.0	1.3	2.7
5-9	0.2	0.2	0.3	0.2	0.1	0.3	0.3	0.4	0.2	0.2	0.2	0.3	0.4	0.8	-
10-14	0.3	0.3	0.3	0.3	0.3	0.3	0.4	0.4	0.4	0.7	1.0	0.4	-	-	-
15-19	0.6	0.8	0.4	0.6	0.8	0.4	0.8	0.9	0.6	0.4	0.6	0.2	1.4	2.4	0.5
20-24	1.0	1.4	0.6	1.0	1.3	0.7	0.8	1.0	0.5	1.4	2.0	0.6	1.6	3.7	-
25-29	0.9	1.3	0.6	0.9	1.2	0.6	1.1	1.7	0.6	0.8	0.8	0.7	1.6	2.6	0.7
30-34	1.1	1.4	0.8	1.0	1.2	0.9	1.6	2.1	1.0	1.7	2.7	0.7	0.9	1.5	0.3
35-39	1.5	1.9	1.1	1.4	1.8	1.1	1.9	2.3	1.5	2.3	3.1	1.4	1.5	2.3	0.5
40-44	2.5	3.2	1.9	2.4	3.1	1.8	2.6	2.8	2.3	3.7	4.9	2.5	2.1	3.6	-
45-49	4.9	6.3	3.4	4.4	5.8	3.0	5.0	5.7	4.4	9.5	11.3	6.5	3.3	3.8	2.7
50-54	7.9	10.5	5.1	6.8	9.2	4.5	9.7	11.4	7.7	13.6	15.9	7.5	10.0	13.8	4.4
55-59	13.6	16.4	10.7	12.7	16.3	9.4	15.1	14.3	16.1	18.4	19.0	16.3	16.3	18.0	13.3
60-64	22.2	28.8	15.6	20.8	28.5	14.3	23.2	23.2	23.3	35.0	37.9	25.0	22.0	25.0	17.5
65-69	34.8	44.9	25.4	32.7	43.5	23.6	47.9	53.5	41.1	46.2	47.9	41.4	40.0	50.0	30.0
70 & over	76.8	86.8	69.4	75.2	86.2	67.8	84.0	83.8	84.1	98.2	102.5	86.7	87.8	77.5	96.0

SOURCE: Singapore Department of Statistics.

years. In fact the tables for 1970 and 1980 show a very steep decline especially in Malay ASDRs. For example Malay ASDR for the age group 0-4 declined by 71 per cent between 1957 and 1970 and again by 43 per cent between 1970 and 1980. The decline was less marked for the other two ethnic groups. Between 1957 and 1970, the ASDR for age group 0-4 declined by 56 per cent and 58 per cent for the Chinese and Indians respectively. For the period 1970 and 1980, the decline was 40 per cent and 22 per cent for the Chinese and Indians respectively. This means that for the age group 0-4, the Malays experienced the most rapid improvement in mortality in the last 23 years. The same pattern persisted also for the other age groups which suggested that the Malay ethnic group as a whole was catching up with the other two groups. By 1980, the mortality picture for the Malays was even better than that for the Indians. The narrowing of the ethnic differentials in mortality among the three ethnic groups is a welcome sign which suggests that there has been concurrently a closing of the gap between the different ethnic groups in socio-economic characteristics as well.

Ethnic Differentials in Life Expectancy

The same trend holds true for expectation of life between the three ethnic groups. In the 1950s, Indian males had the highest average length of life (62.2) and Malay males the lowest (57.4) of all the ethnic groups. Chinese females had the highest life expectancy in 1957 (66.6) followed by Indian females (61.5). By 1970, the life expectancy for the Malay population had caught up with that of the Indians, although it still lagged behind that of the Chinese. Between 1957 and 1970, Malay life expectancy improved 12.5 per cent for males and 12.1 per cent for females compared to 2.7 per cent for Indian males, 6.5 per cent for Indian females, and 7.7 per cent for Chinese males and 6.3 per cent for Chinese females. Between 1970 and 1980, percentage change in life expectancy among the three ethnic groups again showed that Malay life expectancy improved more rapidly than for either the Indians or the Chinese. By 1980, on an average Chinese life expectancy exceeded that of Malay males by less than one year and that of Indian males by 4.2 years. The gap between female average length of life among the three ethnic groups was however wider (between 4 to 5 years). (Refer to Table 2.)

Causes of Death

As the pattern of mortality changes, the structure of death causes also undergoes transformation. In a sense the changes in the

226

cause structure also reflect changing living conditions at the macro and micro level.

One difficulty in the analysis of death causes is the multifarious causes of death as well as the various revisions in the causes of death classification system employed such that comparison over time is not very easy. The most detailed causes of death classification is the International three-digit code classification which lists 1,000 diseases and causes. In the cause of death literature, however, the most commonly used causes of death classification is the abbreviated list of 50 causes. One caution in analysing cause of death data is that one must also be aware of the fact that certain changes in the number of deaths attributed to specific causes may be the result of progress in diagnostic techniques and not necessarily indicative of any shift underlying causes of death structure.

It is clear from the cause of death data that diagnostic techniques in Singapore have improved significantly over the years. In 1948 as much as one quarter of all deaths were classified under the catch-all category of "symptoms of ill-defined conditions". But the proportion of deaths through ill-defined causes declined to about 15 per cent in the mid-1960s, and to less than 5 per cent in the more recent years.

That Singapore's cause of death structure has shifted significantly is also clear. As mortality declines through successful disease control and environmental and health improvements, infections and parasitic diseases cease to be the dreaded killers as in the past. Instead cancer, disease of the circulatory system and respiratory diseases like pneumonia (often "adult" causes of death) have become the major killers. This shift in the cause structure is apparent even if we only examine the cause of death data for the last decade. Table 6 shows only the broad groups of death causes since 1970. Some selected causes are graphically represented in Figure 3. Some causes like deaths through accidents, poisonings and violence have remained rather stable whereas quite obviously the modern killers are cancer and heart and hypertensive diseases. This pattern in the cause structure of deaths, is very similar to that of the more developed countries. Given this pattern, it would seem that further reduction of mortality in Singapore may in fact prove difficult, unless medical sciences can seek cures for such diseases.

Socio-economic Change in Singapore

The mortality decline in Singapore since the end of World War II

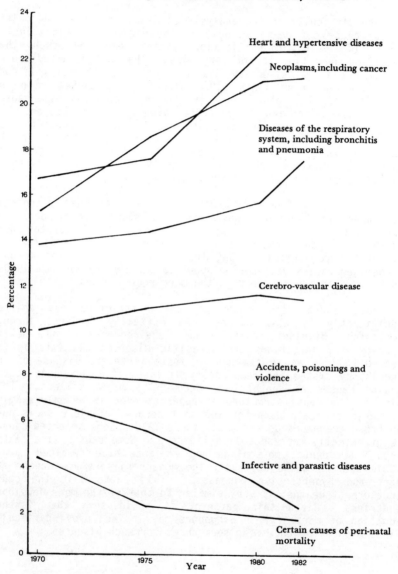

FIGURE 3

Change in Selected Causes of Death, 1970–82

Heart and hypertensive diseases

Neoplasms, including cancer

Diseases of the respiratory system, including bronchitis and pneumonia

Cerebro-vascular disease

Accidents, poisonings and violence

Infective and parasitic diseases

Certain causes of peri-natal mortality

Percentage

Year

SOURCE: Singapore Department of Statistics.

228

TABLE 6

Deaths by Broad Groups of Causes, 1970–82

Causes of Death	1970 Number	1970 %	1975 Number	1975 %	1980 Number	1980 %	1982 Number	1982 %
All Causes	10,717	100.0	11,447	100.0	12,505	100.0	12,896	100.0
Infective and Parasitic Diseases	727	6.8	630	5.5	425	3.3	293	2.2
of which: Tuberculosis	458	4.3	420	3.7	240	1.9	207	1.6
Neoplasms	1,633	15.2	2,123	18.5	2,623	21.0	2,729	21.2
of which: Cancer	1,596	14.9	2,083	18.2	2,561	20.5	2,668	20.7
Endocrine, Nutritional and Metabolic Diseases	250	2.3	375	3.3	359	2.9	397	3.1
of which: Diabetes	134	1.2	259	2.3	319	2.6	361	2.8
Diseases of the Blood and Blood-forming Organs	51	0.5	52	0.4	31	0.2	33	0.3
Diseases of the Nervous System and Sense Organs	173	1.6	133	1.2	131	1.0	121	0.9
Diseases of the Circulatory System	2,899	27.1	3,369	29.4	4,305	34.4	4,430	34.4
of which: Heart and Hypertensive Disease	1,780	16.6	2,000	17.5	2,777	22.2	2,866	22.4
Cerebro-vascular Disease	1,038	9.7	1,244	10.9	1,447	11.6	1,469	11.4
Diseases of the Respiratory System	1,473	13.7	1,632	14.3	1,965	15.7	2,257	17.5
of which: Pneumonia	843	7.9	948	8.3	1,129	9.0	1,375	10.7
Bronchitis	241	2.2	211	1.8	75	0.6	68	0.5

TABLE 6 (continued)

Deaths by Broad Groups of Causes, 1970-82

Causes of Death	1970 Number	1970 %	1975 Number	1975 %	1980 Number	1980 %	1982 Number	1982 %
Diseases of the Digestive System	454	4.2	423	3.7	368	2.9	400	3.1
Diseases of the Genito-Urinary System	239	2.2	311	2.7	366	2.9	319	2.5
Congenital Anomalies	150	1.4	146	1.3	185	1.5	182	1.4
of which: Congenital Anomalies of Heart	76	0.7	76	0.7	111	0.9	101	0.8
Certain Causes of Peri-natal Mortality	463	4.3	254	2.2	227	1.8	215	1.7
Accidents, Poisonings and Violence	836	7.8	887	7.7	899	7.2	966	7.5
of which: Motor Vehicle Accidents	268	2.5	255	2.2	250	2.0	326	2.5
Other Accidents	300	2.8	217	1.9	122	1.0	198	1.5
Suicides	185	1.7	252	2.2	271	2.2	239	1.9
Other Diseases and Causes	1,369	12.8	1,112	9.7	621	5.0	454	3.5
of which: Senility	1,002	9.3	860	7.5	403	3.2	219	1.7

NOTE: Deaths for 1969-78 are classified according to the Eighth (1965) Revision of the International Classification of Diseases while deaths from 1979 are classified according to the Ninth (1975) Revision.

should also be assessed in view of the changes which have occurred in the society at large. From a British colonial outpost, Singapore has been transformed into an independent city-state since 1965. And from an economy highly dependent on trade, it has diversified to include manufacturing and small-scale industries in the late 1960s and early 1970s. In the last decade, it has upgraded its industrial capacity so rapidly and so successfully that together with South Korea, Taiwan and Hong Kong, Singapore is now dubbed an "NIC" (newly industrializing country) in this part of the world. Currently with a per capita GNP second only to Japan in the region, Singapore's economic and social life has been transformed quite dramatically over the last two or three decades.

While Singapore's development goal has been explicitly that of economic growth, it has been commonly acknowledged that progress along the environmental and social front has also not been totally neglected. A few examples of the socio-economic progress of particular interest to the present study has been selected to illustrate this.

Looking at the income side, the level of wages for workers has increased quite substantially, even taking into consideration the effects of inflation. Real income has increased, especially in the last ten years. Average weekly earnings, for example, has increased from S$75.6 in 1972 to S$212.3 in 1982, an increase of some 280 per cent. At the same time, the number of families which require public assistance in the form of welfare doles dropped from 7,881 to 3,297 over the same period, indicating that poverty in Singapore while not totally eradicated is not as pressing a problem as that compared to many Third World countries. Increase in disposable income for the average family has meant that people by and large are able to enjoy a better standard of living particularly better food and better housing both of which are basic conditions for mortality reduction.

Perhaps, more than income rise, the improvements in health and medical services have been significant for mortality decline in Singapore. Elsewhere, it has been found that diffusion of new medical technology and modern medicines has played a crucial role in lowering mortality. In Singapore the early impetus to establish a modern medical service came largely from private initiative indicating that very early on, the people were already aware of the need to provide medical services as a means of controlling illnesses. Some wealthy community leaders at the turn of the century got together to support hospital building. By 1910, two small hospitals were built largely from donated funds. After World War I, the hospital building programme was expanded with increased participation of the public sector.

231

Public health and maternal and child health received attention as early as the 1920s with the opening of the first infant welfare clinics in 1923. At the same time training programmes were started to train public health personnel to deal with the control of infectious diseases and the inspection of food premises, markets and public places. However, significant improvement of public health standards came about only after the 1950s. Travelling dispensaries were set up to give medical attention to people living in areas far from the city centre and the hospitals. In addition, government out-patient clinics were built all over the island to meet the demand for medical services. The out-patient clinics, travelling dispensaries together with the maternal and child health (MCH) clinics formed the network which provided primary health care of a general kind, as well as to meet the specific needs of mothers and children. Subsequently, a school health service was also established. Together with the MCH, it implemented immunization programmes for pre-school and school children.

Table 7.1 summarizes the progress in the provision of health facilities and health personnel since 1957. It can be seen that the number of hospitals grew from 8 in 1957 to 26 (13 private and 13 government) in 1982 which provide both general and specialist treatment. In terms of the supply of hospital beds in relation to population size, there is actually a decline. This is partly because of the change in the disease structure which afflicts the sick over time. Some of the hospitals which had provided specialist treatment for certain infectious diseases, skin and chronic ailments experienced a drastic reduction of patient in-take as these diseases were brought under control. The lowering of demand for such services meant that these hospitals had no need to expand their services and some of these "specialized" hospitals had in fact been recently converted to become "general" hospitals.

The same picture seems to have emerged if we look at the number of out-patient and MCH clinics. The number of such clinics have also declined. This is partly because the MCH services are now being provided by some 30 or so family planning clinics run by the Singapore Family Planning and Population Board. Hence government-run MCH clinics had become redundant and many were closed. Another factor which led to the decline of the number of clinics since 1970 is, ironically, due to the growing affluence of the population. Many people now prefer to seek medical services from private doctors because of their desire to cut down waiting time and to receive more personalized services. Also, in line with the government's philosophy to discourage the continued provision of subsidized services when such can be borne by the members of public themselves, the number of clinics have in fact been reduced, with the existing ones catering only largely to the lower income group.

TABLE 7.1

Medical Facilities

Year	Population[1]	Hospitals	Per 10,000 Population	Hospital Beds	Per 10,000 Population	Outpatient & MCH Clinics	Per 10,000 Population
1957[*]	1445.9	12	.083	6451	44.6	62	.429
1960	1646.4	14	.085	7187	43.6	73	.444[2]
1965[*]	1886.9	16	.085	7676	40.7	90	.477
1970[*]	2074.5	16	.077	7760	37.4	78	.376
1975[*]	2262.6	22	.097	9105	40.2	65	.287
1980[*]	2413.9	26	.108	9579	39.7	56	.232
1982	2471.8	26	.105	9822	39.7	55	.223

[*] Census.
1 Mid-year Population.
2 From 1965, the Singapore Family Planning and Population Board has its own MCH and Family Planning Clinics.

SOURCE: Singapore Department of Statistics.

Medical personnel in relation to population, however, continued to grow (see Table 7.2). The number of doctors per 10,000 population has increased from 4.3 in 1957 to 9.0 in 1982. Similarly, there has been an increase in the number of nurses and midwives in relation to population over the years too. In fact, when it comes to the impact on infant and child deaths the increase in the supply of paramedical personnel and nursing personnel may probably be more pertinent at times. Much of the ante-natal and post-natal care are provided by nurses and midwives rather than by doctors per se. One disturbing trend in the more recent years has been the decrease in the supply of nurses and midwives. This is largely because fewer and fewer people are attracted to the nursing service. Unless, this trend is reversed through the upgrading of the nursing service and improvement of service conditions, Singapore may soon reach the stage where there will be a shortage of nurses and midwives, not unlike the situation in some developed countries in the West.

Together with the upgrading of medical facilities and medical care, over the years there has also been a very significant improvement of the environmental and housing conditions of the general public. Piped water, electricity and modern sanitation facilities are now amenities taken for granted by the population since these are available to practically every household on the island. To a large extent this development was brought about by the concerted and sustained effort on the part of the government. Like many post-war newly independent nation states, the provision of social amenities was regarded not only as an indication of progress, but also a means to gain continued political support and legitimacy. For Singapore, one such deliberate programme was the provision of affordable housing to the low income and lower-middle income segments of the population, the majority of whom were then still living under very overcrowded conditions.

Public housing began in Singapore in earnest in early 1960 with the establishment of the Housing Development Board (HDB). Prior to that, there existed in colonial times a modest public housing programme under the Singapore Improvement Trust (SIT) which was established as early as 1927. But between 1927 and 1959, SIT only built a total of 23,000 housing units as compared to HDB which had completed a total of 55,430 units at the end of its first five-year plan (1960-65). The pace of the construction had further accelerated since then and by the end of 1982, some 400,000 units were built. Together, these house about 75 per cent of Singapore's total population today (see Table 8). Also among the 75 per cent population living in HDB flats today, the great majority own their flats through the home ownership scheme.

Although housing within the HDB estates cannot be described as luxurious, it is generally acknowledged to range from adequate

TABLE 7.2
Medical Personnel

Year	Population[1] (1,000)	Doctors	Per 10,000 Population	Nurses	Per 10,000 Population	Midwives	Per 10,000 Population
1957*	1445.9	619	4.3	1252	8.7	239	1.6
1960	1646.4	640	3.9	1703	10.3	964	5.9
1965	1886.9	919	4.9	2807	14.9	1465	7.8
1970*	2074.5	1363	6.6	4304	20.7	2094	10.1
1975*	2262.6	1622	7.2	5767	25.5	2469	10.9
1980*	2413.9	1976	8.2	7545	31.3	2766	11.5
1982	2471.8	2225	9.0	7534	30.5	2673	10.8

* Census.
1 Mid-year population.

SOURCE: Singapore Department of Statistics.

TABLE 8
Units Constructed and Sold by the Housing and Development Board, 1960–82/83

Year	Number		Percentage of Total Population Living in Public Flats (End of Period)
	Shops and Flats Completed	Flats Sold Under "Home Ownership Scheme"[2]	
1960	1,682	–	9.0
1961	7,320	–	11.4
1962	12,230	–	15.3
1963	10,085	–	18.3
1964	13,028	1,451	22.0
1965	10,085	1,516	23.0
1966	12,659	1,320	24.0
1967	12,098	1,499	26.0
1968	14,135	8,504	29.6
1969	13,096	9,897	32.6
1970	16,115	6,967	35.9
1971	17,143	6,062	38.1
1972	23,024	9,142	43.7
1973/74[1]	30,219	21,189	45.1
1974/75	31,775	18,693	50.0
1975/76	32,954	22,147	54.8
1976/77	32,593	35,121	60.2
1977/78	34,047	42,248	64.7
1978/79	27,187	31,583	69.0
1979/80	26,917	42,900	71.9
1980/81	17,927	32,267	74.1
1981/82	17,120	25,489	74.1
1982/83	22,180	22,620	75.0

NOTES: Figures include units constructed and sold by Jurong Town Corporation and Housing and Urban Development Company.

[1] Refers to financial year 1 January 1973 to 31 March 1974. From 1974 figures refer to April to 31 March.

[2] Home Ownership Scheme started in 1964.

SOURCE: Housing and Development Board.

to comfortable (depending on the size of the apartment and the number of people in the household). The environment is also well maintained and the level of sanitation by and large high.[3] In the context of public health, environmental cleanliness is one major factor in deterring the spread of diseases in densely populated areas and hence does contribute to the general improvement of health of the population.

A general increased awareness of the importance of good health and a good understanding of the nature and causes of illnesses has also come about in Singapore through better communication via the mass media. This to a large extent is due to rising education. Experience in some development countries has shown that even an improvement in basic literacy can go a long way towards better child-care and greater understanding of preventive medicine. For Singapore, although education is not compulsory, it has become for all intent and purpose universal. This can be seen by looking at the literacy rates of the population. Except for the older age groups where illiteracy is still a problem, literacy rates for the under 40 are 90 per cent or more. Looking at the figures regarding educational achievement, the picture is also very encouraging. The proportion of students going beyond primary school education has increased quite markedly over the years. The ratio of students in secondary level and above to the total student enrolment has grown from 16.1 per cent to 40.9 per cent (see Table 9).

Given the rise in education and the small size of the island, the diffusion of information through the mass media has also become much more efficient. This has meant that the population has easy access to information, be it about health, medicine, disease or anything else. That the average Singaporean today is much better informed can also be judged from the greater utilization of mass media facilities (see Table 10). Newspaper circulation has grown from 78.6 per 1,000 population in 1960 to to 264.3 in 1980. This is equivalent to a distribution of one newspaper to less than every four people. Ownership of radios and television is also very high and so too is access to telephones. It is now rare not to find a household without a radio and/or television and a telephone as well. And one of the reasons why Singaporeans (to some observers) seem to respond so readily to any

---

3   The maintenance of cleanliness in Singapore has become a much publicized fact. This is largely achieved by strict law enforcement and the seemingly endless number of campaigns each year to ensure that Singapore maintain this "clean and green" image. Recent campaigns include a "No Spitting" Campaign and an "Anti Killer-Litter" Campaign (that is, the throwing of litter from high-rise flats).

type of government-initiated campaigns (health/environment-related or otherwise) is that it would be difficult for people not to be aware of them via the mass media in one form or another.

The above illustrates only very briefly that Singapore has made significant progress within the socio-economic dimension and health dimension. The question still remains whether and to what extent such progress has affected mortality decline. To examine this, we need to go beyond description and to apply multivariate analysis techniques to demonstrate how and in what ways socio-economic factors influence the mortality decline of Singapore.

Socio-economic Correlates of Mortality Decline in Singapore

As indicated earlier, it is not appropriate for Singapore to use areal-level analysis in its analytical design given the fact that Singapore is too small to have significant areal differentials. For the present study, Singapore has to be treated as a single urban unit. This makes it very difficult to examine socio-economic differentials of mortality using mainly census data or other types of published data because the data are not individual-level data. And although vital registration data pertain to the individual, they do not contain enough information of a socio-economic kind.

TABLE 9
Education

Year	Total Student Population	Secondary Level and above	Secondary Level and above Enrolment Ratio
1957	271367	43755	16.1
1960	352952	67415	19.1
1965	486811	129736	26.6
1970	527668	164150	31.1
1975	532956	204555	38.4
1980	501977	205369	40.9

TABLE 10

Media and Communication

Year	Population[1] (1,000)	Newspaper Circulation[2]	Per 1,000 Population	Radio/TV	Per 1,000 Population	Telephone[4]	Per 1,000 Population
1957*	1445.9	-	-	-	-	29948	20.7
1960	1646.4	129373	78.6	95201[3]	57.8	37113	22.5
1965	1886.9	214030	113.4	140589	74.5	58378	30.9
1970*	2074.5	394204	190.0	236856	114.2	106443	51.3
1975	2262.6	449001	198.4	344690	152.3	201574	89.1
1980*	2413.9	615612	255.0	459449	190.3	523446	216.8
1982	2471.8	653336	264.3	470757	190.5	630357	255.0

* Census.
1 Mid-year population.
2 Daily circulation of all language newspapers.
3 Radio licenses only.
4 Direct exchange only (does not include extensions).

SOURCE: Singapore Department of Statistics.

For Singapore, time serial data are available not only on the demographic dimension, but socio-economic data and environment and health-related data have also been collected and systematically tabulated by the Statistics Department of Singapore. Much of the data are based on the annual returns of the various departments and ministries in the public sector. The series is longest for the demographic data with birth, death rates available for the pre-World War II period. But some of the other types of socio-economic and environment-related data are available only since the 1950s and 1960s. Wherever available the data series runs from 1957-82, a serial run of more than 20 years.

Times series analysis using multiple regression techniques is now increasingly used by social scientists dealing with analysis of change. For time series data, the set of observations on the variables are collected over a period of time. In principle, the data can be handled by regression analysis as long as the data are measured in interval level. However, in practice, some statistical problems can arise, especially that related to the assumption of the independent error terms. The estimation of the error terms can be most problematic in time series analysis which may lead to very unreliable inferences, especially if one were interested in hypothesis testing. However, some of these problems can be overcome and will be discussed later.

The Variables

First we focus on the variables to be used in the analysis. And unless otherwise stated, the variable series run from 1957-80.

Dependent Variables

The dependent variables in the study are of course the mortality variables. These are:

(1) Crude Death Rate (CDR) -- Number of deaths per 1,000 mid-year population.

(2) Infant Mortality Rate (IMR) -- Number of infant deaths under 1 year of age per 1,000 live births.

(3) Neo-natal Mortality Rate (NMR) -- Number of infant deaths under 28 days per 1,000 live births.

(4) Maternal Mortality Rate (MMR) -- Number of deaths due to puerperal causes per 1,000 live births.

240

<u>Independent Variables</u>

The Independent Variables are divided into various categories to reflect the different dimensions:

Economic Dimension

(5)   Income (INC) -- Average monthly income in Singapore dollars, 1972-80.

(6)   Home Ownership[4] (HOMOWN) -- Percentage of HDB flat dwellers who purchase their own flats, 1964-80.

Education Dimension

(7)   Secondary Education (SECED) -- School leavers who completed secondary four education and above per 1,000 population.

(8)   Enrolment Ratio (ENRA) -- Ratio of students in secondary school and above per 1,000 students.

Health Dimension

(9)   Hospital Beds (HOSBED) -- Hospital beds per 10,000 population.

(10)   MCH facilities (MCHMW) -- MCH facilities per 10,000 married women.

(11)   Doctor-Patient Ratio (DOCPRA) -- Doctors per 10,000 population.

(12)   Midwives-Women Ratio (MWWRA) -- Midwives per 10,000 married women.

(13)   Nurses-Patient Ratio (NUPRA) -- Nurses per 10,000 population.

Occupation Dimension

(14)   Proportion Professional/Administrative/Managerial/Technical Workers in workforce (PPAMTW) -- number of

---

4   This variable is to some extent a measure of economic well-being. Since the bulk of the population now lives in HDB flats, the proportion of HDB flat dwellers who also own their flats is an index of wealth. The problem is that the series for this variable is not very long and dates only from 1964.

workers classified as professional, administrative, managerial and technical workers per 100 economically active persons aged 10 and over (1957, 1970, 1973-82).[5]

(15) Proportion Agricultural Workers and Fishermen (PAWF) -- number of workers classified as agricultural workers and fishermen per 100 economically active persons aged 10 and above (1957, 1970, 1973-82).

Media Exposure

(16) Ownership of Radios/TV (OWNRTV) -- Number of households with Radios/TVs per 100 households.

(17) Newspaper Readership (NR) -- Number of Newspaper circulation per 1,000 population.

Demographic Dimension

(18) Crude Birth Rate (CBR) -- Number of Births per 1,000 mid-year population.

(19) Total Fertility Rate (TFR) -- Average number of children born to a woman during her child-bearing years based on the prevailing age-specific fertility rate.

No sanitation variable is included because very few households in Singapore are not equipped with running water and modern flush toilet facilities. And also no rural-urban distinction is made. Change in population density too is not a relevant variable in the Singapore context.

Serial Correlation

Before we subject the data to multivariate regression analysis, first we must discuss some problems with time series analysis. One problem with time series analysis is that there may be present the problem of serial correlation or auto-correlation. In ordinary regression analysis, it is normally assumed the error

---

[5] Labour force statistics have been collected only on an annual basis since 1973 and based on a five per cent sample and projected for the population as a whole and for the census years 1957, 1970, 1980. Because the series is so short, 1981 and 1982 statistics have also been included to increase the sample points.

term has a mean of zero, constant variance over all observations and that the error terms corresponding to different points in time are not correlated. In time series data, the factors at work at some previous point in time may carry forward to affect the subsequent periods thereby creating the problem of serial correlation. If the problem is not serious and if the sample is big, it will not lead to undue error in estimation of the goodness of fit. But given the small size of our present sample and the consistent pattern of increases and decreases of most of the variables, auto-correlation could lead to bias in the estimation of the true variance.

Because of this problem, before the regression analysis is run, the data has to be transformed. The simplest way is to transform the original data into first differences before analysing the data. The first difference is obtained by taking the difference between $X_t - X_{t-1}$ for all independent variables and $Y_t - Y_{t-1}$ for all dependent variables where t refers to the time "t". The "first difference" method is used in this case because there is good reason to believe that the autocorrelation in the present data set is positive given the consistent pattern of increase or decrease over time. In taking the first difference of the variables, the confounding element of time is removed.

Bivariate Analysis

Table 11 shows the correlation matrix of the transformed variables as measured by the Pearson product moment correlation. It can be seen that after the confounding element of time is removed the r values between the mortality variables are not very high although still fairly highly correlated. Take for example CDR (crude death rate) and IMR (infant mortality rate), the r value is only 0.266. This is due to the fact that the annual change in CDR from 1957 onwards has already slowed to a very stable trend especially in the decade of the seventies when CDR has stablized at about 5.2 per 1,000 population. Were only the raw data correlated, auto-correlation will over-estimate the correlation coefficients and all the other estimates derived thereby.

Examining the bivariate relationship between variables, it seems that the shift in the occupational structure is highly correlated to mortality decline. The correlation coefficient between the decline in the proportion of workers in agriculture and fishing is positively correlated with the decline in mortality (r is 0.611 for PAWF with CDR, 0.517 with MMR, 0.695 with NMR). The relationship is less for income, home ownership or the media exposure variables.

TABLE 11
Correlation Matrix[1]

	CDR	IMR	NMR	MMR	INC	HOMOWN	SECED	ENRA	HOSBED
CDR	–								
IMR	.266	–							
NMR	.497	.523	–						
MMR	.207	.496	.503	–					
INC	–.305	–.263	–.253	–.206	–				
HOMOWN	–.271	–.303	–.291	–.191	.429	–			
SECED	–.213	–.296	–.204	–.102	.318	.547	–		
ENRA	–.295	–.314	–.299	–.147	.439	.418	.578	–	
HOSBED	–.300	–.369	–.371	–.214	.437	.289	.314	.322	–
MCHMW	–.201	–.412	–.394	–.200	.222	.171	.300	.193	.436
DOCPRA	–.314	–.302	–.311	–.215	.304	.157	.279	.346	.508
MWWRA	–.096	–.400	–.417	–.196	.172	.091	.301	.212	.401
NUPRA	–.321	–.375	–.402	–.205	.319	.278	.114	.198	.483
PPAMTW	–.517	–.411	–.314	–.293	.527	.302	.462	.307	.319
PAWF	.811	.517	.695	.411	–.418	–.208	–.417	–.274	–.305
OWNRTV	–.321	–.369	–.348	–.118	.393	.445	.338	.419	.377
NR	–.314	–.315	–.341	–.291	.383	.501	.401	.397	.381
CBR	.384	.405	.313	.217	–.387	–.306	–.342	–.395	–.298
TFR	.401	.511	.476	.200	–.499	–.412	.381	–.368	–.315

[1] First Differences.

TABLE 11 (continued)
Correlation Matrix[1]

MCHMW	DOCPRA	MWWRA	NUPRA	PPAMTW	PAWF	OWNRTV	NR	CBR	TFR
–									
.417	–								
.427	.579	–							
.314	.414	.502	–						
.200	.298	.409	.326	–					
-.113	-.276	-.106	-.093	.797	–				
.295	.314	.228	.133	.517	-.487	–			
.378	.421	.251	.295	.560	-.373	.589	–		
.305	-.310	-.588	-.204	-.400	.214	-.222	-.100	–	
-.313	-.522	-.306	-.313	-.313	.349	-.237	-.214	.599	–

245

Among the health variables, the variables MWWRA, MCHMW (midwives to married women ratio and MCH facilities per 1,000 married women) have higher correlation coefficient with IMR and NMR than CDR or MMR. Again MMR and CDR are already so low and stable that improvement or increase in MCH facilities seemed to have little impact on these two variables. The other health-related variables like DOCPRA (doctor-patient ratio), HOSBED (hospital beds per 10,000 population) and NUPRA (nurse-patient ratio) also show the same pattern.

Of the demographic variables TFR and CBR expectedly have a positive relationship with the mortality indicators.

As expected also there is a fairly high degree of correlation between variables on the same dimension. Hence the pattern of increase in home ownership correlates fairly strongly with that of rise in income. The same is true of the education variables.

Multiple Regression Analysis: Standard Regression Analysis

While the bivariate examination of each pair of variables indicates the strength and direction of the relationship, it does not indicate to what extent and in what ways other factors may affect the study variables.

To handle this, multivariate analysis has to be adopted to examine the unique contribution of each factor (or set of factors) after controlling for the effects of other factors. Also, as suggested earlier the objective of the study includes not only the establishing of how socio-economic factors influence mortality change but also as far as possible identify the way particular aspects of socio-economic change, environmental changes or progress in medical and health programmes as well as other demographic-related behavioural changes, impact upon mortality decline.

Different strategies can be adopted to study the effect of exogenous variables on the study on dependent variables. The commonest is to adopt the simultaneous regression (or standard) model in which all the independent variables are treated on an equal basis and are entered into the analysis simultaneously. In which case the resulting regression equation will provide the best linear estimate of Y values taking into account (or controlling for) all the X values.

Another approach is that the researcher is interested in the pattern of relationship, in some ordered fashion one may want to know how a particular variable (or a set of variables) can add to the explanation of variance of the dependent variable, net of all the other variables. In this case the strategy of the analysis is to determine the order of the variables to be studied and analyse the variables in a predetermined order. Because there is a hierarchical order to the analysis, the model is termed hierarchical model of analysis.

For the present study, standard regression analysis is first adopted to study how each set of variables which pertains to a particular dimension is related to the mortality variables.

Four independent mortality variables are included in the study -- CDR, IMR, NMR and MMR.

Tables 12.1-12.6, show the standard regression analysis of each category of variables representing each of the six dimensions. First, standard regression analysis indicate that the demographic factors and changes in the occupational structure in Singapore over the past two decades have the greatest influence on mortality decline, especially infant mortality and neo-natal mortality. Demographic variables (CBR and TFR) account for 26.7 per cent and 22.5 per cent of the variance in IMR and NMR respectively. Its impact on CDR and MMR is much less, accounting for only 12.3 per cent and 9.8 per cent of the variance respectively. Strangely too, the relationship of the fertility variables with maternal mortality is negative. The reason could be that the annual change in MMR was very small in the last ten years with differences sometimes positive, although the actual rate was very low. Such minor changes of signs could have affected the direction of the relationship.

The shift in occupational structure in Singapore corresponds with the change in the economic strategy of the government since independence with people shifting from more traditional activities like market gardening, fruit growing, pig and poultry rearing and fishing to industrial manufacturing and service oriented activities. This has also coincided with the physical transformation of housing patterns in Singapore. With increasing competition of land for housing, many people in the traditional activities have also been resettled in HDB flats thereby leading to significant shifts in the occupational structure. Hence the proportion of workers in agriculture and fishing has now decreased to only a very small group. At the same time, with rise in education, changing demands in the economy, the number of professionals, administrative, managerial and technical personnel is on the increase. Hence these two occupational variables account for a very important part of the variance in mortality. It accounts for 17.4 per cent to 19.2 per cent of the variance of CDR and IMR, 13.8 per cent of NMR but much less on MMR.

247

TABLE 12.1

**Summary Table of Multiple Regression of Demographic Variables (CBR, TFR)
on Crude Death Rate, Infant Mortality Rate, Neo-natal Mortality Rate
and Maternal Mortality Rate**

	Crude Death Rate	Infant Mortality Rate	Neo-natal Mortality Rate	Maternal Mortality Rate
	Beta	Beta	Beta	Beta
CBR	.2176**	.2260**	.2733**	.1438*
TFR	.4283**	.5141**	.5229**	.1945*
Multiple R	.3512	.5170	.4744	.3123
R Square	.1232	.2672	.2250	.0975

** p < .001
* p < .05

TABLE 12.2

**Summary Table of Multiple Regression of Occupation Variables (PPAMTW, PAWF)
on Crude Death Rate, Infant Mortality Rate, Neo-natal Mortality Rate
and Maternal Mortality Rate**

	Crude Death Rate	Infant Mortality Rate	Neo-natal Mortality Rate	Maternal Mortality Rate
	Beta	Beta	Beta	Beta
PPAMTW	-.2361**	-.3145**	.0985**	.0273*
PAWF	.0922**	.1211**	.0768**	.0083*
Multiple R	.4170	.4384	.3718	.1992
R Square	.1739	.1920	.1382	.0397

** p < .001
* p < .05

248

TABLE 12.3

Summary Table of Multiple Regression of Economic Variables (INC, HOMOWN)
on Crude Death Rate, Infant Mortality Rate, Neo-natal Mortality Rate
and Maternal Mortality Rate

	Crude Death Rate	Infant Mortality Rate	Neo-natal Mortality Rate	Maternal Mortality Rate
	Beta	Beta	Beta	Beta
INC	-0.1210*	-.1342*	-.1263*	-.0647
HOMOWN	-0.3893*	-.5113**	-.1044*	-.0217
Multiple R	.3254	.3989	.3410	.2975
R Square	.1059	.1591	.1163	.0885

** p < .01
* p < .05

TABLE 12.4

Summary Table of Multiple Regression of Education Variables (SECED, ENRA)
on Crude Death Rate, Infant Mortality Rate, Neo-natal Mortality Rate
and Maternal Mortality Rate

	Crude Death Rate	Infant Mortality Rate	Neo-natal Mortality Rate	Maternal Mortality Rate
	Beta	Beta	Beta	Beta
SECED	-.1443**	-.2141**	.3161**	.1272*
ENRA	-.0981*	-.0867*	.2118**	.1214*
Multiple R	.2461	.2935	.3010	.1973
R Square	.0606	.0861	.0906	.0389

** p < .01
* p < .05

TABLE 12.5
Summary Table of Multiple Regression of Health Variables (HOSBED, MCHMW, DOCPRA, MWWRA)
on Crude Death Rate, Infant Mortality Rate, Neo-natal Mortality Rate
and Maternal Mortality Rate

	Crude Death Rate	Infant Mortality Rate	Neo-natal Mortality Rate	Maternal Mortality Rate
	Beta	Beta	Beta	Beta
HOSBED	-.1623**	.1640**	-.1492**	-.0643
MCHMW	-.0414	.1522	-.0828	-.0922*
DOCPRA	-.2358**	.1471*	-.0313	-.1271**
MWWRA	-.0041	.3213**	-.1170**	-.1066*
Multiple R	.2503	.3441	.3697	.1905
R Square	.0626	.1184	.1367	.0363

** p < .01
* p < .05

TABLE 12.6
Summary Table of Multiple Regression of Media Exposure Variables (OWNRTV, NR)
on Crude Death Rate, Infant Mortality Rate, Neo-natal Mortality Rate
and Maternal Mortality Rate

	Crude Death Rate	Infant Mortality Rate	Neo-natal Mortality Rate	Maternal Mortality Rate
	Beta	Beta	Beta	Beta
OWNRTU	-.1713**	-.3443**	-.2511**	.2046**
NR	-.1136*	-.1078*	-.0988*	.0362
Multiple R	.4039	.4510	.4183	.2339
R Square	.1631	.2034	.1750	.0547

** p < .001
* p < .01

Media exposure is another very important dimension. Perhaps, increase flow of information over TV and radio and newspapers circulation has increased people's consciousness about health and preventive medicine. In the case of Singapore, given its small size, the strong influence and very paternalistic attitude of the authorities over all types of media network, it is not surprising that a substantial proportion of the programmes and news features are of a "educational" (including health-related) nature. Although it is not clear if people in actual fact watch or read such material conscientiously, it is surmised that frequent exposure could have some conscious or subconscious impact. Moreover, it is felt that health-related information probably receive more attention than other types of "educational" material because there is a self-interest element in knowing more about how the body functions and their relationship to diet, diseases, and medicine.

Compared to these three groups of factors, the economic and education factors seem to have lesser impact, although they are still fairly important for explaining the variance especially for infant mortality and neo-natal mortality. It is suggested that improvement in living standards and education level for the population as a whole had been more gradual and had been taking place over a fairly long period of time (even before the study period) and therefore its influence on mortality decline during the period under study is less conspicuous then some other variables. Income and home ownership is also important for crude death rate (10.6 per cent of the variance).

Health facilities and health personnel again seem to explain a fair proportion of the variance for IMR and NMR but much less so for CDR and MMR. Again health care could have been fairly good already by the late 1950s and therefore subsequent marginal improvement might not be very significant. Nonetheless, the health variables still account for more than 10 per cent of the variance in both IMR and NMR. For medical science to continue to have a major impact on mortality, given the current low mortality levels, there must be major breakthroughs in the tackling of old age diseases and other endogenous causes of death which have still defied present medical knowledge.

Hierarchical Analysis

The purpose of hierarchical regression analysis is to order the variables based on assumptions of structural or causal priority to examine the pattern of contribution to the variance. Because of the fairly high inter-correlation of some of the variables within

251

the same variable set, some variables have been dropped in the analysis. Among the two demographic variables, only TFR has been retained. Similarly among the health variables HOSBED, DOCPRA and MWWRA are used and only PAWF of the occupation variables are retained in the analysis.

The hierarchical regression analysis in Tables 13.1-13.4 show that all the variables account for 52-57 per cent of the variance in IMR and NMR. When all the variables are taken into account, 40 per cent of the variance CDR has been explained. However, the unexplained variance is still quite high for MMR. Total variance explained for MMR when all the variables are considered is less than 19 per cent. This shows that MMR is not very well explained by socio-economic and occupational and health factors. It could be that MMR being already so low, its change is not related to socio-economic, health and occupational conditions any more.

For CDR, R^2 change is highest for the occupation variable and media variables, suggesting that the net contribution of these two factors are considerable. The contribution is smaller for health, education or income.

The results of the regression analysis, however, have to be interpreted with care. Although the transformation of the data has taken care of some of the confounding effects of serial correlation, it has not taken into effect the impact of time lag. Theoretically the independent variables should be lagged to account for any kind of social phenomenon which takes time to have any effect. Also the process of socio-economic change, including the diffusion of health care and improvement of health facilities is already very much in progress before our study period. But our serial data documenting these changes were not available until the late 1950s and early 1960s. As a result we do not have a long enough observation period. Hence our interpretation has to be more cautious with the statistics serving as indices of direction and strength of relationship to mortality change rather than as absolute values.

Summary and Conclusion

Mortality levels in Singapore today are comparable to that of some of the more developed nations in the world. Like other developing countries, the pattern of mortality decline in Singapore is essentially a twentieth century phenomenon, with rates of decline especially rapid only during the last two or three decades. This is to some extent due to the global diffusion and advancement of medical knowledge and the increased consciousness of public health measures in the control of the spread of epidemics and infectious diseases.

Cause of death patterns in Singapore has also shifted. Along with rapid societal transformation, the pattern of diseases has also changed. No longer are epidemics like cholera, typhoid or other types of infectious diseases the major killers. Instead, what has been termed "adult diseases" like cancer and hypertensive diseases now take their toll. Such shift in disease pattern is probably the greatest challenge to present-day medical science which will now have to look for new cures to tackle these diseases and further extend life.

To some extent, the analysis of the time series data for Singapore confirms this. While improvement in health facilities and health personnel may still have some impact on reducing infant mortality and neo-natal mortality, there is already indication that their limits may be reached soon, unless other breakthroughs occur for further prolongation of life for the very old. In some countries this has already occurred where people are rapidly pushing beyond their eighties and nineties.

On the whole, for Singapore, the most significant factors which explain the decline in mortality in the past two decades have been closely intertwined with the change in the economic structure of Singapore, as well as to the increased accessibility and conscientious extension of better housing environment and living conditions to the masses. This has been achieved both through deliberate government planning and as part and parcel of the process of social progress and economic restructuring. As such mortality levels have not only declined very rapidly, there has also been a substantial narrowing of the mortality differentials among the various ethnic groups in the population.

One drawback in the present study, however, is that much of the inferences are drawn only from aggregate data. For the results to be much better substantiated, individual level data will have to be collected and analysed. In light of this, it is really a pity that more socio-economic and background information about the deceased cannot be obtained from the death registration data. If some effort could be made just to include a few more items on the background characteristics of the deceased, the death registration data would provide a wealth of information for mortality studies, especially given their high degree of completeness of coverage and general accuracy. This is one point perhaps the Registrar of Births and Deaths should consider.

TABLE 13.1

Summary Table of Hierarchical Regression Analysis of
Crude Death Rate by Order of Variables

	Regression					
Independent Variables	1	2	3	4	5	6
	Beta	Beta	Beta	Beta	Beta	Beta
1. DEMOGRAPHIC						
TFR	.1141**	.1478**	.1448**	.1007**	.0917*	.0919*
2. HEALTH						
HOSBED		-.0923*	-.0817*	-.0819*	-.1145*	-.1007*
DOCPRA		-.1114	-.1438*	-.2113*	-.1936*	-.1913*
MWWRA		-.0512	-.0527	-.0514	-.0516	-.0447
3. ECONOMIC						
INC			-.1756*	-.1778*	-.1212*	-.1143*
HOMOWN			-.3141**	-.1782**	-.1996**	-.1981**
4. EDUCATION						
SECED				-.0413	-.0484	-.0386
ENRA				-.0598	-.0311	-.0278
5. OCCUPATION						
PAWF					.2686**	.1986**
6. MEDIA						
OWNRTV						-.2140**
NR						-.1008*
R^2	.1011	.1432	.1970	.2385	.3171	.4033

* $p < .05$
** $p < .01$

TABLE 13.2

Summary Table of Hierarchical Regression Analysis of
Infant Mortality Rate by Order of Variables

Independent Variables	Regression					
	1	2	3	4	5	6
	Beta	Beta	Beta	Beta	Beta	Beta
1. DEMOGRAPHIC						
TFR	.2031**	.1782**	.1217**	.0949*	.1027*	.1332*
2. HEALTH						
HOSBED		-.2417**	-.2147**	-.1871**	-.1396**	-.1423**
DOCPRA		-.3410**	-.3148**	-.1933**	-.1174**	-.1278**
MWMRA		-.4483**	-.3497**	-.2414**	-.2512**	-.4210**
3. ECONOMIC						
INC			-.0947*	-.0833*	-.1001*	-.0891*
HOMOWN			-.0747*	-.0822	-.0486	-.0733
4. EDUCATION						
SECED				-.0778*	-.0371	-.0071
ENRA				-.0791*	-.0104	-.0055
5. OCCUPATION						
PAWF					.4314**	.1938**
6. MEDIA						
OWNRTV						-.2237**
NR						-.0913*
R^2	.2015	.3118	.3971	.4117	.5295	.5721

*   p < .05
** p < .01

TABLE 13.3

Summary Table of Hierarchical Regression Analysis of
Neo-natal Mortality Rate by Order of Variables

Independent Varibles	Regression					
	1	2	3	4	5	6
	Beta	Beta	Beta	Beta	Beta	Beta
1. DEMOGRAPHIC						
TFR	.3493**	.2941**	.2473**	.1896**	.2315**	.2043**
2. HEALTH						
HOSBED		-.1599*	-.1400*	-.1498*	-.1073*	-.0993*
DOCPRA		-.1521**	-.1375**	-.1334**	-.0941**	-.1319**
3. ECONOMIC						
INC			-.1973*	-.1736*	-.1497*	-.1212*
HOMOWN			-.0994*	-.0790*	-.0536*	-.0676*
4. EDUCATION						
SECED				-.0631	-.0328	-.0071
ENRA				-.0171	-.0098	-.0055
5. OCCUPATION						
PAWF					.1911**	.1072**
6. MEDIA						
OWNRTV						-.2014**
NR						-.1719**
R^2	.1537	.2341	.3170	.3926	.4722	.5261

* $p < .05$
** $p < .01$

TABLE 13.4

Summary Table of Hierarchical Regression Analysis of
Maternal Mortality Rate by Order of Variables

Independent Variables	Regression					
	1	2	3	4	5	6
	Beta	Beta	Beta	Beta	Beta	Beta
1. DEMOGRAPHIC						
TFR	-.1112*	-.0793*	.0745*	.0686*	.0877*	-.0663*
2. HEALTH						
HOSBED		-.1212*	-.0918*	-.0832*	.0876*	-.0675*
DOCPRA		-.1721*	-.0878*	-.0583	-.0548	-.0698
MWRA		-.1993**	-.1707**	-.1899**	-.1017*	-.0993*
3. ECONOMIC						
INC			-.1912*	-.1012*	-.0644*	-.0672
HOMOWN			-.0996*	-.1011*	-.1293*	-.0808*
4. EDUCATION						
SECED				-.0836	-.0471	-.0361
ENRA				-.0926	-.0223	-.0384
5. OCCUPATION						
PAWF					.3176**	.3062**
6. MEDIA						
OWNRTV						-.2017**
NR						-.1544*
R^2	.0505	.0713	.1128	.1334	.1627	.1821

* $p < .05$
** $p < .01$

References

Barclay, George W. _Techniques and Population Analysis_. New York: John Wiley & Sons, Inc., 1958.

Box, George E.P. and G.M. Jenkins. _Time Series Analysis_. San Francisco: Holden-Day, 1970.

Cohen, Jacob and Patricia Cohen. _Applied Multiple Regression/Correlation Analysis for the Behavioral Science_. New Jersey: LEA Publishers, 1975.

Goldscheider, Calvin. _Population Modernization and Social Structure_. Boston: Little Brown & Co., 1971.

Nie, Norman H. et al. _Statistical Package for the Social Sciences_, 2nd ed. McGraw-Hill Book Company, 1975.

Ostrom, Charles W. Jr. _Time Series Analysis: Regression Techniques_. Sage Quantitative Applications in the Social Sciences, No. 9. Beverly Hills: Sage Publications, 1978.

Pressat, Roland. _Demographic Analysis. Methods, Results, Applications_. Translated by Judah Matras. Chicago: Aldine-Atherton, 1969.

Saw Swee Hock. _Singapore Population in Transition_. Philadelphia: University of Pennsylavania Press, 1970.

Singapore. _Report on Registration of Births and Deaths_. Registrar-General of Births and Deaths. (Several Years).

_____. _Demographic Trends in Singapore_. Census Monograph No. 1. Singapore: Department of Statistics, 1981.

_____. _Report on the Census of Population, 1957_. Singapore: Singapore Government Press, 1964.

_____. State of Singapore. _1957 Census of Population Releases Nos. 1-17_. Singapore Printing Office, 1958.

_____. _Report on the Census of Population 1970_. Singapore: Department of Statistics, 1975.

_____. _Census of Population 1980, Singapore Administrative Report_. Singapore: Department of Statitics, 1983.

_____. _Census of Population 1980, Singapore Releases Nos. 1-9_. Singapore: Department of Statistics, 1981.

_____. _Economic and Social Statistics_. Singapore: Department of Statistics, 1983.

Ueda Kozo. Recent Trends of Mortality in Asian Countries. SEAMIC Publications
    No. 34. Tokyo, 1983.

United Nations. Foetal, Infant and Early Childhood Mortality, Vols. 1 and 2.
    Population Studies No. 13. New York: Department of Social Affairs,
    Population Division, 1954.

_____. World Population Trend and Prospects by Country, 1950-2000. New
    York, 1979.

Wrigley, E.A. An Introduction of English Historical Demographic from the
    Sixteenth to the Nineteenth Centuries. London: Weidenfeld and Nicolson,
    1966.

Suchart Prasithrathsint
Kanikar Sookasame and
Laddawan Rodmanee

Introduction

Despite the fact that mortality is one of the most important components of population change, it is the least known and researched demographic phenomenon by the Thai demographers. Mortality data help to identify a country's current demographic situation, indicate its immediate demographic future, and serve as an important indicator of social and economic progress. Mortality levels are also closely related to other variables of social concern, such as labour productivity and fertility. All these make the study of mortality deserving of greater attention.

One of the commonly used mortality measures is the crude death rate (CDR) in a particular year, that is, deaths in all ages combined divided by the total mid-year population. CDR is known to be a rough indicator of mortality levels because it disregards the age composition of a population. A more refined measure of mortality which takes age mortality differentials into consideration is life expectancy at a particular age. Infant mortality rate is another measure of mortality of great significance. In less developed countries, due to the deficiencies of registration data, mortality studies until recently have relied largely on the use of Regional Model Life Tables, developed by Coale and Demeny. These Regional Model Life Tables, have four different patterns of mortality, designated as North, East, South and West. Although the West Model life tables are most commonly used for Thailand, recent research by John Fulton indicates that the North Model Life Tables may be more appropriate (Knodel and Chamratrithirong 1978). The issue of appropriate model life tables for the country has not yet been settled.

Vital registration in Thailand began in 1917 in the Registration Section of the Department of Public Health. In 1936, the Section of Statistical Compilation and Analysis and the Division of Vital Statistics were established. The basis for the compilation of vital statistics was the information from the certificates of births and deaths which include still births, deaths at all ages, and deaths of children under one year of age in all provinces. According to the official procedures, at the end of each month, vital records are to be sent from the Provincial Health Officers to the Division of Vital Statistics where the official vital and health statistics are compiled. However, the registration of the vital statistics competes with other responsibilities of the medical and health officials and consequently it is assigned a low priority. The general public also do not recognize the significance of vital registration despite the fact that they are legally required to do so. Hence deaths continue to be greatly under-registered.

A Review of Mortality Studies

Crude Death Rate

Bourgeois-Pichat (1974) estimated crude death rates in Thailand from 1920-55, which showed CDR had steadily declined from 31.3 in 1920 to 18.0 in 1955. It was also observed that CDR increased during World War II (1942 to 1946). Thereafter, the country has experienced a decline in CDR. Before 1948 CDRs were about 30 per 1,000 (Table 1). Rungpitarangsi (1974) estimated mortality trends in Thailand from 1937 to 1970 by using Brass' new technique and found that the values of life expectancy in 1937, 1947, 1960 and 1970 were 39, 40, 51 and 56 for males and 42, 44, 55 and 56 for females, respectively. The values were too low compared to the findings of the 1974-76 Survey of Population Change (National Statistical Office 1978). The official crude death rates from the vital statistics during 1950-75 also showed CDR was on the decline. In 1950, CDR was 10. It dropped to 7.1 in 1965 and 5.6 in 1975. Table 1 shows estimated and registered CDRs from different sources, revealing that CDRs from the Vital Statistics Office are lower than the other sources. Nonetheless, the data show a clear trend of decline, faster in the earlier period and slower in the later period.

Infant Mortality

Infant mortality rate has often been regarded as a sensitive

261

TABLE 1

Registered and Estimated Crude Death Rates in Thailand 1945–86

Year	Registered Crude Death Rate	Estimated Crude Death Rate									
		1	2	3	4	5	6	7	8	9	10
1945	-	30.9	29.9	24.0							
1946	-	32.2	29.5	23.2							
1947	-	30.2	26.6	21.4							
1948	-	27.3	21.0	17.3							
1949	-	26.6	17.8	16.9							
1950	10.0	24.6	16.5	15.9							
1951	10.4	23.4	16.5	16.1							
1952	10.0	22.2	15.6	14.3							
1953	9.5	20.3	14.3	13.8							
1954	9.8	19.6	13.3	13.9							
1955	9.4	18.0	12.6	12.9							
1956	9.1			13.2							
1957	9.5			13.7							
1958	8.3			12.5							
1959	8.0			11.9							
1960	8.4			12.2	M14.3* F13.6**	15.2		12.0			12.0
1961	7.8			11.2							
1962	8.0			11.3							
1963	8.2			11.4							
1964	7.9			10.9							
1965	7.1			9.9			10.8				
1966	7.6			10.3			12.2				
1967	7.2			0.0			11.6				
1968	7.1			9.7			11.5				
1969	7.2						11.8				
1970	6.5			8.8	M9.0* F8.0**	10.3	10.6	10.0			9.5

TABLE 1 (continued)

Registered and Estimated Crude Death Rates in Thailand 1945-86

Year	Registered Crude Death Rate	Estimated Crude Death Rate									
		1	2	3	4	5	6	7	8	9	10
1971	6.4						10.5				
1972	6.5						11.2				
1973	6.0						10.6				
1974	6.1						10.6				
1975	5.6						8.9				
1980	-								8.0		
1983	-								7.0		
1986	-									4.3	

1   Bourgeois-Pichat (1974).

2   Estimated by United Nations (1982).

3   Population of Thailand Country Monograph No. 3, Table 50 (1976).

4   Rungpitarangsi (1974, p. 55), (estimates of death rates by death distribution techniques).

5   Leoprapai and Wanglee (1978).

6   Krongkaew (1979), (adjusted registered death rates for under-registration estimated from the Survey of Population Change 1964-65 and 1974-75).

7   U.S. Bureau of Census (1978, Table 3).

8   Population Reference Bureau. 1980 and 1983 World Population Data Sheets.

9   Working Group on Population Projection. Population Projection for Thailand: Whole Kingdom and Regions 1970-2005.

10 National Statistical Office, Survey of Population Change, 1964-65, 1974-76. (1969 and 1977).

*   M -- Male

** F -- Female

indicator of socio-economic differentials at both macro and micro levels. Previous studies have demonstrated that the proportions of children dying during the first year of life are closely associated to national levels of socio-economic development (Shin 1975). The variables that produce lower rates of infant mortality in developing countries have not yet been clearly established. They include more effective systems of water supply, electricity, better medical care and better education. A higher standard of living and better household environment are clearly more conducive to better health and a greater probability of survival. Demographic variables are also found to have significant influence in mortality.

In addition infant mortality can also be explained by environmental influences as well as by variables related to parental resources and choices (Simmons et al. 1982). Infant mortality declines that have occurred in Thailand during the past few decades have been attributed to both general socio-economic development and special government programmes in training midwives to provide better maternal and child health service in remote areas (Economic and Social Commission for Asia and the Pacific 1976).

Studies of infant mortality rates for Thailand are mainly based on survey data due to incomplete registration of vital statistics. The 1974-75 Survey of Population Change shows about 56 infant deaths per 1,000 live births. The Life Tables for Thailand for 1969-71, calculated for the United Nations Model Life Tables, based on death registration statistics corrected for under-registration, gives an infant mortality rate for both sexes of about 70 per 1,000 live births. Based on these figures, it was estimated that the infant death rate had declined by approximately 1.6 per cent per year between 1947 and 1969-71 (United Nations 1982).

Data from the first Survey of Population Change (SPC) indicate that Thailand had an infant mortality rate of 84.3 in 1964-65. By 1974-76, the second SPC reported that the infant mortality had fallen to 51.9 (National Research Council 1980). Indirect estimates of infant mortality, based on the children ever born data from both the 1970 census and the second SPC, confirmed that the infant mortality rate declined from more than 100 during the mid-1950s to less than 60 during the early 1970s (Knodel and Chamratrithirong 1978). They indicate that the North and Northeast regions had higher infant mortality than the Central and South regions in Thailand, while urban areas had substantially lower infant mortality than rural areas but the declining trend in infant mortality over this period of time was evident in all four regions and in both urban and rural areas.

Hill et al. (1979) used the Feeny method to estimate infant-child mortality from the 1974-76 Survey of Population Change. The estimates of the derived infant mortality provide information on time trends beginning approximately 15 years prior to the survey. The results showed a regular decline in infant mortality in Thailand and in each geographical region during a period beginning approximately 15 years prior to the survey through about two years prior to the survey. The most recent estimate for the whole kingdom which refers to approximately two years prior to the 1974-76 survey indicates a level of about 57 infant deaths per 1,000 births, close to the direct 1974-76 SPC estimate of about 52.

Data on infant mortality have been available only since 1960. Table 2 shows infant mortality from various sources by years and by region during 1964-80, which includes infant mortality rate from the 1974-76 SPC, the 1970 census and estimates based on Trussell's technique using the North and West Model Life Table systems.

Table 2 demonstrates a more recent steady decline in the infant mortality rate over the last ten years, from about .0701 in 1970 to .0477 or .0433 in 1980. This trend is expected to continue. Regional differentials in the levels and trends of infant mortality show that mortality situations seem to be considerably worse in the North and Northeast than in the South and the Central. However, in all four regions, infant mortality declines are quite evident. The pace of the declines does not differ very much among the four regions. The North has the highest infant mortality rate and Bangkok the lowest.

In summary, studies using various techniques have confirmed that crude death rate and infant mortality rate of Thailand have been declining over the last two decades. There are significant differences among the regions: Bangkok, the Central and the South have lower mortality levels than the North and the Northeast.

Expectation of Life

Like in most countries, the expectation of life among Thai females is higher than males. Life expectancy in Thailand has steadily increased during the period of 1947 to 1980-85 when the life expectancy at birth rose from 48.50 to 61.05 for males and from 51.38 to 64.86 for female (Figure 1). Data from other sources generally support this rise in life expectancy. Between 1947 and 1964, Thai males gained about 7 years of life expectation and their female counterparts about 10 years and from 1964-65 to 1980-85, the former gained an expectation of life of about 6 years while the latter gained only 3 years.

TABLE 2

Estimated Infant Mortality Rates from 1964 and 1974 SPC,
1970 and 1980 Censuses by Regions

	1964 SPC+	1970 Census*	1974 SPC*	West Model** 1980 Census	North Model** 1980 Census
Thailand	.0843	.0701	.0611	.0477	.0433
Central	.0940	.0554	.0354	.0390	.0356
North	.0965	.0814	.0774	.0578	.0524
Northeast	.0834	.0789	.0414	.0528	.0479
South	.0485	.0547	.0600	.0394	.0360
Bangkok	-	-	.0170	.0265	.0253

+ Committee on Population and Demography 1980, "Fertility and Mortality Changes in Thailand 1950-1975", Report No. 3.

* Knodel and Chamratrithirong, 1978.

** Population Survey Division, National Statistical Office, Infant Mortality Rates: Estimated from 1980 Population and Housing Census of Thailand. September 1983.

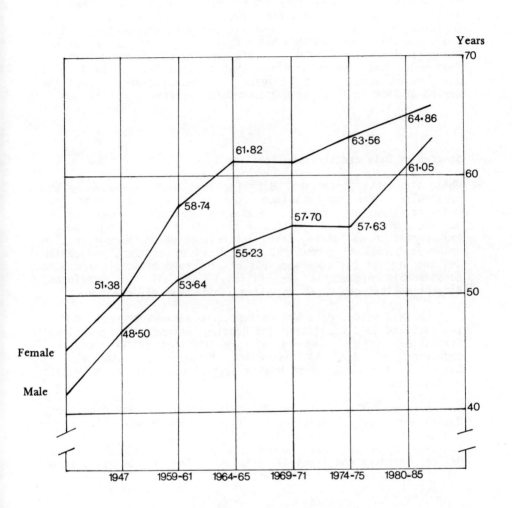

FIGURE 1
Life Expectancy for Thailand

SOURCE: Institute of Population and Social Research, "Population and
Development Data Sheet". Bangkok: Mahidol University, 1982.

4

In Table 3, data from the 1974-76 SPC show that the average life expectancy in Bangkok is almost 1.4 years longer than that for the whole country. The Central region, excluding Bangkok, has the highest life expectancy of 67 years and the North has the lowest, 57 years. Data from the 1970 census show that the Southern region has the highest average life expectancy of 62.7 years while the North has the lowest of 55.9 years. Rungpitarangsi's estimates of life expectancy at birth for the Thai males and females indicate that between 1937 to 1960 males and females gained about 12 years in life expectancy. From the period of 1960 to 1970, both gained 5 more years.

Sources of Data and their Reliability

While the vital statistical data for the country as a whole and particularly for the provinces are defective and suffer from under-registration, they are relatively accurate in major cities because of the availability of health services, better transportation and strong level enforcement of death registration prior to burial or cremation. The level of citizens' education and the statistical consciousness of concerned officials are also considerably higher in the cities. Of all the provinces, Bangkok's vital registration system is the most efficient.

In this study, data are derived from various sources such as the 1970 and 1980 Population and Housing Censuses of the National Statistical Office, Reports of the Division of Registration, Department of Local Administration, Ministry of Interior, and Reports of the Division of Health Statistics, Ministry of Public Health.

Data on health variables for this study are taken from Rural Health and Health Statistics Divisions. Infant mortality rates are estimated from the 1980 Population and Housing Census of Thailand by Population Survey Division, National Statistical Office, based on the Trussell technique. They are believed to be robust and sufficiently reliable.

Statistical Methods of Analysis

Insofar as the statistical methods of analysis are concerned, this study uses hierarchical regression analysis to determine the strength of each set of social, economic and demographic variables on mortality as measured by CDR and estimated IMR, and to analyse

TABLE 3

Expectation of Life for Thailand by Region

	1970 Census[a]	1974 SPC[a]	1937[b]	1947[b]	1960[b]	1980[b]
Thailand	58.7	61.0	Male 38.94 Female 41.73	Male 40.19 Female 43.45	Male 50.93 Female 55.08	Male 55.53 Female 59.80
Central	62.6	67.3				
North	55.9	56.9				
Northeast	56.5	59.1				
South	62.7	61.3				
Bangkok	-	74.8				

a John Knodel and Apichat Chamratrithirong, "Infant and Child Mortality in Thailand: Levels, Trends and Differentials as derived through Indirect Estimation Techniques". Paper of the East-West Population Institute, No. 57 (1978).

b Benjawan Rungpitarangsi, Mortality Trends in Thailand: Estimates for the Period 1937-1970. Bangkok: Institute of Population Studies, 1974.

the effects of change in the independent variables on the dependent variable(s). Path analysis is also used to analyse the postulated causal inter-relationships of all the independent variables and their relationships with the dependent variable(s). Table 4 presents the description of the variables used in the analyses. The means of these variables are shown in Table 5.

The analysis is divided into three parts. The first part uses hierarchical regression analysis of cross-sectoral data with time lag on some of the independent variables. The second part employs hierarchical regression analysis of change in the values of the independent and dependent variables. The final one uses path analysis of the causal ordering of all the variables involved. Two path models are analysed. One has, in addition to other variables, two health variables and the other has one combined health variable.

The Findings

Cross-lag Hierarchical Regression Analysis

This section presents the findings based on hierarchical regression analysis of mortality, using cross sectional provincial data with time-lag on some of the independent variables. There are two models of analysis; the first one treats the ratios of population to physicians and nurses as two separate health service variables. The second one uses the ratio of the population to the number of health facilities as the only health variable. Each of the two models is used to analyse the variance of three dependent variables, namely, crude death rate and the two estimates of infant mortality rates based on the North and West Regional Model Life Tables.

With the available data, the independent and dependent variables are causally ordered as shown by the temporal differences among them. The kind of analysis is known as cross-sectional or cross-lag analysis.

Table 6 shows the zero-order coefficients of all the variables involved indicating that none of the independent variables is strongly correlated with one another but are moderately inter-related. The simple correlation coefficient between GNP80 and POPUR77 is .480, GNP80 and ELEC78 is .449, ACNONAG80 and NURSE79 is -.423, and between EDU80 and NURSE79 is -.451. The rest are lowly inter-correlated.

TABLE 4
Description of Variables Used in the Analysis

Variables	Description
HEALTH	
HEALTH79	– Population per Hospital and Health Station in 1979
NURSE79	– Population per Nurse in 1979
PHY79	– Population per Doctor in 1979
HS79	– Population per Health Station in 1979
HP79	– Population per Hospital in 1979
RURAL-URBAN ENVIRONMENT	
POPUR77	– Percentage of Provincial Population Living in Urban Areas in 1977
POPDEN77	– Population Density in 1977
EDUCATION	
EDU80	– Percentage of Population Completed Secondary Education in 1980
STUD80	– Number of Students in Secondary School Divided by Population aged 12–19 years in 1980 (that is, Ratio of Students in Secondary School)
ECONOMIC	
ACNONAG80	– Percentage of Economically Active Population in Non-Agricultural Occupation (excluding mining) in 1980
GNP80	– Per Capita Income in 1980
HOUSEHOLD ENVIRONMENT	
PIPEW80	– Percentage of Dwelling with Piped Water in 1980
ELEC80	– Percentage of Dwelling with Electricity in 1980
ELEC78	– Provincial Income from Public Utility in 1978
DEMOGRAPHIC VARIABLE	
CBR80	– Crude Birth Rate in 1980
DEPENDENT VARIABLES	
CDR80	– Crude Death Rate in 1980
NORTH	– Infant Mortality Rate: North Model
WEST	– Infant Mortality Rate: West Model

TABLE 5
Means of the Variables Used in the Study by Region (1970-80)

Variable	1970	1977	1978	1979	1980
HEALTH					
1. Population per Nurse	–	7346.42	2235.87	2211.26	6428.22
Central	–	4540.93	1617.70	1800.94	3954.38
North	–	8718.53	2509.89	2434.98	7528.06
Northeast	–	10273.78	3408.95	3164.62	7909.57
South	–	8729.64	2385.95	2294.88	7632.43
Bangkok	–	590.41	477.31	528.66	518.50
2. Population per Doctor	–	23978.85	24306.32	23556.31	22225.16
Central	–	15004.83	15850.42	16559.17	15272.06
North	–	27086.37	25400.62	23053.31	22079.62
Northeast	–	31277.75	31981.82	26828.82	29137.64
South	–	29860.79	31028.83	31021.94	27550.03
Bangkok	–	1567.34	1251.74	1228.68	1256.74
3. Population per Health Station	–	11766.05	10331.87	10364.89	9930.98
Central	–	9549.77	9164.75	9218.74	8435.54
North	–	11576.34	10948.40	10850.85	11034.42
Northeast	–	12012.81	10351.10	10321.58	10354.90
South	–	11251.69	11034.53	11177.65	10538.83
Bangkok	–	79046.23	–	–	–
4. Population per Hospital	–	78127.44	87164.47	78458.95	78249.22
Central	–	52662.52	58811.30	55651.19	54350.30
North	–	90014.82	97745.31	85182.58	94131.32
Northeast	–	102711.06	113414.48	103819.79	101341.13
South	–	90399.50	103372.42	91682.53	86534.47
Bangkok	–	45169.28	41275.50	42012.73	44430.19
RURAL-URBAN					
1. Population Density	–	154.64	157.66	161.23	164.92
Central	–	181.96	184.06	186.87	189.99
North	–	57.96	59.23	61.12	63.97
Northeast	–	78.97	80.92	82.42	84.13
South	–	95.23	97.37	99.34	101.53
Bangkok	–	3023.30	3104.70	3197.50	3285.40

TABLE 5 (continued)
Means of the Variables Used in the Study by Region (1970-80)

Variable	1970	1977	1978	1979	1980
2. Percentage of Population in Municipal Areas	-	9.54	9.82	.9.87	9.80
Central	-	10.02	10.24	10.27	9.94
North	-	6.71	6.68	6.82	6.80
Northeast	-	4.56	4.51	4.53	4.66
South	-	8.53	9.19	9.20	9.32
Bangkok	-	100.00	100.00	100.00	100.00
EDUCATION					
1. Percentage of Population Completed Secondary Education	1.35	-	-	-	2.90
Central	1.60	-	-	-	3.44
North	1.06	-	-	-	2.73
Northeast	0.75	-	-	-	1.62
South	1.33	-	-	-	2.58
Bangkok	4.00	-	-	-	8.10
2. Ratio of Student in Secondary School					0.1629
Central	-	-	-	-	0.1463
North	-	-	-	-	0.2833
Northeast	-	-	-	-	0.0703
South	-	-	-	-	0.1140
Bangkok	-	-	-	-	0.2430
SOCIO-ECONOMIC					
1. Per Capita Income (Baht)	-	10537.65	11289.68	12464.56	14730.13
Central	-	12874.21	15943.67	16664.29	19412.08
North	-	6244.12	7557.35	8527.94	9753.12
Northeast	-	3778.33	4302.67	5248.83	6270.33
South	-	12296.29	10260.96	11883.83	14492.96
Bangkok	-	25799.00	29655.00	35825.00	43423.00

TABLE 5 (continued)
Means of the Variables Used in the Study by Region (1970-80)

Variable	1970	1977	1978	1979	1980
2. Percentage of Active Population in Non-Agricultural Occupation	20.63	-	-	-	26.79
Central	29.47	-	-	-	38.70
North	13.67	-	-	-	18.88
Northeast	7.32	-	-	-	10.22
South	16.64	-	-	-	21.80
Bangkok	91.30	-	-	-	94.80
HOUSEHOLD ENVIRONMENT					
1. Percentage of Household with Piped water	16.15	-	-	-	14.02
Central	21.25	-	-	-	18.46
North	12.71	-	-	-	10.39
Northeast	8.82	-	-	-	11.32
South	11.97	-	-	-	10.15
Bangkok	88.70	-	-	-	78.00
2. Percentage of Household with Electricity	26.06	-	-	-	40.39
Central	32.67	-	-	-	55.49
North	20.11	-	-	-	35.72
Northeast	11.42	-	-	-	19.75
South	24.24	-	-	-	31.44
Bangkok	92.20	-	-	-	95.90
DEMOGRAPHIC					
1. Crude Birth Rate	-	23.63	22.82	22.94	23.51
Central	-	21.61	22.02	21.34	22.03
North	-	19.43	19.53	19.63	20.94
Northeast	-	27.83	26.53	27.18	27.73
South	-	27.33	24.79	25.63	25.77
Bangkok	-	29.40	28.20	27.80	23.20

TABLE 5 (continued)
Means of the Variables Used in the Study by Region (1970–80)

Variable	1970	1977	1978	1979	1980
DEPENDENT VARIABLES					
1. Crude Death Rate	–	5.55	5.67	5.53	5.71
Central	–	5.98	5.98	5.67	6.21
North	–	5.21	5.73	5.64	5.96
Northeast	–	5.60	5.50	4.83	5.17
South	–	5.35	5.39	5.51	5.20
Bangkok	–	5.50	5.20	5.20	4.90
2. Infant Mortality Rate (West Model)	–	–	–	–	.0477
Central	–	–	–	–	.0390
North	–	–	–	–	.0578
Northeast	–	–	–	–	.0528
South	–	–	–	–	.0394
Bangkok	–	–	–	–	.0265
3. Infant Mortality Rate (North Model)	–	–	–	–	.0433
Central	–	–	–	–	.0356
North	–	–	–	–	.0524
Northeast	–	–	–	–	.0479
South	–	–	–	–	.0360
Bangkok	–	–	–	–	.0253

TABLE 6

Simple Correlation Coefficient, Means and Standard Deviations of the Variables Used in the Analysis

Variable	NURSE 79	PHYE99 79	HEALTH 79	POPDEN 77	POPUR 77	ELEC 78	GNP 80	ACNONAG 80	EDU 80	CBR 80	CDR 80	NORTH	WEST
PHYE79	.590												
HEALTH79	.511	.232											
POPDEN77	-.145	-.197	-.100										
POPUR77	-.436	-.302	-.267	.303									
ELEC78	-.025	-.162	-.034	.445	.138								
GNP80	-.275	-.090	-.321	.256	.480	.449							
ACNONAG80	-.423	-.280	-.394	.126	.501	.018	.512						
EDU80	-.451	-.358	-.306	-.044	.406	.111	.311	.638					
CBR80	.014	.173	-.118	-.373	.168	-.219	.051	.040	-.101				
CDR80	-.361	-.189	-.387	.060	.217	.144	.191	.320	.233	.267			
NORTH	.168	.085	.162	-.381	-.482	-.134	-.501	-.485	-.280	-.088	.028		
WEST	.171	.087	.164	-.389	-.485	-.137	-.505	-.484	-.280	-.084	.027		
x̄	2234.96	23870.79	8897.06	114.24	8.26	52.52	14326.00	25.84	2.82	23.51	5.72	.042	.047
S.D.	1103.15	16276.20	4191.38	106.03	5.52	143.94	12910.49	16.10	1.31	5.46	1.22	.011	.012

Crude Death Rate

According to the first model of analysis, Table 7 shows that among the independent variables included in the analysis, the availability of nurses has a negative effect on crude death rate but not the availability of physicians. The findings are consistent with the fact that the ratio of physicians to population is too low to have any significant impact. Data also show that CDR is significantly and positively related to crude birth rate of the same year indicating the adverse effect of high fertility on mortality. It is generally known that deaths during the first year of life constitute a sizeable proportion of all deaths. A negative regression coefficient between the percentage of the economically active population engaged in non-agriculture and the crude death rate implies the contribution of non-agricultural development to a decline in mortality.

In addition, the second model of analysis confirms a general expectation that the availability of health facilities significantly contributes to mortality reduction.

Infant Mortality Rate

Analysis of infant mortality rate using Trussell's method and based on the North Regional Model Life Tables (shown in Table 8) shows only slightly different results from the analysis of crude death rate. The health variables in both models significantly affect the variance of infant mortality rate. Other social and economic development variables such as percentage of urban population, population density, the engagement of labour force in non-agricultural activities, and GNP per capita are all negatively related to infant mortality. The coefficients of the health variables are smaller than those of the social and economic ones. This indicates the stronger impact social and economic development variables have on the decline in infant mortality and therefore implies the greater sensitivity of infant mortality to social and economic development compared to crude death rate.

Analysis of the estimated infant mortality rate based on the pattern of mortality of the West Regional Model Life Tables (shown in Table 9) shows similar results to that of the previous analysis and the findings can be similarly interpreted.

277

TABLE 7
Hierarchical Regression Analysis of Crude Death Rate, 1980

Independent Variable	Step 1	2	3	4	5	6
			Beta Coefficients			
Model I						
PHY79	.05068	.03203	.06423	.09732	.09248	-.02665
NURSE79	-.37086*	-.37009*	-.39009*	-.35410*	-.37390*	-.36891*
POPUR77		.10510	.12380	-.01581	.04056	-.33610
POPDEN77		-.22505	-.40277	-.41887	-.47702	-.15271
ELEC78			-.23215	-.30898	-.34726*	-.35905*
GNP80				-.11067	-.13617	-.12036
ACNONAG80				-.29323	-.37227*	-.33774*
EDU80					-.13237	-.03049
CBR80						.32769*
R^2	.117	.136	.163	.201	.208	.287
Model II						
HEALTH79	-.38726**	-.35493*	-.35685*	-.32232*	-.32735*	-.28142*
POPUR77	77	.12606	.12505	.07084	.09224	-.03563
POPDEN77		-.01365	-.08084	-.08812	-.10442	.07087
ELEC78			-.15106	-.22540	-.24209	-.24630
GNP80				-.15119	-.16276	-.17513
ACNONAG80				-.23743	-.27612	-.24793
EDU80					-.06144	.06647
CBR						.32578*
R^2	.150	.164	.182	.216	.218	.289

* $p < .05$
** $p < .01$

TABLE 8
Hierarchical Regression Analysis of Infant Mortality Rate (North Model)

Independent Variable	Step					
	1	2	3	4	5	6
	Beta Coefficients					
Model I						
PHY79	-9.098E-03	-.03861	-.04719	.03262	.03323	.04185
NURSE79	.20188	.06560	.07106	-.10121	-.09871	-.10002
POPUR77		-.57221*	-.57781	-.08341	-.09054	-.04119
POPDEN77		.22891	.27743	-.10294	-.09559	-.13808
ELEC78			-.06338	-.19124	-.18640	-.1848
GNP80				-.43032*	-.42709*	-.26825
ACNONAG80				-.26278*	-.27278	-.26825
EDU80					.01674	3.387E-03
CBR80						-.04204
R^2	.039	.160	.162	.362	.363	.364
Model II						
HEALTH79	.16241	.03062	.03004	-.10769	-.11146	-.13923
POPDEN77		-.25311**	-.27855*	-.30535**	-.31756*	-.42355**
POPUR77		-.39613**	-.39643**	-.16184	-.15256	-.07524
ELEC78			-.04597	-.17670	-.18920	-.18666
GNP80				-.33786*	-.34653*	-.33905*
ACNONAG80				-.23774*	-.20875	-.19170
EDU80					-.04603	-.12337
CBR						-.19700
R^2	.026	.294	.296	.438	.439	.465

*   Significant at 0.05 level.
**   Significant at 0.01 level or less.

279

TABLE 9
Hierarchical Regression Analysis of Infant Mortality Rate (West Model)

Independent Variable	Step					
	1	2	3	4	5	6
	Beta Coefficients					
Model I						
PHY79	.14776	-.03328	-.04719	.03386	.03444	.0423
NURSE79	.14776	.06851	.07405	-.09843	-.09603	-.09722
POPUR77		-.56607*	-.57124*	-.07760	-.08444	-.03950
POPDEN77		.21621	.26589	-.11760	-.11056	-.14925
ELEC78			-.06424	-.19365	-.18001	-.18760
GNP80				-.43541*	-.43232*	-.43420*
ACNONAG80				-.25763*	-.26721	-.26309
EDU80					.01604	3.887E-03
CBR80						-.03909
R^2	.040	.164	.166	.367	.267	.268
Model II						
HEALTH79	.16447	-.03101	.03132	-.10601	-.11004	-.13742
POPUR77		-.39610**	-.39651**	-.16217	-.15237	-.07615
POPDEN77		-.26595*	-.28661*	-.31359*	-.32648*	-.43097**
ELEC79			.04646	.17885	.19205	.18954
ACPOPAG80				-.23382	-.20322	-.18641
GNP80				-.34138*	-.35054*	-.34317*
EDU80					-.04859	-.12484
CBR						-.19419
R^2	.027	.301	.303	.444	.446	.471

* Significant at 0.05 level.
** Significant at 0.01 level or less.

Hierarchical Regression Analysis of Change

This section deals with the analysis of change in the independent variables, measured by the difference in their values at two periods of time, and the impact of such changes on mortality. Table 10 presents the matrix of simple correlation coefficients of all the variables and their means and standard deviations. The negative changes in the ratios of population to nurses and health services indicate a positive increase in the number of nurses and health services, and a positive change in the ratio of population to physicians indicates a worsening situation.

The definitions of and the measurement of change in the variables are as follows:

NURSERC — Change in population per nurse between 1978-77

HSRC — Change in population per health station between 1978-77

PHYRC — Change in population per physician between 1978-77

HPRC — Change in population per hospital between 1978-77

POPDENC — Change in population density between 1978-77

POPURC — Change in percentage of population in urban area between 1978-77

GNPC — Change in per capita (GNP) between 1978-77

CBRC — Change in crude birth rate between 1978-77

PIPEW80 — Percentage of dwelling with piped water in 1980

ELEC80 — Percentage of dwelling with electricity in 1980

EDU80 — Percentage of population completed secondary education in 1980

CDR — Crude death rate in 1980

NORTH — North Model infant mortality

WEST — West Model infant mortality

The results of the hierarchical regression analysis of crude death rates and infant mortality rates are shown in Table 11. The

281

TABLE 10

Simple Correlation Coefficients, Means and Standard Deviations of the Variables Used in the Analysis

Variable	NURSERC	HSRC	PHYRC	HPRC	POPDENC	POPURC	PIPEW80	ELEC80	GNPC	EDU80	CBR80	CDR80	NORTH	WEST
NURSERC	1.000													
HSRC	.111	1.000												
PHYRC	.314	.105	1.000											
HPRC	-.089	-.055	-.043	1.000										
POPDENC	.059	.117	-.002	.002	1.000									
POPURC	.132	.022	-.009	.014	.010	1.000								
PIPEW80	.216	.076	.106	-.175	.080	.025	1.000							
ELEC80	.321	.137	.019	-.136	.009	.024	.660	1.000						
GNPC	.0001	-.006	.048	-.061	.072	.011	.064	.142	1.000					
EDU80	.395	.153	.070	.003	-.042	.112	.468	.611	-.069	1.000				
CBRC	.182	.041	.066	-.018	-.030	.047	.111	.094	.110	.072	1.000			
CDRC	.319	.085	.229	-.172	-.089	-.019	.230	.284	.123	.256	.072	1.000		
NORTH	-.284	-.141	-.166	-.124	-.070	-.153	-.388	-.287	.040	-.298	.030	.069	1.000	
WEST	-.289	-.141	-.168	-.122	-.072	-.155	-.320	-.284	.041	-.289	.031	.068	1.000	1.000
x̄	-5250.761	-418.628	341.695	9446.901	1.935	.294	12.870	39.109	752.628	2.819	-.799	5.665	.042	.046
S.D.	4281.865	1311.511	13306.956	22686.262	4.436	1.803	7.251	17.123	11616.106	1.325	5.868	1.130	.011	.012

TABLE 11
Hierarchical Regression Analysis of Crude Death Rate and Infant Mortality Rate (North and West Models)

	CDR						North Model					
	Step						Step					
	1	2	3	4	5	6	1	2	3	4	5	6
	Beta Coefficients						Beta Coefficients					
POPDENC	0.096	0.089	0.082	0.082	0.084	0.020	-0.065	-0.046	-0.052	-0.005	-0.062	-0.036
POPURC	-0.016	-0.023	-0.024	-0.023	-0.024	-0.032	-0.150	-0.142	-0.143	-0.084	-0.087	-0.083
PIPEW80		0.078	0.084	0.085	0.082	0.062		-0.240	-0.234	-0.151	-0.157	-0.201
ELEC80		0.242	0.227	0.230	0.232	0.240		-0.120	-0.136	0.149	0.153	0.113
GNPC			0.083	0.083	0.078	0.062			0.081	0.005	-0.005	0.001
EDU80				-0.004	-0.008	-0.104				-0.431*	-0.439*	-0.309
CBRC					0.042	0.005					0.083	0.112
HPRC						-0.103						-0.196
NURSERC						0.200						-0.147
HSRC						0.014						-0.070
PHYRC						0.150						-0.098
R^2	0.010	0.100	0.107	0.107	0.108	0.197	0.027	0.137	0.143	0.206	0.213	0.279

* Significant at 0.05 level.

TABLE 11 (continued)

Hierarchical Regression Analysis of Crude Death Rate and Infant Mortality Rate (North and West Models)

West Model

	Step					
	1	2	3	4	5	6
	Beta Coefficients					
POPDENC	-0.066	-0.047	-0.053	-0.067	-0.063	-0.038
POPURC	-0.152	-0.145	-0.145	-0.086	-0.085	-0.084
PIPEW80		-0.236	-0.231	-0.146	-0.153	-0.196
ELEC80		-0.119	-0.134	0.156	0.160	0.120
GNPC			0.081	0.004	-0.006	-0.0004
EDU80				-0.439*	-0.446*	0.316
CBRC					0.084	0.113
HPRC						-0.193
NURSERC						-0.152
HSRC						-0.069
PHYRC						-0.098
R^2	0.028	0.135	0.141	0.207	0.213	0.280

* Significant at 0.05 level.

changes in the majority of the independent variables are not sufficient to have any significant impact on the general mortality rate. However, insofar as infant mortality is concerned, educational change or positive improvement in the percentage of population who have completed secondary education is the only change that has a significant negative correlation coefficient with the dependent variables, implying that the improvement in the Thai educational system has a significant contribution to the reduction in infant mortality rates. The independent variables explain about 19.7 per cent of the variance of crude death rate and 27.9 per cent of the estimated infant death rates.

Path Analysis

Two path models are used in analysing the inter-relationships of the dependent and the independent variables. The differences between the two models is that the first model uses the ratios of population to medical personnel (ratios of population to nurses and of population to physicians) while the second model uses the ratio of population to health facilities (the number of hospitals and health stations).

The variables used in the path analysis are:

POPDEN77   - Population density in 1977

POPUR77   - Percentage of population in urban area in 1977

NURSE79   - Population per nurse in 1979

PHY79   - Population per doctor in 1979

HEALTH79   - Ratio of population 1979 to the number of hospitals + health stations in 1979

ELEC78   - Income of the province from electricity and piped water in 1978

ACNONAG80   - Percentage of active population in non-agricultural occupation in 1980

GNP80   - Per capita (GNP) in 1980

CDR80   - Crude death rate in 1980

NORTH   - North Model infant mortality

WEST   - West Model infant mortality

EDU80   - Percent of population completed secondary
                education in 1980

Figures 2.1-2.3 show conceptualized and statistical inter-
relationships of the independent variables and the three dependent
variables (CBR, North Model infant mortality and West Model infant
mortality). The significant path coefficients have asterisks.
The results of the analysis are as follows:

The degree of urbanization is moderately correlated with
population density or vice versa.   Population density is
positively related to the degree of electrification of the
provinces, reflecting a general practice of the electricity
authority in giving priority for the provision of electric power
to a more densely populated area. However, it is important to
note the significant positive path coefficient between electricity
and GNP, which implies a positive contribution of electricity to
subsequent provincial economic growth.

The degree of urbanization is also found to be negatively
related to the ratios of population to medical personnel (nurses
and physicians). That is to say, the more densely populated the
area, the lower the ratios of population to medical personnel as
most medical personnel prefer staying in the urban to the rural
areas.   The degree of urbanization is also related to the
percentage of economically active population engaged in non-
agricultural occupation which is in turn positively related to GNP
and the percentage of population who have completed secondary
education.   The percentage of economically active population
engaged in non-agricultural activities, the percentage of
population who have completed secondary level education and GNP
are all negatively related to infant mortality, implying a strong
inverse relationship between infant mortality and the level of
social and economic development.

It is noteworthy that the ratios of population to medical
personnel are not significantly related to mortality, especially
infant mortality, as expected, even though the sign of relationships between them is in the expected direction. This is probably
due to the fact that the ratios are too low to have any
significant impact on mortality. What is equally interesting is
the finding that while the ratio of population to nurse is
significantly related to death rates, the ratio of population to
physicians is not.   The finding substantiates the argument that
there must be a critical level of medical service before it could
have any significant impact on the reduction of mortality.

It is significant to point out at this juncture that the

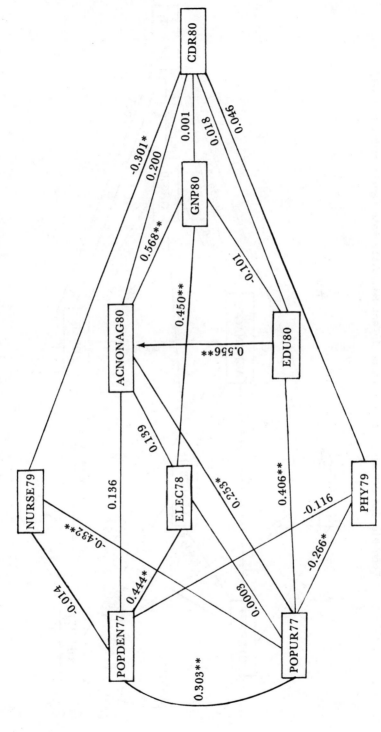

FIGURE 2.1

Path Diagram Illustrating Results of Empirical Assessment of Effects of Social, Economic and Demographic Factors on Crude Death Rate: Model I

* Significant at 0.05 level.
** Significant at 0.01 level.

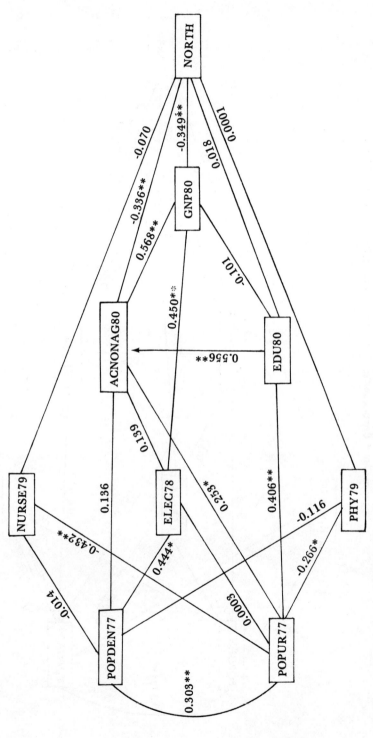

FIGURE 2.2

Path Diagram Illustrating Results of Empirical Assessment of Effects of Social, Economic and Demographic Factors on Infant Mortality Rate (North Model): Model I

* Significant at 0.05 level.
** Significant at 0.01 level.

FIGURE 2.3

Path Diagram Illustrating Results of Empirical Assessment of Effects of Social,
Economic and Demographic Factors on Infant Mortality Rate (West Model): Model I

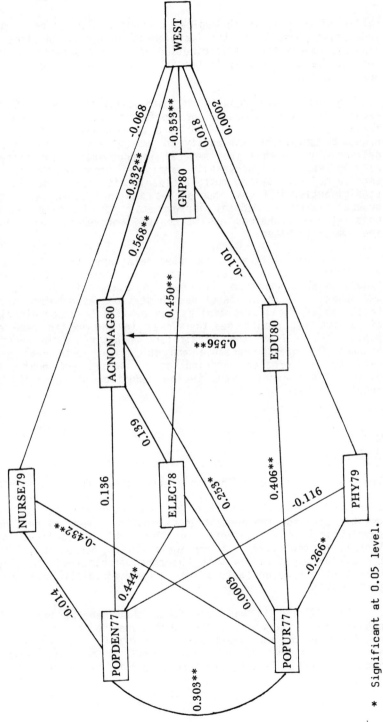

* Significant at 0.05 level.
** Significant at 0.01 level.

ratios of population to medical personnel also conceal the most problematic barrier to the improvement in health services in the country, namely the maldistribution of medical personnel. Doctors concentrate more heavily in the urban areas than nurses and public health nurses.

In brief, the results of path analysis show that in the recent past the reduction of mortality in general and infant mortality in particular is due more to improvements in social and economic conditions and partly to improvements in health service delivery system than just medical improvements. The differences between medical improvements and the improvements in health service delivery system must be clearly distinguished. They imply significantly different approaches to the improvements of the general public. Medical improvements may be only clinics or hospital based whereas public health improvements are education and community based.

A clearer picture of the inter-relationships of the dependent and independent variables is shown in Figures 3.1-3.3 where a single health variable is used in place of the two health variables. The inclusion of health stations as a component of the total health facilities implies the availability and distribution of nurses and public health nurses in the health care of the population. Thus the significant negative path coefficient between the health variable and the crude death rate probably reflects the greater contribution of nurses and public health nurses than the physicians in the reduction of mortality at the provincial level.

Conclusion

The results of data analysis presented above lead to the conclusion that social and economic development in recent years have made a significant contribution to mortality decline far greater than the improvement in the ratio of medical personnel to population. Improvements in the Thai educational system, increasing employment in non-agricultural occupations, and the process of urbanization with the concomitant provision of public utilities are major factors that effect mortality decline in the past decade.

In addition it has been found that general improvement in public health services contributes more to a recent mortality decline than the improvements in the medical field per se. It has also been argued that the improvement in medical service will become a crucial factor affecting a decline in mortality only when

FIGURE 3.1

Path Diagram Illustrating Results of Empirical Assessment of the Effects of Social,
Economic and Demographic Factors on Crude Death Rate: Model II

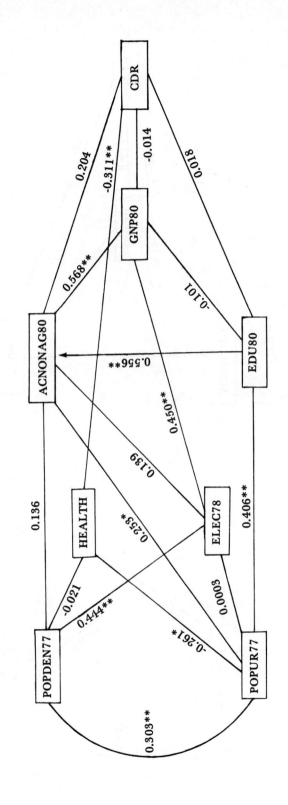

* Significant at 0.05 level.
** Significant at 0.01 level.

FIGURE 3.2

Path Diagram Illustrating Results of Empirical Assessment of the Effects of Social,
Economic and Demographic Factors on Infant Mortality Rate (North Model):   Model II

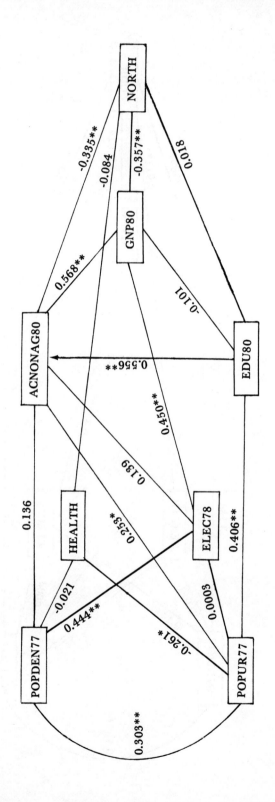

*   Significant at 0.05 level.
** Significant at 0.01 level.

FIGURE 3.3

Path Diagram Illustrating Results of Empirical Assessment of the Effects of Social,
Economic and Demographic Factors on Infant Mortality Rate (West Model): Model II

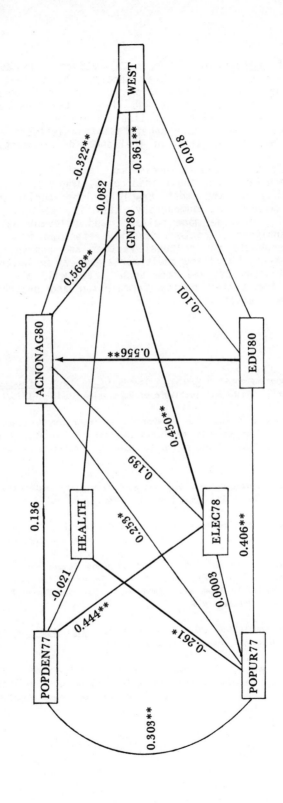

* Significant at 0.05 level.

** Significant at 0.01 level.

it is of a sufficiently critical volume and has an adequate coverage to benefit the rural people. At present the ratio of medical personnel to population is too low to reach the great majority of the Thai people who live in the rural areas and thus to effect a significant decline in mortality. Investment in public health yields more benefits than investment in the medical field at the present stage of Thailand's development.

Since all analyses presented in this paper are based on available data, given their inadequacy, there is a dire need for a field study of the most crucial, long neglected and policy relevant aspects of demography, that is, mortality. The field survey will provide more reliable and relevant data for a more serious analysis of factors causally affecting mortality. Various social, economic and cultural factors and health practices that affect infant, child and adult mortality can be better identified. The conclusions derived from such survey will definitely be more reliable for better policy formulation and programme implementation and evaluation.

References

Benjawan Rungpitarangsi. Mortality Trends in Thailand: Estimates for the period 1937-1970. Bangkok: Institute of Population Studies, 1974.

Bourgeois-Pichat, Jean. "An Attempt to Appraise the Accuracy of Demographic Statistics for an Under-developed Country: Thailand". Perspective on Thai Population Research Report No. 1. Bangkok: Institute of Population Studies, 1974.

Committee on Population and Demography. "Fertility and Mortality Changes in Thailand 1950-1975". Report No. 3. 1980.

Economic and Social Commission for Asia and the Pacific. Population of Thailand. Country Monograph Series No. 3. Bangkok: United Nations, 1976.

Hill, Kenneth, Arjun L. Adlakha, and Chintana Pejaranonda. "The Survey of Population Change 1974-1976". Special Report on Fertility, Nuptiality and Infant Mortality Measures. Bangkok: Population Survey Division, National Statistical Office, 1979.

Institute of Population and Social Research. Population and Development Data Sheet. Bangkok: Mahidol University, 1982.

Knodel, John and Apichat Chamratrithirong. "Infant and Child Mortality in Thailand: Levels, Trends, and Differentials as Derived through Indirect Estimation Techniques". Papers of the East-West Population Institute, No. 57, 1978.

Krongkaew, Medhi.   "The Distribution of and Access to Basic Health Service in Thailand". Bangkok: Faculty of Economics, Thammasat University, 1979.

Leoprapai, Boonlert and Anuri Wanglee.   "Estimates of Vital Rate by Stable Population Analysis of the Age Distribution for Thailand 1960 and 1970". Paper presented at the Pattaya Workshop, Thailand, 19-23 June, 1978.

National Research Council.   "Fertility and Mortality Changes in Thailand, 1950-1975". Committee on Population on Demography, Report No. 2. Washington D.C.: National Academy of Sciences, 1980.

Population Reference Bureau.   1980 World Population Data Sheet.   New York: Population Reference Bureau, 1981.

_____. 1983 World Population Data Sheet. New York: Population Reference Bureau, 1984.

Population Survey Division.   "Infant Mortality Rates: Estimated from 1980 Population and Housing Census of Thailand". Bangkok: National Statistical Office, 1983.

Prasithrathsint, Suchart.   "Implications of the Relationship between Fertility, and Mortality for Family Planning and Economic Development of Thailand". Journal of Social Sciences. Vol. 10, No. 1 (January 1973): 88-101.

Shin, Eui Hang.   "Economic and Social Correlates of Infant Mortality: A Cross-Sectional and Longitudinal Analysis of 63 Selected Countries". Social Biology, 22 (1975): 315-25.

Simmons, George B., Celeste Smucker, Stan Bernstein, and Eric Jensen. "Post-Neonatal Mortality in Rural India: Implications of an Economic Model". Demography, Vol. 19, No. 3 (August 1982).

Thailand.   The Survey of Population Change 1964-67.   Bangkok: National Statistical Office, 1969.

_____. The Survey of Population Change 1974-75. Bangkok: National Statistical Office, 1977.

United Nations.   Levels and Trends of Mortality since 1950.   New York: United Nations, 1982.

U.S. Department of Commerce, Bureau of Census.   "Country Demographic Profiles: Thailand". Washington D.C: U.S. Department of Commerce, 1978.

Working Group on Population Projection.   Population Projection for Thailand Whole Kingdom and Region 1970-2005.   Bangkok: Working Group on Population Projection, 1979.